The Great War
in the
Argonne Forest

The Great War in the Argonne Forest

French and American Battles 1914–1918

Richard Merry

Pen & Sword

MILITARY

AN IMPRINT OF PEN & SWORD BOOKS LTD
YORKSHIRE – PHILADELPHIA

First published in Great Britain in 2020
and reprinted in this format in 2021 by
PEN & SWORD MILITARY
An imprint of Pen & Sword Books Ltd
Yorkshire – Philadelphia

ISBN 9-781-52679-781-0

Typeset by Concept, Huddersfield, West Yorkshire, HD4 5JL
Printed and bound in England by CPI Group (UK) Ltd, Croydon, CR0 4YY

Pen & Sword Books Ltd incorporates the Imprints of Aviation, Atlas, Family
History, Fiction, Maritime, Military, Discovery, Politics, History, Archaeology,
Select, Wharncliffe Local History, Wharncliffe True Crime, Military Classics,
Wharncliffe Transport, Leo Cooper, The Praetorian Press, Remember When,
White Owl, Seaforth Publishing and Frontline Publishing.

For a complete list of Pen & Sword titles please contact
PEN & SWORD BOOKS LTD
47 Church Street, Barnsley, South Yorkshire, S70 2AS, England
E-mail: enquiries@pen-and-sword.co.uk
Website: www.pen-and-sword.co.uk
or
PEN & SWORD BOOKS
1950 Lawrence Rd, Havertown, PA 19083, USA
E-mail: uspen-and-sword@casematepublishers.com
Website: www.penandswordbooks.com

This book is dedicated to
George Robert Merry
Croix de Guerre
1873–1920
&
Harry Rupert
1946–2019

Contents

List of Maps

List of Plates

Clermont en Argonne, *c.*1900.

Clermont en Argonne, *c.*1914: the ruins.

Passavant en Argonne, *c.*1900: memorial to the massacre of the *Mobiles*.

Passavant en Argonne, *c.*1914: the headless memorial.

Uncle Bob in his uniform.

Uncle Bob sitting in his car with (*left*) André Citroën.

Lieutenant Erwin Rommel, 1915.

General Henri Gouraud, 1915.

General von Mudra, 1915.

Nicole Manguin, 1915/16.

German bodies being put in the Poincaré family plot at Nubécourt.

Bruno Garibaldi dying, 1914.

Garibaldi funeral in the forest, 29 December 1914.

A hand-drawn card depicting a French post in the Argonne forest, Christmas 1914.

Joan of Arc depicted rising from the ruins of Rheims Cathedral.

French *Poilus* fighting in the forest, *c.*1914/15.

German soldiers fighting in the forest, *c.*1914.

German soldiers in a trench, spring 1915.

French *brancardiers* in a trench, spring 1915.

Bois de la Gruerie, 1915.

A German cemetery, 1915/16.

A French cemetery of 1916/17, with Cocarde.

Crown Prince Wilhelm giving out medals after the summer 1915 offensive.

Acknowledgements

I would like to thank both my grandparents Bert and Rene Merry and my parents David and Eileen Merry for safeguarding Bob's shoebox with his correspondence and photos for over seventy years; Rose Walter for her hours of translation of French into English for both this book and the display we put on at the Abbey Lachalade in 2014 for the centenary of the outbreak of the First World War, and her friend Maria Caterina Coates for translating Italian into English and vice versa for both this book and the centenary display.

I thank Christina Holstein for her encouragement and support in writing the book and fact checking; my old friend Dr Frank Ellis for translating old German script into English for me; Jean-Paul de Vries at his Romagne 14–18 Museum for encouraging me to write; similarly Maarten and Didi Otte at 14–18 Nantillois Museum for their encouragement; the Franco-German Committee at Moreau Valley Camp for their tireless work in maintaining the German rest camp and working with young people to understand the epic struggle that took place around the Argonne Forest; Mikaël Embury for his tireless work in the Argonne Forest, maintaining the First World War sites, commemoration ceremonies and arranging for new signage, including English translation; and the other volunteers whose names I know not, who keep the Main de Massiges trenches and tunnels at Vauquois open and safe for the public. Also Douglas Mastriano and his volunteers for keeping alive the memory of Sergeant York, and for maintaining the trail which over 100 years later enables visitors to 'follow the footsteps' in Châtel Chéhéry.

Thanks are also due to the many American friends I've made over the last six years, particularly Mike Cuna and his regular podcasts on the First World War, and battlefield tour guide Randy Gaulke; and to Nicola Ayrton at the National Army Museum, who asked me to speak on removing the dead from the Argonne Forest after the First World War. As a result of that talk I met Rupert Harding from Pen & Sword Books, to whom I'm indebted for helping to publish this book, along with the editor, Sarah Cook.

Lastly I thank my friends and neighbours in the Argonne Forest, be they French, British, American or Dutch, especially Mike and Patricia, Dave, John, Janine and Erwin, Catherine and Ludovik, Georges and Marie, Rieky and Jean Marie, who have always been on hand, whether it be for a chat and a cup of tea, or donations of garden vegetables and forest mushrooms, through to help clearing snow and stacking logs.

Preface

This is the story of my great-uncle Bob, and countless thousands of Germans, French, Italians, Americans and even men from the former Czechoslovakia, who discovered the Spirit of the Argonne in the First World War. Somehow they endured, as did a few women, and carried on in conditions that are inconceivable today. It also tells a story that is little talked about: the clearing-up of the postwar battle front and the reburial of the dead, and how the local population set about rebuilding their ruined villages and lives.

The publication of this book brings to an end a thirty-year odyssey, during which fate has played its hand and not always kindly. In the early 1990s my parents gave me an old cardboard shoebox. My father said it was some stuff belonging to his Uncle Bob, not that he had ever met him, but family talk had it he was a bit of a cove, shipboard romancer and chancer who had come to a sticky end before the First World War. I gave it no more than a perfunctory glance. Inside were old postcards, sepia prints and a manila envelope. I made a mental note to investigate further at some unspecified point in the future. In the meantime I had a career to burnish and two young children to occupy my spare time. So the shoebox went up into my attic, just as it had been in both my parents' attic and my grandmother's attic for the previous seventy years.

At start of the twenty-first century I changed career and found myself working shifts, which now gave me some free time to work on my family history. Slowly I began to add flesh to the box's contents. Bob was born in 1873 in Chelsea, the second son of a senior official in the Admiralty. Soon after he was born, his father retired to south-east London and begat a larger family with his young wife. Four girls and Albert Merry, my grandfather, followed. There is no record of Bob's education; his next appearance is as a member of the famous Catford Cycling Club. Here he became a well-known and reasonably successful cyclist, at one point holding a national title. He started travelling to Europe with his cycle, racing in Holland, and later he took part in the exhibition races at the official opening of the *Stade Buffalo*, Paris's new velodrome. About 1896 he left for

Holland, working for the Birmingham-based Dunlop Rubber Tyre Company. In 1900 he returned briefly to Balham in London, to marry on Boxing Day a bride he'd brought with him from Holland. Not long after, he returned home to Amsterdam. Later my grandfather, then aged 12, began to spend his school holidays with Bob, working with him at Dunlop. This continued for a couple of years until my grandfather was forced to return to London: in quick succession tuberculosis had claimed his mother and three of his sisters, and my grandfather now had to look after his ageing father.

At some point Bob's wife died and he too changed career. In 1908 he arrived in Paris, then in thrall to *La Belle Époque*. France was then the largest car exporter in the world. He joined André Citroën at the sports car company Mors. Once a premium sports car brand, it had hit the doldrums. Citroën, with his mechanical genius and marketing skills, revived the brand. Ships' records show Bob crisscrossing the world – South America, India, Ceylon, Thailand, Singapore – selling Mors sports cars. In 1913 he travelled once more to London to marry a young French woman. In April 1914 he returned from his final voyage to South Africa.

When war was declared in August 1914 Bob knew he was too old to return to London to join the British Army. But fate played its hand and the French government changed the terms of enlistment for the French Foreign Legion (FFL). Bob's enlistment papers show he entered the FFL central Seine recruiting office on 30 August 1914. He was now signed up for the duration. The enlistment paperwork has little on it, and they certainly weren't looking at his age as they had an upper age limit of 40. Bob was older than this. He opted to enlist under his real name and was not given another identity.

It was on a later visit to the Public Record Office in Kew, London (now the National Archives), that the final shocking pieces of Bob's story fell into place. Finally the truth emerged as I turned the dusty pages of a ship's log book and saw his British Army service record. My father, who had believed another story for seventy-odd years, was even more shocked when confronted by the real story.

In 2013, after many, many hours using Google translate, I finally arrived in the Argonne to see where Bob's war had really taken place. He had never mentioned the forest by name, or if he did, it was removed. Here I first met Harry Rupert, a Dutchman who was a guide at Camp Moreau, and we became firm friends. Our friendship developed later as we walked over old battlegrounds. His area of interest was Sergeant York and Chatel-Chéhéry, where he lived with his wife Rieky. He began to plan an exhibition for the Sergeant York centenary in 2018.

In 2014 I returned with an exhibition of Bob's story, and that of the Garibaldis, which was placed in the Abbey at Lachalade. At the First World War centenary commemorations in the Argonne, the French Veterans Minister was somewhat surprised by my presence and by the exhibition. As well as a wreath for Bob, I laid one on behalf of King's Canterbury, Bruno Garibaldi's former school. French Foreign Legionnaires stood either side of the Garibaldi Memorial as we placed our wreaths.

In 2016 Harry and I both took part for a few days in the inaugural walk of the *Via Sacra*, along the length of the Western Front. The then British Prime Minister David Cameron had wanted a legacy project to follow the four years of First World War commemorations. Sir Anthony Seldon, one of his advisers, had come across the idea of a *Via Sacra* earlier when looking at First World War letters from pupils at his school. British Army officer Douglas Gillespie wrote home in the summer of 1915 to his old schoolmaster:

> When peace comes, our government might combine with the French government to make one long avenue between the lines from the Vosges to the sea ... I would make a fine broad road in the 'No-Man's Land' between the lines, with paths for pilgrims on foot, and plant trees for shade and fruit trees, so that the soil should not altogether be waste. Then I would like to send every man, woman and child in Western Europe on a pilgrimage along that *Via Sacra* so that they might think and learn what war means from the silent witnesses on either side.

With Gillespie's death at the front later in 1915, and the continuation of the war for another three years, the idea disappeared from the British public conscience for another hundred years. (Further details are available at https://www.thewesternfrontway.com.)

Fate now played a strange hand as we assembled in Verdun, setting out to follow the old *Poilus*' route up to the battleground above the city. The BBC had brought in a film crew and presenter to film us for the day. The aim was to publicise the walk that was planned to reach the Somme for 1 July 2016, the day of the centenary of the opening of the joint French–British offensive. Our guide for the next two days was the Verdun expert Christina Holstein, who has published five books on Verdun. Up and back down we trudged like the Grand old Duke of York's men. Each time as the camera framed us another car sped by and back down we went. The story only received a brief mention that night on the BBC news. It was 24 June 2016 and the result of the referendum for Britain to leave the European Union had just been announced. There was only one thing the media wanted to talk about with Sir Anthony, as a well-known biographer of recent British Prime Ministers and with a book about to be published on David Cameron, and it wasn't the *Via Sacra*.

Fate was kinder to me personally; Christina had seen the exhibition on Bob in the Abbey at Lachalade and had made a note to find the person behind it. When better acquainted with Bob's story, she felt there was a book in it. So for the next three years I scribbled away during the winter and spent the summers with Harry visiting the sites.

In early 2018 Harry suffered an aneurysm, but incredibly he survived. By the early summer of that year he was miraculously fit enough to launch his centenary exhibition. On display in Chatel-Chéhéry were hundreds of pictures of the German occupation, Sergeant York and the village's liberation late in the war. For the rest of the summer he sat greeting people from all over the world at his wonderful exhibition.

In January 2019 I was asked to speak at the National Army Museum in London about the digging-up of the dead in the Argonne sector after the First World War. In the audience was Pen & Sword commissioning editor Rupert Harding and, as they say, the rest is history. On 18 May 2019 I made my way out to France, having spoken to Harry only about some walks we had planned a couple of days earlier. I was saving my good news about the book having a publisher until we met. But when I arrived in the Argonne late that afternoon, there was a flurry of emails from our American friends. Harry had died during the previous night/early morning, probably from another aneurysm.

Introduction

For keen students of military history in the Argonne in the First World War, this book offers no new or original material, with one exception: it contains excerpts from Bob's correspondence from the front. However, where this book differs from the better known and more authoritative sources used is that it brings together a number of narratives. Necessarily most published accounts of this campaign cater for a constituent group, whether German, Italian, French or American, in their own language. Here I hope you will find for the first time in English a continuous narrative from before, during and after the First World War, with many eyewitness accounts from all the protagonists over the four-year campaign. Also, unlike most books about the First World War, this one does not end after a battle or on 11 November 1918. Here the story continues. I look at the thankless task of clearing the battlefield, digging up and reburying the dead, and rebuilding the destroyed villages. After twenty years of reconstruction, and just when normality was returning to the area, once again the German Army swept through the region. Although spared the destruction of the First World War, this time there was no safe area behind the lines. France was partially and then entirely occupied for four years.

The Argonne Forest is in Lorraine in north-eastern France and today the area is a quiet rural idyll, renowned for the quality of its pure air, its miles of underused forest footpaths and cycle tracks, and its sparse population. Wildlife and birds proliferate amid the great oaks, beeches and hornbeams that dominate the forest. It wasn't always thus; in the latter part of the eighteenth century, and through the nineteenth and early twentieth centuries the area frequently found itself at the epicentre of French history.

The forest is situated between the cities of Rheims and Verdun, straddling a north–south linear ridge line. Along this ridge runs an old Roman road, the *Haute Chevauchée* ('High Road'). The porous *gaize* (rock) subsoil permits the large oaks, beeches and hornbeams to draw water from deep underground. The ground drops away on either side of the *Haute*

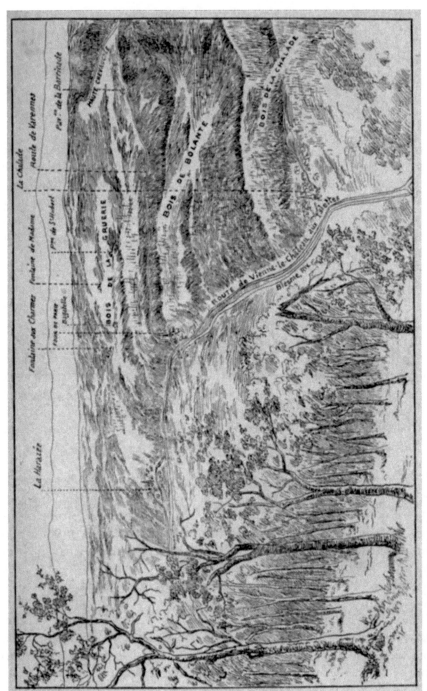

A topographical postcard of the Argonne forest.

Chevauchée into impenetrable thickets and dense forestry, which hide steep ravines and gulleys. For centuries the forest had provided a buffer between France and the Holy Roman Empire, and later Germany. Until the 1920s French Army engineers oversaw any large-scale tree-felling and widening of roads and tracks to ensure no invading army could gain any advantage. The wood provided an abundant resource for local woodcutters and charcoal-burners. In turn they supplied the fuel for the glass and pottery kilns that once prospered around the forest periphery. *Gaize* was also an essential constituent in these industries, which dated back to Roman times.

In 1789, during the French Revolution, King Louis XVI fled the Jacobin '*sans culottes*' ('without breeches': working-class French revolutionaries) in Paris with his Austrian wife Marie Antoinette and headed towards Montmédy. At the village of Varennes en Argonne, in the centre of the forest, they were apprehended by recently invigorated *Citoyen* and taken back to Paris under escort. In 1792 the advancing armies of Austria and Prussia under the Duke of Brunswick found a gap in the forest defences. Once through the gap, they advanced towards Paris, only to find the French Army behind them at Valmy, just west of the Argonne. Here the French general Kellerman rallied his makeshift force by the old Valmy Mill, above the Plateau of the Moon. As battle commenced, Kellerman rode up and down the lines raising his hat and shouting '*Vive la Nation*'. In turn the inspired army sang two famous revolutionary songs, *La Marseillaise* and *Ca Ira*. The French won the day. The famous German poet, philosopher and statesman Johann Wolfgang von Goethe had accompanied the invading army as an observer. He commented, 'On that day and at that place began a new era in the history of the world and you can say you were there.' The new French government, having won its first decisive military victory, proclaimed the First Republic on the following day, 21 September 1792. Soon after, King Louis XVI and Marie Antoinette were arrested and subsequently executed.

In 1842 the French author Victor Hugo, later famous for his novels, *Les Miserables* and *The Hunchback of Notre Dame*, wrote one of the world's first travel guides, *Le Rhin*, which featured many descriptions of the Argonne region. Clermont's name had derived from the hill being clearly viewable:

From Sainte Ménéhould to Clermont en Argonne, the road is lovely. A continual orchard. On both sides of the road a chaos of fruit trees whose beautiful green leaves feast on the sun, and spread on the road their shadow, cutting into the Chicory. The villages have something Swiss and German. Houses of white stone, half clad with planks, with large roofs of hollow tiles which overhang the wall 2 or 3 feet. Almost cottages, we feel the mountains ... Clermont is a beautiful village, which is situated above a sea of greenery with its church on its head, like the Le Tréport [a French seaside resort] over a sea of waves.

In 1870 France was mainland Europe's major military power but the unification of Germany threatened the status quo; sensing a shift in the balance of power, France declared war on Germany on 16 July. The Germans responded with two military firsts: the mass mobilisation of a conscript army, which was brought by train to the front. Not long after the German troops crossed the border, they were involved in a notorious Argonne incident.

On 25 August 1870 a group of French National Guard *Mobile* were on the road from Vitry-le-Francois to St Ménéhould when they were intercepted by elements of the 6th Prussian Cavalry, which charged them with lances, killing and injuring many of the *Mobile*. The remainder were disarmed and made prisoner, and taken to Passavant en Argonne. What happened next was subject to some conjecture; either the Prussians believed they were under attack, or one Prussian shot another Prussian by mistake. Whatever happened, it caused the Prussian cavalry to panic, along with the soldiers already billeted in the village. This led to a massacre of forty-nine of the *Mobile* prisoners by lance, sword and rifle fire, although it was claimed many more died of their wounds while fleeing the village.

The Germany Army continued its advance to Paris, where it laid siege to the city. On 28 January 1871 Paris surrendered. German troops now occupied the north-east of France, including the Argonne, until the French government paid financial reparations to them. Sensing that the French at some point in the future would seek revenge, the Germans annexed Alsace and part of Lorraine to act as a buffer between the two countries.

Revanchism (reclamation of the lost land) became the French public and political mantra. Books, paintings and political debate all served to promote the concept of revenge for the defeat of 1870–1 and the need to reclaim the two lost provinces. Military planners from both sides worked away in earnest. Germany was also watching with alarm the growing strength of Russia. The resulting German Schlieffen Plan was intended to knock out France in a quick six-week campaign, before moving on to attack and defeat Russia before the Russians could establish an army large enough to alter the balance of power in their favour. In early June 1914 von Moltke, the German Chief of General Staff, said, 'We are ready, the sooner the better for us.'

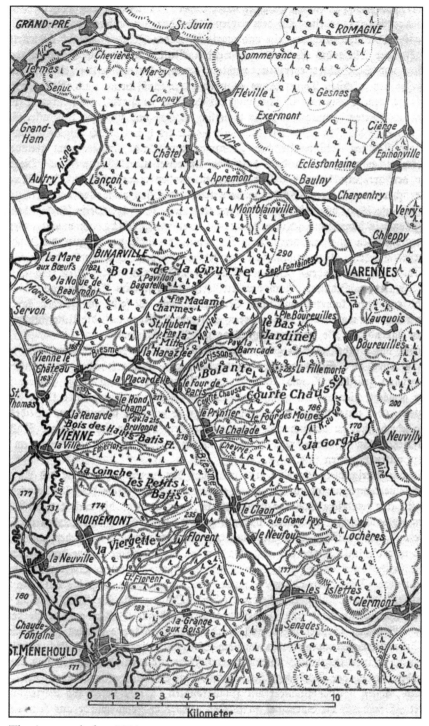

The Argonne before 1914.

Mainland Europe was now a tinderbox: all that was required was the match. This was duly struck on 28 June when Archduke Ferdinand and his wife were assassinated in Sarajevo. The archduke was the heir to the Austro-Hungarian Empire, Germany's principal ally. Now the cat's cradle of alliances, and the need for military planners to mobilise, in many cases usurping the political process, which had not been fully focused on the gathering storm clouds either, allowed the likelihood of a major European land war to gather momentum. It was a war that France and Germany had been preparing themselves for, for over forty years.

Britain, then the world's super-power, was largely reliant on its over-whelming naval fire-power. This Germany had disregarded in its planning, believing the war would be land-based and a naval confrontation with Britain therefore unlikely. Britain's standing army was far smaller (*c.*250,000) than those of the behemoths of Germany and France and was primarily used to police its Empire. Although British Army planners at the behest of government had been involved with their French Army counterparts in scoping out likely scenarios in the event of a confrontation with Germany, their political masters had not been willed the means. The Royal Navy continued to garner a disproportionate share of financial resources, despite the growing likelihood of a land-based war. In short, Britain was totally unprepared for a large-scale European land campaign. Neither had the public been prepared for a potential clash of titans involving Britain on mainland Europe; even as late as the end of July, they were reassured that it was a 'continental European affair' and unlikely to involve Britain.

The United States of America stood even further back, having been governed by the 'Munroe Doctrine' for nearly a century. Former President James Munroe was the fifth President of the United States of America, from 1817 until 1825. The Congress of Vienna in 1814/15 had seen Europe set aside hundreds of years of animosity and agree to live peaceably. The USA became increasingly nervous that a Europe at peace might once again nurture colonial aspirations towards America. In 1823 Munroe set out what later became known as the 'Munroe Doctrine', in which he stated that any further efforts by European nations to take control of any independent state in North or South America would be viewed as 'the manifestation of an unfriendly disposition toward the United States'. He also stated that the USA would not interfere with European colonies and would not meddle in the internal affairs of Europe. Over the next eighty to ninety years this became a central tenet of American foreign policy and for the most part it held firm. The policy also enjoyed widespread public support from millions of new American immigrants by the end of the nineteenth century. As many of them were fleeing from Europe, they wanted no part in any form of European intervention. A new free America was their future, not the old Europe with its despotic monarchies, conscription, wars, and religious and political persecution.

Meanwhile back in Europe, a remark made in 1888 by Otto von Bismarck, united Germany's first Chancellor, was about to come true: 'One day the great European War will come out of some damned foolish thing in the Balkans.'

From the autumn of 1914 to the autumn of 1915 a number of grim and bloody battles took place amid the trees of the Argonne. Much of the forest and most of the surrounding villages were destroyed in the chaos of battle. For the next three years the war moved to other fronts. On 6 April 1917 America joined the war against Germany, and in the autumn of 1918 the largest American army in history assembled in the Argonne region.

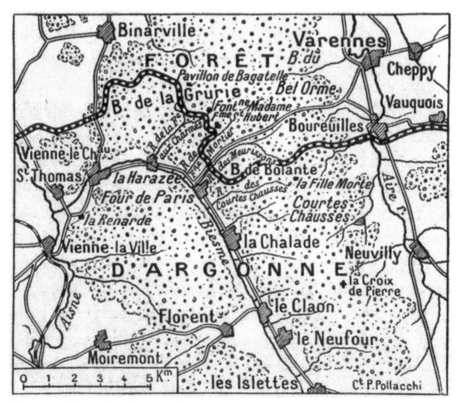

The general front line for most of the war.

The Meuse–Argonne offensive was (and still is) the largest American military campaign ever mounted.

It's now over a hundred years since the guns fell silent. The forest has regrown, the soil healed and the last of the veterans who fought in the epic battles of the forest are now dead. It is fitting perhaps that one of the men who prevents the campaign from slipping from public memory is one of literature's greatest fictional characters, Jay Gatsby, from F. Scott Fitzgerald's classic, *The Great Gatsby*. He claimed to have fought in the Argonne Forest, even alluding to service in America's famous 'Lost Battalion'.

Chapter 1

1914

While high-stakes political manoeuvring took place among the European capitals during the final week of July 1914, in the area surrounding the Argonne Forest all was quiet. The area's only connection with these grand political events was that the Deputy for the Meuse Department, Raymond Poincaré, had been elected President of France in 1913. His family seat was in Nubécourt en Argonne, at the southern end of the forest. Any impending war, it was assumed, would be fought somewhere over the eastern horizon. Most villagers then had very little comprehension of life outside their commune, let alone what the lost lands in the east, Alsace and part of Lorraine, actually looked like.

Late on 1 August the reality of the current situation was brought home when the *Tocsin* (church bells) rang to call villagers in from fields and workshops to hear their mayor announce mobilisation. From their pulpits on Sunday morning, 2 August, priests exhorted men to do their duty and God's work. Afterwards, men stood around in groups outside town halls or sat in cafés waiting for the details of mobilisation to be posted by the mayor. Husbands, fathers and sons scoured homes for their army books, which outlined their requirement on mobilisation. Conscription had been a bedrock of national policy since the 1870–1 Franco-Prussian War. Over the next two weeks men packed their few possessions in a small case or knapsack. Last meals were eaten silently with their families, and men took what for many would be one final look over their shoulder at their village, home and family. After the arrival of their mobilisation orders they walked or rode through the dust to the railway stations of Aubréville, Clermont, Les Islettes or St Ménéhould. Most men stood in their Sunday best, as men did when leaving their village, but men recalled from leave stood resplendent in uniforms more suited to the army parade grounds of the nineteenth century than to the impending clash of military titans. Along-side them horses stood tethered to railings; they had also unwittingly been called up.

The pivotal day was 3 August. In London Parliament sat, despite it being a Bank Holiday, as Sir Edward Grey, the Foreign Secretary, outlined Britain's position, Britain's treaty obligations and the likelihood of being unable to stand aside in the event of a war in Europe. Belgium had refused to allow German troops to enter the country, and that evening Germany declared war on France, alleging that French planes had flown over Belgium to bomb Germany and in so doing, they had violated Belgian neutrality. France responded similarly. That evening Sir Edward Grey remarked, 'The lamps are going out all over Europe; we shall not see them lit again in our lifetime.'

The following day, 4 August, was to be no less turbulent, as the German invasion of Belgium began early in the morning. The Belgian Army did not stand aside, but fought the Germans. During the morning Britain urged Germany to continue to respect Belgian neutrality but Germany maintained its position, that it was merely pre-empting a French invasion. At midday the Belgian government asked Britain and France to come to their aid. Britain's request to Germany to respect Belgium's neutrality later become an ultimatum to be responded to by midnight European time. Meanwhile in France mobilisation continued apace. During the afternoon Britain formally mobilised its army and reserves, and the Empire rallied behind Britain with pledges of support. As darkness fell, German troops continued their advance across Belgium. At 11pm Big Ben struck; it was midnight, European time. With no response received to the ultimatum, Britain declared war with Germany.

An air of excitement prevailed for the most part at the railway stations around the Argonne as men met old friends and waited for their trains. For some, they were about to become part of history, helping to reclaim the lost provinces of Alsace and Lorraine, and obediently bending to the will of the state. For others, who were living on life's periphery around the forest, the chance of regular pay and three square meals a day was sufficient enticement. Some young men relished the opportunity for combat, although the general consensus was that they would simply take over the duties of the current army, freeing the soldiers to fight, while the reserves undertook garrison or support duties. Many of the young men assumed it would all be over in a few months, by Christmas at the latest. Older and wiser heads could see that a clash on this scale was more likely to stretch into years. All the same, it was a fine adventure and a chance to miss the backbreaking work of summer harvest.

Trains carried the men, east, west, north and south to their allotted assembly areas all across France. Women and children were left on the platforms, weeping and waving at the disappearing trains. Home they trudged, back along the dusty summer roads, past crops ripening in the fields. Back at the *foyer* (home and hearth), time for tears was short. The need to harvest was upon the villages; with only old men and children left, the bulk of the work would now fall to the women. With the majority of the horses gone as well, the work would be even harder and they would now have to walk everywhere. Most of the men from the Argonne, despite their initial reservations, would see action before August had ended. The French Army's casualties in that month were appalling: 2,500 men killed and a further 5,000 a day injured or posted missing.

The two great armies of France and Germany, each initially more than two million men strong, wheeled into action. The Germans, following the Moltke-modified version of the Schlieffen plan, started to push the bulk of their army through Belgium. The French Commander-in-Chief, General Joffre followed his Plan XVII to attack Alsace and Lorraine, to reclaim its lost territory. It did not go to plan, and on 24 August the French Army went into *La Grande Retraite* to the River Marne, after a series of defeats. Meanwhile, in Belgium German troops now clashed unexpectedly with the Belgian Army and the recently landed, small but professional British Expeditionary Force (BEF); both offered stiff resistance. The anticipated German timetable of reaching Paris in six weeks was now starting to look increasingly difficult to keep.

The German Fifth Army under Crown Prince Wilhelm, the Kaiser's eldest son, advanced steadily towards the Argonne. On 21 August they approached Dun sur Meuse, with the aim of capturing Bar-le-Duc and surrounding the fortresses and vital railway junction at Verdun. By the end of August the occupants of the Argonne villages were hastily evacuated to the south and west. Horse-drawn carts and handcarts were all piled high with what precious few portable possessions the villagers could hastily gather. Dragging behind this sorrowful procession in the heat and dust came the old, the children and the animals. The Argonne villages were now occupied by only a handful of people, who either refused to leave or were unable to, and French troops. The forest with its dark and impenetrable thickets persuaded both French and German troops to avoid it. The German advance swept southwards on either side of the forest, preceded by heavy shelling. Villages that had been built up and watched history pass by for hundreds of years were now destroyed in a matter of hours.

Varennes fell on 3 September. After seven hours of shelling, much of the town was reduced to rubble. Gone were the historic buildings where the great drama of the flight of Louis XVI and Marie Antoinette had taken

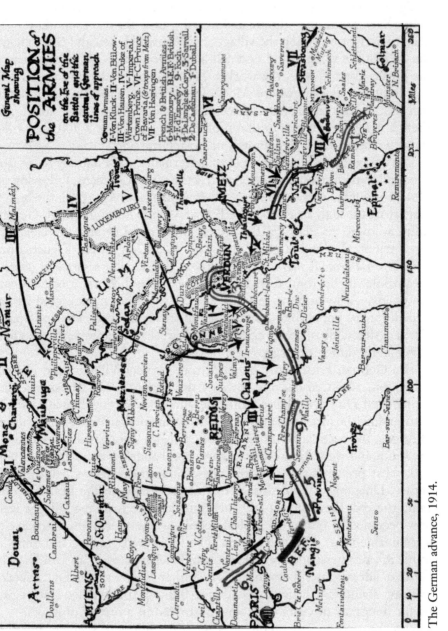

The German advance, 1914.

place; gone were the historic clock archway and gate where they were initially stopped and Monsieur Sauce's house where they sat, still hoping to be saved. The wooden houses surviving the shelling soon succumbed to fire. Chickens, ducks, guinea fowl and calves, in fact almost any remaining livestock, animal or fowl, was either eaten or carried away by the Germans to be eaten elsewhere. St Ménéhould fell on 4 September to the German Fifth Army, which had split either side of the forest. It was spared, for the most part, the destruction by artillery inflicted on the smaller villages on the eastern side of the forest. The town, though, was looted and used as a base for German soldiers. Rheims fell the same day, to the Third Army; this was to prove the western limit of the German advance.

During the evening and night of 3 September trains evacuated wounded French soldiers from the hospital in Clermont, run by the Sisters of Saint Vincent de Paul. The following morning horse carriage ambulances removed the last of the wounded soldiers, leaving about forty infirm villagers in the hospital. Sister Gabrielle Rosnet insisted that she was unable to leave her patients and volunteered to remain with two elderly nuns to look after them and a wounded French soldier she had found.

During the morning of 4 September the villages of Boureuilles and Neuvilly on the eastern side of the forest fell to artillery fire and the advancing German troops of the Fifth Army. Soon the fighting spread to Auzéville, Aubréville and Brabant. By early afternoon the German artillery gunners had Clermont in their sights. Despite the French troops leaving after lunch, for five hours shells fell on real or imagined targets. The French artillery batteries responded, adding to the carnage in the village. Two-thirds of the houses, shops and other businesses in Clermont were destroyed. The few remaining villagers took to their cellars in terror as their houses and shops collapsed around them.

By evening the shelling had abated and the townspeople waited nervously for the imminent arrival of the Germans. During the early hours of 5 September the Germans entered the all-but-destroyed village of Clermont. In the cellar of the hospital, still under the care of the redoubtable Sister Gabrielle, lay the infirm and sick. The Germans tried to enter the hospital but were confronted by Sister Gabrielle, who in no uncertain terms told the German commanding officer, 'You are here in a house devoted to suffering, you will not enter further.' She eventually permitted them to enter, but only under her terms, to see how they could utilise it for a hospital themselves. Soon a German nursing unit was working alongside Sister Gabrielle, looking after wounded German soldiers.

For such a short campaign the Schlieffen Plan expected the German Army to be living off the land, rather than being resupplied. This process was supposed to be accompanied by requisition and payment notes for local suppliers. The reality soon became apparent to the remaining Clermont villagers as the Germans now began looking for food, drink and any other booty they could lay their hands on. Searching with lit torches, it was not long before fires started in several of the remaining wooden houses and spread quickly from one building to another. With only a few able-bodied men left, the villagers were unable to operate the fire appliances, not that there was enough water pressure left to pump water since the water mains had been damaged at the start of the German shelling. The Germans sat on the hilltop above the village and watched the houses burn. Soon the Church of St Didier was ablaze too. The destruction of Clermont was nearly complete. The hospital was one of the few buildings that remained untouched, but with flames all around it, and the wooden outbuilding starting to smoulder, its destruction appeared imminent.

Again Sister Gabrielle confronted the German commander at the hospital, showing him how near the flames were and insisting, 'Your officers had given me their word that the hospital would be spared. They denied it. Never would a French officer act in this way.' She also pointed out that the destruction of the hospital would obstruct the route to Bar le Duc, the next destination for the Germans. The Germans then produced a fire vehicle and soldiers began to create a fire-break around the hospital. Meanwhile the few remaining villagers could only cover their faces and run through the fire and smoke, taking refuge on the grassy hill of St Anne above the village. There they stood or sat and wept as much of what little was left of their village after the shelling burnt down. On 6 September the few remaining Clermont villagers were forced to start pulling down the walls of their burnt-out houses. Dead people and animals, killed in the shelling, and the remains of animals that had been eaten by dogs were buried by villagers and soldiers and the roads cleared to allow the German Army to pass through.

Later in the day a German sentry was shot, suffering a minor flesh wound. The German commander went to see Sister Gabrielle and told her that the whole population was about to be shot in reprisal, old men, women and children. She appealed to him about the cruelty of his intentions, and said, 'If you think that it takes human life to compensate your soldier's wound, take mine, I am ready, but do not massacre innocent people.' At one point she was placed against the wall, awaiting execution, but was spared; despite the experience, she continued working with

German patients. After waiting a further twenty-four hours, the commander renounced his execution plans. Again Clermont owed a debt to the
redoubtable Sister Gabrielle. Meanwhile the German artillery batteries
outside Clermont started shelling the towns and villages further to the
south and west, in advance of their army. Their fate was sealed as surely as
Clermont's had been, with death and destruction raining from the skies.
No sooner had the Germans arrived than they made a list of demands for
vital supplies from the few remaining villagers, which they were unable
to meet. Meanwhile furniture and other usable goods that had been
recovered from the ruins of Clermont and other villages were transported
away by the Germans in the direction of Varennes to the north.

A small German airfield was set up between Clermont and Auzéville, to
fly reconnaissance missions over the battlefront. During the day villagers
in Clermont could hear the sound of continuous fighting. At night the
distant skyline was crimson red and the stars were obscured by smoke, as
other villages suffered a similar fate to theirs. Crown Prince Wilhelm, the
German Fifth Army commander, was a regular visitor to the village, from
his forward headquarters further north in Varennes.

Les Islettes fell on 5 September, escaping large-scale damage but not
the looting. Later the same day the German Fifth Army swept south from
Clermont. First it was President Poincaré's brother Lucian's house in
Triaucourt-en-Argonne that was looted and his furniture and family
paintings carried away in trucks. Next the old family home in Nubécourt
was shelled, and then the doors to the Gillon-Poincaré family plot in the
church were broken open and dead German officers brought in and laid to
rest next to his parents and grandparents. The German Fifth Army soon
reached its most southerly advance position, Revigny-sur-Ornain, which
now lay destroyed, just like Clermont.

Four opposing armies now held the front line south of the Argonne
Forest: the German Fourth Army under Albrecht, Duke of Württemberg,
held the line from Vitry-le-François to Revigny, where it linked up with
the German Fifth Army under Crown Prince Wilhelm, stretching north-
east towards Verdun. Here, from 6 to 10 September, these combined
forces sought to drive a wedge between the French Third Army in the west
under General de Langle de Cary and the French Fourth Army in the east
under General Sarrail. The final battle of the offensive took place overnight on 9/10 September when 150,000 men of the German Fifth Army
attacked across a 20km front from Louppy-le-Chateau stretching north-
east to Heippes. It was an attack that Moltke had disapproved of, but he
relented when the Crown Prince threatened to go over his head to his

father the Kaiser and seek his approval. The epicentre was at the small farm and railway halt of Vaux-Marie on the edge of a vast plateau. This halt stood astride the main railway route from Clermont to Bar-le-Duc. At 2am on 10 September thousands of Germans prepared their rifles and fixed bayonets to attack across the whole front. Among the Germans advancing that night was Lieutenant Erwin Rommel (later the 'Desert Fox' and Afrika Korps commander of the Second World War); his regiment, the 124th Württemberg, was tasked with taking Côte 287, about 500 metres north of Rembercourt aux Pots.

Later on 10 September the enigmatic Lieutenant Colonel Hentsch visited the Crown Prince. Hentsch was the 'go between' from Moltke, based in the remote German High Command, *Oberste Heeresleitung* (OHL), located in a school in the suburbs of Luxembourg City, and the army field commanders. The Crown Prince reported that the progress made across the front could be sustained, despite his suffering 15,000 casualties in ten days. Hentsch, though, said that the Crown Prince should now retreat. The Crown Prince refused, insisting he would only do this on direct orders from OHL, and sent Hentsch back to Luxembourg. Hentsch's tour of the front-line generals finally brought Moltke to the front. Moltke knew that all across the German front casualties were now at an unsustainable level. There were insufficient reserves to replace them immediately and a broad French counter-attack was widely anticipated. The German Fourth Army's preferred line of defence was the St Méné-hould to Clermont road stretching east towards Verdun. The Crown Prince argued that this left his German Fifth Army with too long a line to defend and he thought there was better and narrower ground to defend to the north of the forest, using the hilltops of Vauquois and Montfaucon as strongpoints. Throughout 10 and 11 September Rommel and his men endured endless pounding by the French artillery 75mm cannon. Ammunition for German artillery was in short supply but the French fired with impunity. Moltke was seen in the vicinity of Rheims on 11 September and was observed to be a broken man; he was replaced shortly afterwards.

It was, though, French General Foch's Ninth Army attack on the remnants of the German Third Army near Châlons that saw the German Fourth and Fifth Armies start their retreat north, fearing their right flank would be left exposed. Across the whole German front men recognised that their position was difficult and in places untenable, yet they were not a defeated army. They looked at each other in disbelief, tears rolling from their eyes as their sacrifices and those of their dead comrades were about to be thrown away. During the early hours of 12 September the general retreat was firmly in progress, and later that day Vaux Marie was back in French hands. The stone memorial to the massacred *Mobile* at Passavant en Argonne had its head hacked off by retreating Germans. Rommel and his men were ordered to retreat back to Triaucourt. On 13 September fresh orders came, and they moved back from Triaucourt to Brizeaux.

The German Fifth Army retreat was now a sorry procession of vehicles, equipment, horses and carts. Once-jubilant men now dejectedly marched north back towards Clermont for several days. The casualties suffered on the retreat were enormous; the worst were treated in the hospital at Clermont, which still functioned, thanks to the earlier efforts of Sister Gabrielle. Once treated, casualties were moved back towards Varennes.

Early in the morning on 14 September the last Germans left St Méné-hould, Les Islettes and Clermont, and the first French troops re-entered the wrecked villages. It was the ruins and remnants of Clermont, not Hugo's 'beautiful village' that returning French troops now saw.

The French public also now became aware of the burial of Germans in the Poincaré plot and it caused public outrage. Poincaré initially helped fuel the anger, commenting, 'I have some trouble, however, to divert my thoughts from these horrors.' Later he was more sanguine: 'When my father died he wanted to be buried next to my mother in our family plot at Nubécourt. They were sleeping there when the Germans came in with a few of their own dead whom they laid next to ours. I dreamed, that day, that my father said to me: "Do not get annoyed, leave them alone. Unfortunately they will not wake us".'

* * *

As with the advance two weeks earlier, the retreating German Fifth Army split either side of the forest, but in the confusion of the retreat and the speed of the French advance, the German Fourth Army became inter-mingled with the Fifth. So whether the Crown Prince won the defensive line argument, or the 'fog of war' simply enveloped both armies, they both now retreated to a defensive line at the northern end of the forest, rather than the southern end.

Little had changed in the interceding seventy years to alter Hugo's description of these quaint picturesque villages. But now, after just a few short weeks, the 'chaos of fruit trees' was now a vast apocalyptic vista. Each army's dead lay where they had fallen, in varying degrees of decomposi-tion. Some were half-buried or had been temporarily buried. Dead animals of all kinds – military, farming and domestic – lay rotting under the sun. Burnt-out carts, vehicles, piles of destroyed cannon and other weapons lay everywhere. The booty, which only a few days earlier had seemed so important, now lay broken or discarded. The roads were lined with smashed and empty bottles of wine, beer and champagne.

Meanwhile Rommel and his men marched on in the dark with only short breaks, through Les Islettes, Le Neufour, Le Claon and Lachalade to Varennes, arriving at midnight on 13 September. They were then ordered to move further on to Montblainville, arriving there exhausted on 14 September, having covered 30 miles in twenty-four hours.

To the west of the forest the French had advanced to just south of Binarville by 15 September. In mid-September the French Tenth (Paris) Division leading the advance northwards was taken over by the charismatic General Henri Gouraud, who had forged a reputation for himself as a successful commander in France's North African Empire. He was joined at the Divisional Headquarters in the recently retaken Cistercian abbey in the village of Lachalade by a somewhat unlikely character in the shape of George Robert Merry, a 41-year-old Englishman, a former car salesman based in Paris. Now he was 8318 Legionnaire G.R. Merry of the *2ème régiment de marche du 1er étranger*. He had walked into the central French Foreign Legion recruiting office in Paris on Sunday, 30 August 1914, changed his age and signed up 'for the duration'. Speaking fluent French and German, he was now assigned to Gouraud as translator and chauffeur. He drove a 17/20hp Mors sports car, the same type of car he had so recently been selling, under pre-war Mors boss André Citroën. The number stencilled on the car bonnet (RM455) indicated it was an early government-requisitioned car for the Ministerial Reserve in Paris. This was my great-uncle Bob.

By 21 September the French east of the forest were just short of Montfaucon. Now the Germans counter-attacked and what little was left of the pretty eastern Argonne villages fell to the renewed German artillery barrages. On the morning of 21 September the Germans reoccupied the shattered remnants of Varennes. By the 24th they had advanced as far as Vauquois, a hill town further south.

After a few days' rest, Rommel and the 124th Württembergs started to push south again. On the night of 22/3 September they took part in the attack on the Bois de Bouzon. Having routed the French, they marched south through the forest as far as the Varennes–Four de Paris road. They were now in the vicinity of the forest crossroads where the old *Haute Chevauchée* cut through the centre of the forest and crossed the main road. On the morning of 24 September Rommel and his men crossed the main road into French territory. Seeing men moving through the dense under-growth, Rommel was unsure whether they were friend or foe. Moving closer, he saw they were French and immediately opened fire on them; when he ran out of ammunition, he charged them with his bayonet fixed. An accomplished bayonet fighter in peace time, he was confident he could rout them. But as he charged, he slipped on the muddy ground, giving the French an opportunity to open fire, hitting him in the thigh. The French took flight and Rommel was evacuated to a field hospital at Montblain-ville. For his action he was awarded an Iron Cross, Second Class. His wound refused to heal, so he was sent back to Germany to recover.

In Varennes all the men left in the village under the age of 60 were declared civil prisoners on 8 October and were sent 500 miles east to an internment camp at Zwickau in Saxony for the duration of the war. The rest of the villagers eked out an existence of sorts among the caves and cellars, with little food and in constant fear of bombardment. In February 1915 the Germans decided the remaining sixty inhabitants must leave. They sent them on an appalling journey that took forty days, travelling through Germany and then Switzerland before finally crossing back into France at Annemasse, on the Swiss–French border.

To the west the Germans advanced south again, ending up just north of Vienne-le-Château. The French had placed a small screening force just inside the forest, on each side, to prevent the German Fourth and Fifth Armies entering and joining forces. To the west and north-west of the Argonne the front lines consolidated as the 'race to the sea' began. In order to protect themselves from shellfire, which had now become the biggest threat to life, the men dug trenches. As the autumn rains fell, the French soil turned glutinous. Germany was now fighting a war on two fronts and Paris had not fallen. For the Germans, the Schlieffen Plan was now dying in the autumn rain and mud. Military historians have debated the failure of the plan for over a century now. The reasons vary: the plan was a failure from the minute Germany opened the campaign on the Western Front and simultaneously found itself fighting the Russians on the eastern front, or it was just down to plain bad luck; all great and suc-cessful generals need luck on their side and Moltke had none. Whatever the reason for the failure, new war objectives and plans would have to be devised by the incoming German Chief of the General Staff, General Erich von Falkenhayn, the former War Minister and Prussian officer, the personal choice of the Kaiser. Each army's new weaponry had proved a success, but the casualties were appalling on all sides. The combined casu-alties of all the armies were over a million men killed or injured in the first few months alone. The ordinary Austrian, Belgium, British, French, German, Hungarian, Italian, Russian and Serbian soldier had paid a heavy price for their commanders' implacable belief in frontal assault against the full panoply of modern weapons. In addition, hundreds of townspeople and villagers had been killed, many of them murdered in cold blood, and thousands more displaced. The landscape along the newly forming front line was bleak: a panorama of destruction on a scale never seen before of smashed and destroyed property, land and forests. Barbed wire marked the spreading front lines, and in between lay the newly christened 'No Man's Land'.

The Germans' new blue-grey uniform, which a witness described as 'an endless grey mist' as they advanced, had provided some camouflage, as did the British khaki uniform. It was the French with their nineteenth-century blue coats and red pants who were the most conspicuous. Even their blue *kepis* had a red top that could be identified by German aircraft.

In the Argonne Forest little stirred, but a new and vicious war was about to break out as each side sought to consolidate and build a line across the forest. French troops were the first to seize the initiative and take the war to the Germans. With the help of local hunters and foresters, they were able to penetrate the dark thickets and wage a guerrilla war on the few Germans who ventured inside. The Germans, lacking local knowledge, largely remained outside on the main roads and tracks. Here the French were able to ambush them unexpectedly and then retreat back inside the depths of the forest.

Communication between groups on both sides was by means of a century earlier, hunting horn, bugle or drum. Unlike on the rest of the Western Front, the campaign in the forest was initially fought with little artillery support. Lines of sight were limited by the dense, high, forest canopy and scrub, so exact locations were hard to pinpoint. Elaborate ladders were built up the tallest trees on hilltop positions, where men sat on platforms hidden in the foliage. From there they passed signals down to the ground, which meant that initially at least, bringing down accurate fire was more a triumph of hope over expectation. Soon, though, more sophisticated planes and balloons appeared with observers to guide the artillery fire.

Each side pushed into the forest and cleared land around their positions to provide clear sight lines; this enabled aerial observers to better locate enemy positions and bring down more accurate artillery fire. Soon each side was hastily erecting improvised camouflage to extend and protect their established positions from aerial observation.

During the autumn months of September and October 1914 each side probed further into the forest seeking information on the enemy. Although accurate maps of the forest existed, there was no information on exactly where the enemy was. During this early phase it was the French who had the upper hand; with local knowledge they could move around freely in the forest looking for the German locations. For the Germans it was a different story: the French would allow German troops to approach and then open fire at short range, just 5 to 10 metres. The French would then withdraw and, as the Germans resumed the advance, they would once again be ambushed. What follows is a German account of a patrol:

> We tried in the days ahead to penetrate the dense forest, but everywhere we came under fire. It was as if the forest was bewitched and cursed. It caught many a brave and fearless German soldier. A scream of death would sound in the dense bushes and a corpse never to be discovered would decay in the undergrowth.
>
> Smaller formations in columns that were supposed to penetrate a bit more deeply, using fire breaks and hunting trails, encountered wire obstacles and barricades. The unseen enemy, like a garden spider in a web, waited everywhere in ambush. Then all about there were wild flashes and banging. Aroused by the malevolent manner of the attack, the riflemen surged forwards. Flashes of red trousers could be seen in the dense undergrowth. Forwards! But they had already disappeared as if the earth had swallowed them up. Move on after them! The thorny undergrowth tore clothing to shreds, legs tripped over concealed wire, the hazel bush branches struck you in the face and fire was already blazing once again from a hundred barrels.
>
> Orientation was partly lost. In rows and groups the infantry painstakingly worked its way forwards. Minor encounters against smaller enemy sections broke up the lines completely. Isolated groups of French soldiers fired into the rear, adding to the general sense of unease. Here and there prisoners were taken. Losses occurred which increased the insecurity.

The French pushed troops forward of their main positions to break up German attacks before they could build up any momentum and snipers were placed in high trees to kill advancing Germans below. The French also became adept at disguising themselves as Germans to lure unsuspecting soldiers into ambushes. For both sides another hazard was artillery shells, which randomly hit tree tops in mid-flight and exploded, killing or injuring anyone, friend or foe, in the immediate vicinity.

Despite their difficulties, the German campaign was still essentially an offensive one. They needed to break through the forest and decisively engage the French Army and cut off the railway and road access at Les Islettes and Clermont to Verdun in the east, thus driving a wedge between the French Fourth Army of Champagne and General Sarrail's Third Army, guarding the fortresses above Verdun. They also hoped to link up with German troops in the St Mihiel salient, a major bulge in the French front line, south of Verdun.

On 29 September the French started to construct what was to later become their third line of defence. Using an east–west forest track, a defence line was built on the northern side of the forest from Lachalade in the west towards Boureuilles and Neuvilly in the east. Known as *abatis* in earlier centuries, the obstacles comprised felled trees, with sharpened branches facing towards the enemy. These were placed three deep across the width of the forest and the line was completed on 9 October 1914.

It was not long before the Germans, who also lacked modern materials to build defences, began doing the same. Each side selected the best ground it could and slowly but surely built a haphazard line of scrapes and trenches stretching from the east to the west of the forest. Steep ravines, gulleys and all manner of natural obstacles prevented the lines from being in any way straight. From the English Channel to Switzerland, what had previously been mobile warfare had now been replaced by positional war-fare (*Stellungskrieg*). This transition on the Western Front from mobile to static was not one that was brought about intentionally; rather it arose from force of circumstances and therefore occurred almost unconsciously.

One early arrival in the Argonne was Marc Bloch, who later went on to become one of France's most distinguished historians. Sergeant Marc Bloch served in the French 272nd Infantry Regiment and arrived very early in October. He had already taken part in both the initial French advance and the subsequent retreat in August 1914. He wrote about the early days in the Bois de la Gruerie (West Argonne), where chaos and confusion reigned over a poorly equipped army that had not trained for this type of combat. French military doctrine had cherished dash and élan out in the open, not defence in trenches amid the deep cover of the forest. Bloch now saw the war in different terms; Carole Fink's beautiful trans-lation gives us an eerie understanding of what it was like for the men in the front-line trenches:

It was the nights that terrified the *Poilu* [French soldier; lit. 'the hairy one']. The thickness of the undergrowth made the night all the blacker. Night is not silent in the forest. The rustling of the branches, the light grating of the dry leaves, tossed to the ground by the wind, and the occasional sounds of wings and paws, all this music of the shadows, so faint, so incessant, disturbed us. We were afraid we would not hear the Germans in time if they advanced.

Digging tools were either unavailable or of too poor a quality to enable men of either side to dig down through the *gaize*. These initial 'trenches' were no more than shallow shell scrapes, not joined, just scattered along a rough line and connected by footpaths. In the dark men had no contact with anyone other than their comrade in the scrape with them. Barbed wire was also almost non-existent in this sector, and at night men strung ordinary wire between scrapes so they knew where their comrades were. To the front of their positions, tin cans containing stones were suspended from trees, bushes and wire to provide early warning of any potential German advance. Men would not put their heads over a trench parapet for fear of being shot. German machine guns chewed away the parapet tops, which had to be built up as men could not then dig down deeply enough. If men failed to stick their heads up occasionally and return fire, then the Germans would break down the parapet and creep in under the fire, jumping into the French shell scrapes and killing the occupants.

One event that all men feared was coming up into the line and occupying a new position. Here they were disorientated and knew nothing of the enemy's disposition. At such times they were very vulnerable time to attack, and the Germans lay waiting for such opportunities. Dangers were everywhere for both sides, and the randomness of death from a stray round or shell was ever-present. Even in the rear areas, where in theory men were safely away from the front line, a stray round could still kill.

Nights became busy for the troops at the front as better tools and wire started to arrive, so now each army could really dig down, out of sight of the other. Days were spent sleeping, with some men on watch and others repairing any bomb damage and correcting work done in the night. Both sides worked that way. Slowly but surely the men dug down and the shell scrapes joined together into a trench network, which grew deeper and longer.

By the end of October 1914 each side had established a rough front line with a network of support trenches, and second and third defensive lines across the forest. The war, though, was now entering a new and even more deadly phase. Autumn was turning to winter and men now had to fight not only each other but the elements as well. In the Argonne bubbling streams became raging torrents in minutes; ground previously firm underfoot now became a quagmire. Constant heavy rain collapsed trench walls and shelters, burying men alive. Trenches filled with water; uniforms rotted on men; food went off, in particular bread, a staple part of the diet for both French and German soldiers. Weapons and ammunition rusted and became unserviceable without constant maintenance. What few roads and tracks there were to resupply the front lines became all but impassable. They had to be rebuilt with log surfaces.

Although Uncle Bob drove round the front in his car, the bulk of the transport work was done by horses, which pulled everything from artillery pieces to ambulances. Donkeys and mules carried loads up the narrow tracks into the forest and casualties back out. High death rates among the four-legged beasts of burden meant France was soon scouring the French countryside, as well as Spain, Portugal and North Africa, for replacements. It wasn't long before, with Britain, they turned to the USA to buy horses and mules to meet the insatiable demand for animals at the front. Britain had already established strong links with American horse traders a decade earlier. The Boer War of 1899–1902 had created an insatiable demand for horses and mules for front-line duty.

*   *   *

As more accurate artillery fire smashed down the trees on the front line, leaving stumps, and the leaves fell away in the autumn from the few remaining trees, cover became sparse so that men could now see each other clearly for the first time. In some places the trenches were only yards apart, and here elaborate cricket-style nets had to be rigged above the trench parapet walls to prevent grenades and bombs being casually lobbed into opposing trenches.

The eeriness of the new landscape developing along the whole Western Front was dramatically described by Frenchman Louis Barthas:

> Nothing by which to orientate oneself, no landmarks, no trees, after having travelled several hundred metres of this ravaged landscape, our impression at the limit of the horizon was of unmeasurable annihilation. We felt we were lost in the middle of an immense desert; it was impossible for us to judge where we were going, or whence we had come; cowering in a shell hole, we both sought vainly to fix a sense of direction by means of the flares or the reports of guns.

Gouraud oversaw the consolidation of the French positions and put fire into the defending troops, earning himself the nickname 'the Lion of

Argonne'. In early October 1914 Bob wrote in a brief note to his family: 'I'm right in the thick of it with General Gouraud fighting every day, bullets and shells all around us. I'm driving and interpreting for the general who goes everywhere and sees everything. It is awful! We do not know what a bed is, no time to take our clothes off for days.'

For the Germans, the arrival in mid-October of General Bruno von Mudra, XVI Corps commander, brought about a much-needed improvement in troop morale. Mudra's XVI Corps was part of the Fifth Army, which was now responsible for the entire forest frontage. Both Gouraud and Mudra endeared themselves to their men by becoming regular visitors to the front-line troops, sharing their hardships and dangers.

Mudra realised that an advance through the forest and a decisive engagement with the French Army was now extremely unlikely. New tactics would need to be employed. Particularly with unity of command, all arms would now have to work together in order to first break through the French forest fortresses and defences. These were becoming more impregnable by the day. Mudra noted that once the enemy was engaged, leadership quickly dissolved in the dense forest thickets. He needed to devolve leadership down to small groups, away from the traditional German hierarchical military chain of command. He also acknowledged that the men on the front line had a far better understanding of the ground than the generals in remote HQ châteaux, miles away. These generals, Mudra thought, should issue general strategy and directional orders but leave the detail of the operations to the men at the front.

In order to breach the French defences it was now imperative for German infantry and sappers to work together. This happened in two ways. The first involved engineers tunnelling under the enemy trenches to place mines; when these were blown, the infantry rushed through the newly created gaps. The second method involved Pioneers driving *saps* (trenches) forward, towards the enemy front line, and then rushing the position. Mudra insisted that every attack had to be planned meticulously. He wanted the new group of junior leaders to show boldness and initiative in their attacks. He was also hopeful that a regular pattern of raids and actions would keep the men's fighting spirit up; otherwise he was afraid they would become defensive-minded and prefer the security of their trenches. The anxiety of constantly awaiting an attack was for many on both sides worse than an actual attack.

On 23 October Mudra's new style of leadership and devolved operation to junior ranks bore fruit. At 7.45am a small attack by men from the

34th Infantry Division left the German trenches with no preparatory artillery or mortar fire. They simply rushed the French front line; such was the surprise and confusion that the French were quickly overwhelmed. Other adjacent units, seeing the success of the attack, quickly surged forward without waiting for orders and a whole section of the French front fell quickly into German hands. Later in the war Mudra's newly formed small volunteer assault groups would became known as Stormtroopers, a role that evoked the spirit of medieval German mercenary pikemen known as *Landsknechte*, who were feared across Europe for their formidable fighting skills, discipline, sacrifice, comradeship and bravery.

Once either side had breached an enemy trench, 'rolling up' was the normal practice; that is to say men dispersed to both left and right of the breach, to expand the sector of trench held. Once trenches were stormed and 'rolled up', sandbags were built up at the furthest point of penetration to provide cover from a counter-attack. Both the Germans and French always tried to counter-attack rapidly before the positions became impregnable. In the confines of the trenches the weapon of choice was not the rifle but the bomb or hand grenade. German troops improvised a small wooden bat with explosives attached that could be hurled at advancing or retreating French troops. These were later developed into the more widely used *Stielhandgranate*, better known as the 'potato masher' or stick grenade. It was in the Argonne forest that such new tactics were born, and from here they later made their way into the mainstream German Army.

The French had begun the war equipped with the 1847 ball grenade, which was difficult to ignite and had poor fragmentation, creating more bang than real damage. The main problem with it, though, was that when it rained the grenade became damp and for the most part would then fail to explode. The French troops responded with improvised wooden 'pétards' or 'hairbrush grenades'. An imported Italian grenade, 'the Besozzi', supplemented these in early 1915. It was not until later in 1915 that the Model F1 grenade appeared, which encompassed the much-needed improvements in ignition, fragmentation and weather-proofing.

After any action, both sides rapidly repaired damaged defences as quickly as they could. Men arrived carrying more wire and stakes, and the Germans brought in their 'body shields', heavy iron bullet-proof screens that were placed on top of the sandbags and provided valuable cover. Many of the sandbags also contained concrete; once in position, water was added to 'set' them in place. Men could now watch for the enemy or fire back in relative safety. For men holding a newly taken position, the tension could become unbearable as they waited for a counter-attack or, as they were now in a known position, for enemy artillery fire that could rain down quickly and accurately. Their worst nightmare was that the position would be tunnelled underneath and mined, and they would all be blown to kingdom come.

The walking wounded from any attack or explosion were the lucky ones. They could make their own way back for treatment through the labyrinth of support trenches to an aid station. French front-line casualties who were blinded, had lost a limb or were unable to move on their own depended on the bravery and skill of the *brancardiers* (French Army stretcher-bearers). These men were usually the regimental musicians. They would crawl forward into no man's land, often under fire or at night, to recover the wounded, literally dragging them back into the trenches.

The trench system did not follow straight lines but zigzagged, to stop shrapnel from blasts travelling along them and making them more defensible once the enemy had penetrated them. Carrying a wounded man on a stretcher along the zigzagging trenches was out of the question; they either had to be carried 'piggy back' or were loaded into canvas sheets and carried/dragged along the trench network. Only when they were clear of the support trenches could the injured men be loaded onto proper stretchers and transported on two-wheeled carts or, in many cases, wheelbarrows. These conveyed them to an aid post where first dressings could be administered. After this they would be placed in the back of a horsedrawn carriage and taken back 3km to Le Claon. Here, out of artillery range, they would be assessed and in many cases given morphine for their pain for the first time. From here motorised ambulances would carry them to a network of field hospitals well behind the lines. Some 28,000 *blessés* (injured men) passed through the Les Islettes *ambulance* (military hospital) before Christmas 1914. This process was time-consuming and extremely painful for severely wounded men, and the death rate was very high. It takes little imagination to see why so many died in the chaos that reigned during the first few months of the war as each side in turn advanced and then retreated, with no real system in place for treating the injured on either side.

Early in November 1914 Bob wrote:

I'm pleased to think I'm doing my share for my own country and France. I have long been waiting the opportunity and now it has come. My fifteen years as a manager for Dunlop's on the continent is very useful as I know Europe and speak several languages. My trips overseas to India, Siam and Straights Settlements, Surinam and Ceylon for Napiers and South Africa for Mors, have been good training for this war, as they taught me much about motoring under all sorts of difficulties. My first day of service totalled 400 miles, in ten hours. Then 900 miles without stop. My total miles to date, 14 October, is 18,000 miles. The motor service plays a most important part in this war. Armies and towns are moved by motorcar. The French Army have no fewer than 45,000 motor vehicles, so many with each Army Corps, each with their supplies and travelling repair shops and staffs almost ready to build a new car if necessary.

It is a new arm of the service, but it will be quite believed that in this respect the French are quite up to date. The repair trains are always full of work, for the service is much too severe for many cars. Take my own car, for instance. Without consideration of the distance covered. I have run my car for days and nights practically without a stop of any importance and frequently over roads so frightfully cut up that I have had to cover miles and miles upon first and second speeds and six times in two days hauled out of morasses by horses.

We have received sets of hauling ropes, Parsons Chains and glycerine for the radiators; it looks like we are in it for the winter. I am more than lucky to be driving General Gouraud as I have to take him into the very thick of it, sometimes too thick. One night I shall not forget in a hurry we drove most of it through a huge forest without any lights as the Germans were thick about. In addition to much road obstruction, we are frequently held up by the prone bodies of the dead and wounded lying all over the road, to say nothing of the artillery trains, troops, and transport.

Dead horses, too, are not a nice sight at night; the poor animals are having a very bad time of it, but thanks to motorcars they are spared a lot of it. Motorcars supply us with light, post, telegraph, food etc and indeed, the progress would be slower without them, but sometimes they are too fast. One night the Germans brought a few thousand troops forty-two miles by means of motorcars. We have captured many German cars, but they now find it very hard to get any of ours, as we are advancing all the time now. But even when we were retreating we carried the broken-down cars with us.

I am more pleased than I can tell you to be in the French Army and to wear a French uniform as I get a big reception everywhere. My French comrades always offer to share anything they have to eat or drink, or half their straw when they are resting, but, in addition, I have thoroughly acquired the art of getting quite a refreshing sleep in a car. I am beginning to feel I have almost seen enough of the horrors of this war, and like many others, I shall be more than glad when we arrive at the finish, which must be Berlin. Destruction reigns wherever the Germans have passed, and we have shot many of their spies left behind.

The German shells are terrible enough, but from what I have seen the French shells are even more effective. I will not give any details, as they are too horrible to mention. It is a fearful thing to see your officers and friends struck down all around you. But notwithstanding all these trials everybody is as bright and happy as possible, borne out by the cheering thought of attaining in due course the great end we have in view.

Life at the front followed a similar pattern for men on both sides. Most spent a fixed period on the front line, usually five to seven days, before being relieved. The Germans in 1914, though, had to spend up to three or four months at the front with little or no relief, as there were simply no replacements for them. When reinforcements did arrive, the rest camps built to the rear in the forest became known as Hüttenlager ('hut or cabin camps'). These over time grew to include cinemas, delousing and hot shower blocks, canteens and beer gardens and in the odd case even a swimming pool. At the camps behind the lines, men cleaned up, rested and re-equipped and waited for replacements for the men killed, and men returning from leave or from injury. Burial services were held for those who had died in the line. There would also be parades and inspections, and medal ceremonies attended by visiting generals. When a big push was imminent, they would move further back to training areas.

Behind the front lines, the French rest camps (*cantonments*) lay scattered in the forest and surrounding villages, such as Vienne le Chateau, where men, previously Germans and now French, wandered around wearing fezzes, which were manufactured locally for France's North African Army. The villages of La Harazée, La Placadelle, Florent-en-Argonne, Le Claon, Le Neufour and Les Islettes also served as army *cantonments* or garrisons.

In the forest itself settlements appeared as both sides dug into the reverse slopes of hills, so that shells would pass over the top of them. To create the illusion of home, they acquired shop-like fronts, which also enabled men to stand up or sit in some degree of comfort. The main shelters dug into the hillsides only permitted crouching and sleeping. These shopfronts were made from all manner of battlefield detritus. Stone and brickwork were reworked and used for walls, topped by windows and doors salvaged from destroyed buildings in nearby towns and villages.

Trees along the front lines were destroyed by shelling, mines or being shot to pieces. Behind the lines, though, tree-felling was forbidden as they provided vital cover from aerial observation as men and supplies were brought up to the front. Wood, which was needed urgently at the front, had to be felled in forests further back, out of artillery and aircraft observation range. In the rear areas forests were designated for specific wood requirements, such as providing prop shafts for mines, walls and duckboards for trenches, supports for *abris* (underground shelters) and other shelters, fuel and charcoal. Sawmills were established nearby in Les Sennards, Aubréville, Auzéville and Lochères and in the Biesme valley to mill the wood into shape. The wood was initially transported on narrow gauge railways, then pulled by horse to stores in St Pierre Croix and Les Islettes, before being moved by man and mule up to the front line.

In mid-December 1914 Bob wrote:

It is a trying time, especially for men in the trenches, but we are fighting in the right cause, and that gives us courage and perseverance. The roads as you can understand are worse than ever, and we are having very rough work with our cars; but it is wonderful what they stand, when put to it. The war is long and getting hard, but I do not regret giving up a comfortable berth to do my bit against these bandits. It is a great moral satisfaction to me and will bring its own reward after victory, if I pull through. It's a near thing many times a day, but a miss is as good as a mile, n'est pas? I'm right in the thick of it with General Gouraud.

I have been present at some magnificent battles, although horrible, for it is all artillery and underground work now. The war in the air is frost [a Victorian and Edwardian term for 'lacking' or 'a poor show'] and has not given the results expected. On the other hand, we have this morning blown up lots of '*boches*' in their trenches by a mine. What a war!

As Christmas 1914 approached, so did the coldest winter in living memory. Snow fell thickly, covering the forest; the men's uniforms and boots were covered in mud and frozen stiff. Snow settled on the Garibaldis' kepi peaks, freezing their beards and moustaches as they stood around camp fires and in trenches. Men shivered in frozen trenches and desperately waited for relief to go back into the dark underground *abris* where they could huddle over a smoking fire; condensation ran down the walls and the air was asphyxiating, but it was better than standing in a trench.

My great-uncle was not the only person to rally to France's cause. On 3 August, the day Germany declared war on France, the French government changed the terms of enlistment for the French Foreign Legion from five years to 'the duration of the war'. More than 60 per cent of the current French Foreign Legion's soldiers were German and Austrian; they were left to guard the desert fortresses of France's North African Empire. To bring the Legion back up to strength, new recruits had to be brought in and trained by trusted and experienced men coming from North Africa. Thousands of men waited patiently to enter the recruiting offices when they opened on 30 August 1914. Among them were 2,000 Italians.

On 5 November 1914 the *4e régiment de marche du 1er étranger* was officially gazetted and its commander, Peppino Garibaldi, given the rank of lieutenant colonel. He was to be assisted by Frenchman Jean-Baptiste de Duplaà de Garat. The Red-Shirted Garibaldis had endeared themselves to the French by rallying to France's cause in the 1870–1 Franco-Prussian War, when Peppino's father Ricciotti had captured the Pomeranians' standard – the only one captured in the war. The regiment's 2,000 Italian men were divided into three battalions, the 1st, 2nd and 3rd, with Peppino's five brothers (Ezio, Ricciotti Jr, Sante, Bruno and Costante) distributed among the three battalions. On 10 November the regiment was finally assembled at Camp Mailly, where the troops underwent an intensive period of training in preparation for the front. On 17 December the Garibaldis left Camp Mailly and marched north to join the war. On 20 December they were assigned to General Gouraud and his 10th Division in the Argonne. The 2nd Battalion was sent to the army *cantonment* at Florent and the 1st and 3rd Battalions to *cantonments* at Le Neufour and Le Claon.

Orders were received on 24 December to march to Lachalade and from there up into the forest to assemble at Maison Forestière (an old forester's house). The snow lay thick on the ground as the hungry men trudged along the glutinous forest tracks. Their food for Christmas Eve had been sent for earlier in Les Islettes, but had not arrived before their departure. Gouraud briefed Peppino that the Garibaldis would take part in an attack the following day, Christmas Day, on the German line at Fille Mort on the Bolante plateau near Abri de l'Ètoile. There would be no 'Christmas Truce' in the Argonne.

As midnight neared on Christmas Eve, Gouraud, the Garibaldis and Bob assembled in the snow-covered clearing at Maison Forestière for midnight Mass, conducted by a Jesuit priest. Above, the ghostly moon threw a dim light over the eclectic gathering. Old ammunition boxes were stacked to create a makeshift altar, over which was draped the Tricolour of the *4ème régiment de marche*. One witness described the sight of Gouraud's candlelit silhouette and the icicles hanging from trees and the altar as one he would never forget. After the service, men exchanged Christmas greetings and small presents in wooden clogs, in the Italian-French tradition. Despite the intense French artillery salvo into German lines, the attack was postponed. Men spent the day in their saps and *abris*, resting on newspaper as condensation ran down the walls.

Peppino had decided that they would have their Christmas lunch after the attack, so for now men made do with tinned rations. Christmas Day consisted of order and counter-order, gossip, rumour and waiting: the staple of every army prior to a battle. Ricciotti Jr allowed the men to brew some alcohol to warm their cold, numb bodies. That evening the men of the 1st and 2nd Battalions made their way through the winding support trenches to the front line. The 3rd Battalion also moved forward but would remain in reserve, except for Bruno Garibaldi, who had managed to get himself attached to the attackers.

It was the Garibaldis' first sight of the front, as they shuffled passed rows of graves, dead bodies waiting to be buried, others dismembered and scattered after shells had blown them from their graves. In the communication trenches they squeezed against the frozen walls to allow the injured to pass by. The floor was a mixture of frozen snow and icy, glutinous mud. The French *Poilu*, poorly clothed for such cold, had just his pipe for warmth. Now it was part of the smell of the front: a mixture of tobacco, cordite and rotting flesh. Everyone froze as a flare, fired from the trench opposite, suddenly illuminated the night sky. The steady rat-a-tat of machine-gun fire and the crump of artillery rounds flying overhead and occasionally landing nearby brought the reality of their new situation home. As the Garibaldis filed their way into the front line, the Germans began to taunt them. Their impending attack would be no surprise to the enemy.

At 6am on 26 December a deafening artillery salvo from the French 75mm guns began, the shells flying overhead into the German front-line and support trenches. The Garibaldis climbed up the ladders and went over the top, shouting '*Avanti, Viva La France, Viva Italia*'. Peppino had said the men must use their bayonets, so hardly anyone fired. The artillery preparation had not cleared enough of the dense German barbed wire and the advancing men were forced to use what small gaps had been made –

directly into the mouth of withering German machine-gun fire. Lieutenant Trombetta was among the first to be killed, along with Chief
Warrant Officer Borgnis and the bugler Gallo.

Bruno Garibaldi was injured in the arm and made his way to the rear;
after his wound was dressed, he insisted on returning to the fray. The
Garibaldis fought their way into the first line of the German trenches,
and then into the second. The Germans, though, were past-masters of
defence; their overlapping machine guns laid down fire into the occupied
trenches and soon counter-attacks were mounted. For several hours the
battle ebbed to and fro until the Garibaldis were eventually forced to
retreat. Bruno was injured for a second time; this time he was hit twice.
Taken to the shelter of a nearby tree, there he embraced Private Oretti
and whispered to him, 'Embrace my father and brothers for me.' He died
shortly after.

By late afternoon the fighting had died down and the Garibaldis
assembled at Pierre Croissée, a nearby forest marker. Four officers including Bruno and forty-four men had been killed, and one hundred and twelve
injured; many more were missing or captured. Many of the injured still lay
in no man's land, including Bruno, and that night men crept back out into
no man's land to try to recover the dead and injured. Trying to recover
Bruno's body cost yet more men's lives as they searched for him, with the
Germans again taunting them. Bruno was eventually located, but it was
not safe to carry him back safely, so the men began to drive a *sap* forward
to reach him. After nearly two days' digging, Corporal Salgemma climbed
out, lifted Bruno into the *sap* and carried him back to the French line.
Bruno was hit again in the head by a bullet as he was carried along the *sap*.

On 29 December a burial service was held for the Garibaldis in the
clearing opposite Maison Forestière – the same place where only four days
earlier they had attended midnight Mass. Bob wrote, 'Everything is done
to pay a last tribute to the heroic dead. Gouraud pays tribute to the dead
and Peppino Garibaldi says he and his brothers are ready to die in the cause
for which their brother had already fallen.' Bruno Garibaldi, a former pupil
at Kings School, Canterbury, was killed on 26 December 1914 and his
body was brought to St Ménéhould railway station on 3 January 1915.
Although body removal from France had been forbidden by this time, an
exception was made for Bruno. Accompanied on his final journey by two
of his brothers, Ezio and Sante, he was repatriated to Rome by train. As
the train crossed the Italian border, crowds thronged the stations en route
to salute Bruno as he passed through.

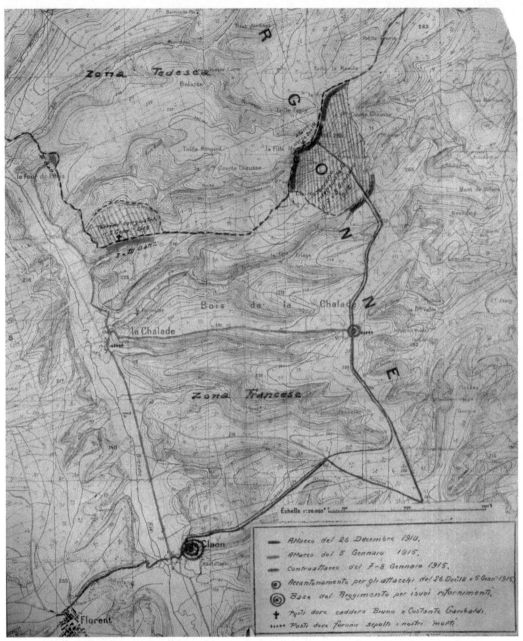

Attacks by the Garibaldis, 1914 and 1915.

After the burial service on the 29th, the remaining Garibaldis busied themselves in their dugouts, making repairs and enjoying the food, drink and warmth. Gouraud now gave Peppino the authority to plan the next attack. Engineers would dig mines under the German front line at Ravin des Courtes-Chaussés. Fresh Italian reinforcements arrived to help replace the men killed, injured or missing following the attack on 26 December.

The village of Le Neufour was a *cantonment* used by troops for rest and recuperation. As it was out of artillery range, large amounts of ammunition and explosives were also stored there. On 29 December oxyacetylene equipment was delivered for experiments in cutting through the German wire. Colonel Cabaud, a newly arrived engineer officer, was due to oversee a cutting demonstration on 30 December. However, at 8.45am on 30 December the ammunition dump exploded, for reasons that were unclear. The Garibaldis of the 2nd Battalion, just back from the front, were billeted in the village and were immediately called to assist in putting out the fires. Two NCOs were killed and another fourteen injured. The centre of the village was totally destroyed.

* * *

A French verb and theatrical term, *camouflage*, was about to enter the army lexicon of new words thrown up during the war in 1914, to join *Poilu*, Tommy, *Boche*, no man's land, front line, trench warfare, etc. Not long after the war started, the little known French stage designer Louis Guingot painted a canvas uniform jacket sent him by Eugène Corbin, an entrepreneur. For inspiration Guingot used the painting styles of the Impressionist School and produced the first camouflaged jacket, known as the 'Leopard'. This he sent to French Army HQ in Paris, hoping it would provide protection for French troops. Sadly, the army chiefs rejected the world's first camouflaged jacket.

However, Lucien-Victor Guirand de Scevola, another well-known painter then serving as a gunner, was about to revolutionise camouflage. In September 1914 he painted a canvas screen to disguise a gun emplacement. While the need to hide French soldiers in their blue jackets and red trousers didn't seem to worry the army chiefs, the need to obscure gun emplacements from aerial observation did. So impressed was Joffre that early in 1915 de Scevola was placed in charge of the newly formed Section de Camouflage at Amiens. Soon he was recruiting artists and their students and they were busy with projects as diverse as artillery screens and observation points disguised as trees to be placed in no man's land. The little known French theatrical term *camouflage* (literally meaning to make up for stage) had now entered the mainstream British and French military vocabulary.

* * *

To stiffen the French public's resolve for what was turning into a long hard slog, propaganda became key. It would not need much effort, though, given the long-standing French enmity towards Germany, dating back to the 1870–1 Franco-Prussian War. Germans were now labelled as *boche* (a German soldier who is slow or a cabbage head). Newspapers and postcards conveyed a steady flow of imagery and stories from the front portraying the lack of culture and barbarism of the *boche*. Popular post-cards sent from the Argonne front included the now headless memorial to the massacre of the 1870 *Mobile* at Passavant, and Hugo's beautiful, but now ruined Clermont, particularly the Church of St Didier. Other post-cards depicted the valour and sacrifice of the Garibaldis in the forest.

For Britain, having failed to warn the public of the likelihood of war, convincing the public that Germany was now the enemy was even more of a challenge. As far as most people were concerned, the Germans had been allies the last time Britain fought on the continent, against Napoleon at Waterloo in 1815. Added to this, the royal family had strong Germanic links. For much of 1914 the British propaganda effort had centred on Germany's invasion of neutral Belgium, the very reason for Britain's arrival on the continent in August. A steady flow of news and pictures depicting 'the rape of Belgium' was drip-fed to the public back in Britain. One particularly shocking story that circulated was that the bodies of the dead were boiled down by the German Army and made into soap.

In August 1914 the propaganda war was helped by a story that entered British Army and public folklore. During the retreat from Mons, the BEF was saved by the ghosts of Henry V's archers of Agincourt, who rained down thousands of arrows on the Kaiser's army, killing them without leaving a mark. Likewise, in September 1914 a fictional short story was printed in the *London Evening Standard*; written by the mystic Arthur Machen, 'The Bowmen' added fuel to the story that became better known as 'the Angel of Mons', which again saved the BEF.

For the French a similar apparition appeared to aid the propaganda war, and entered army and public folklore. Joan of Arc appeared in clouds lit at night by German searchlights, lifting *Poilu* spirits. Joan of Arc was born in 1412, during the Hundred Years War, in the small village of Domremy, south of the Argonne, in Lorraine. At about the age of 13 Joan said she had heard voices and had a vision in her father's garden. She claimed to have seen St Catherine, St Margaret and St Michael, who told her to drive out the English and bring the Dauphin to Rheims for his coronation. The English occupied Rheims to prevent this happening. By 1429 Joan had convinced both King Charles VII and the Catholic Church that she was not a heretic and could lead the country to drive out the hated English. A horse and other military equipment was donated to her. She arrived outside Orléans with the French Army on 4 May 1429 and her arrival brought about a miraculous change in fortune for the army. On the morning of 7 May she was hit by an arrow and retired from the battlefield; later she returned with her banner, on which was the Cross of Lorraine, to inspire victory. The next day the English retreated and the victory was credited to Joan, now known as the Maid of Orléans. With Joan in the vanguard, and her reputation going before her, the French Army swept up the Loire valley, defeating the English all the way. On 16 July 1429 Joan and the French Army entered victorious into Rheims. Charles VII was crowned King of France the following day, with Joan standing next to him with her Lorraine banner. Later Joan was captured by the Burgundians and her ransom paid by the English; now cast by the clerics as a relapsed heretic, she was tried and sentenced to death by burning at the stake. Her stake was built high so the crowds could all see the heretic burn. On 30 May 1431 in the Vieux Marche, the old square of Rouen, aged just 19, Joan was burnt clutching her cross; her last words were heard to be 'Jesus, Jesus'.

It was defeat in the 1870–1 Franco-Prussian War, with the seizure of Alsace and part of Lorraine, that saw Joan of Arc become the rallying point for *Revanchism*. Later, in the Dreyfus affair, a Jewish French army officer was falsely convicted of selling secrets to Germany. The pair became symbolic of the miscarriage of French justice. Comparisons were drawn, that both were innocent victims of a political machine that had scant regard for individual rights. Statues of Joan began to appear in village squares all over France. However, after the passing in 1905 of the French Law on the Separation of the Churches and State, whereby for the first time in France's history the state became secular, politicians had to be a bit more circumspect about using her for propaganda. In 1909 Joan of Arc was beatified. In 1912 her fame was such that British suffragettes used her image on a poster, with the word Justice written across her breast.

Joan of Arc now appeared on propaganda cards and posters, rising from the ruins of Rheims Cathedral, which had been shelled by the Germans in September 1914. Wearing knight's armour, with sword and banner, she embodied not only the spirit of France but also the fight against the invader, the tenacity of the French fighter, *Revanchism*, the sacrifice of French women and ultimate victory. Later she crossed international borders, featuring on posters advertising British War Savings Certificates intended to appeal to women. In 1916 Hollywood sought her out, in a Cecil B. de Mille movie entitled 'Joan the Woman'. Madam Guérin dressed as her while fund-raising in the USA. Once America entered the war, Joan encouraged American women to buy war savings stamps. In the spring of 1918 she featured on the front of a French magazine, between Generals Pétain, Foch, Haig and Pershing, pointing her sword at a map of the Western Front.

In late 1914 French and British soldiers started carrying amulets to ward off evil and death. For the British these ranged from small black cats to Bibles, which would stop a round, if carried in the left breast pocket. For the French by far the most popular was a pendant given by their loved ones, depicting Joan of Arc on one side and Pope Benedict XV (1914–1922) on the reverse.

*　*　*

By late 1914 the dead scattered along the front were becoming an increasing problem. For the French, fighting on 'home ground', the vexed issue of the dead and their burial was to give the government even more headaches. It was made more complicated by the complex French mourning process, in which great importance was attached to there being a physical body to mourn. In the chaos of the early months of the war, amid the ebb and flow of the battle, French families or their representatives had simply located the body of a loved one and arranged to take it home.

Although official permission was required to reclaim a body, and paperwork was necessary, it could still be arranged, especially from hospitals away from the front. In order to bring clarity to the situation, General Joffre, Commander-in-Chief of the French Army, prohibited the transfer of corpses on 19 November 1914 from the Zones of the Armies. He justified this decision to disgruntled families on the basis of equality of mourning (only wealthy families could afford to make the removal arrangements) and a concern for public health.

*　*　*

As 1914 came to an end, the war of attrition continued unabated in the Argonne forest. Lines were consolidated and becoming ever more impregnable. The hopes of 'It being over by Christmas' lay dead amid shattered tree stumps and corpses across no man's land, which now stretched from the Belgian coast to the Swiss border.

Chapter 2

1915

In early January 1915 Uncle Bob wrote:

I enclose a photograph of my car [sadly missing], in which I am always driving General Gouraud, showing the means taken to disguise it from the view of enemy aircraft, when we are within range of their artillery. They always concentrate their fire on any motor car they can distinguish, as motor cars near the fighting line indicate headquarters staff, and are, if detected, welcomed at once by a storm of shells, which is rather too warm a reception even for a general. The spot where the photograph was taken is 400 yards from the German trenches, near enough not to be comfortable.

I spent quite a remarkable Christmas. I was present with my General on Christmas Eve at a midnight service in the middle of the big forest, held amid the roar of the guns and under shell and rifle fire. We stayed there until nine o'clock on Christmas day, and my lunch consisted of two slices of sausage with some bread and coffee, but I had my beef and plum pudding when I got back to headquarters. It was late but better late than never. War, when you are at home by a nice fire, with your slippers on, and smoking a big Henry Clay [pipe], accompanied by a large whisky and soda, reading the latest news, is not easy to realise to its fullest extent. It is more conclusively brought home when you have to sleep in the mud with cold feet and an empty stomach; but on the other hand, you enjoy your pipe all the more when you get it. As a rule we have more food than we want, but there are exceptions at times. My experience since the conflict began suggests to me that most of us eat too much in time of peace, and it is quite good to starve oneself occasionally, but very distressing at first until one gets used to it.

It is wonderful what the human body can stand. I never realised until I experienced this war. This is the most remarkable in connection with the wounded, who are often found alive after three or four days and nights out in the cold and rain, without having had anything to eat or drink. Very often a sap has to be driven to reach the wounded and to protect the rescuers from the enemy's fire.

All civilised countries in the world ought to feel themselves in duty bound to take a hand in stopping these barbarians with as little delay as possible, particularly the United States, who are standing out in a very short-sighted way, as if the Allies went down before the Huns, it would be their turn next, and Germany would blow the Munroe Doctrine to smithereens. As it is I see the United States are grousing because they are not permitted to send the enemy munitions of war. At the same time we are too many for the Germans already, but the more the better so that the end may arrive all the sooner.

You should see the wounded come back after we have taken a trench, dishevelled beyond description. A bayonet charge is a grand thing to witness and I have seen a few, but it is horrible work. When I am in a warm corner and want shelter from the German shells, I find a very good place is with the French Battery; as the Germans try very hard to bombard our batteries, one is safer there than half a mile away. Their artillery is better against towns where there are women and children to be killed. I see, with regret, that you have already experienced this at home, but it will give you more courage than ever.

My General asked me if I would like to be transferred to the British Expeditionary Force, as he has received a signal from General Joffre that Lord Kitchener wished this, but left me free to decide. I am so happy with my General and his staff that I have decided to remain with them to the end, and I hope my friends in England will think I've resolved correctly, as do General Gouraud and my French comrades.

I have just returned from a very impressive ceremony. It was the decoration of a soldier with a *Médaille Miltaire*, which is the equivalent of our Victoria Cross. A military band played during the investment, which greatly added to the impressiveness of the scene, particularly as the function took place on the battlefield with the usual accompaniment of German shells. I hope 'the Boches' heard the music, although I don't suppose they like dancing to it.

Funerals at which the General is present happen alas! only too frequently, but everything is done to pay a last tribute of respect to the heroic dead. One sees graves everywhere, but the only effect is to whet one's appetite more and more for revenge. I was yesterday with the General at the funeral of Lieutenant Bruno Garibaldi, grandson of Italy's great hero and patriot, who joined the volunteers with his five brothers. In the funeral oration over the dead body of his brother, Colonel Garibaldi said 'He and his remaining brothers were ready to die in the cause in which their brother had already fallen.'

I hope, as they say, that the war in the air will deliver better results, but I still consider it a frost. The bombs that I have seen dropped have done very little damage, and do not expedite matters. The only use aviators have proved up to present has been by way of obtaining information, and the services so performed, at any rate so far as they have come within my personal knowledge, have not been of very brilliant character.

I have not been near the British Force for over four months; indeed I have not seen an Englishman during all that time. I am glad to say that I received my copy of *The Autocar* yesterday.

* * *

On 4 January 1915 new orders arrived and the 2nd Battalion of the Garibaldis moved by way of Florent and La Placadelle to La Harazée to await the order to attack. That night the men sat writing what for many would be their last letters. They would attack in the vicinity of Four de Paris and create a diversion to the rear of the main attack by the 1st and 3rd Battalions at the Ravin des Courtes-Chaussés, further south.

At 3am on 5 January the men made their way into the front line, taking over from French troops. At 5am with a deafening crescendo the French 75mm guns poured rounds into the German front and support trenches. At 6am the Garibaldis of the 2nd Battalion climbed over the parapet and charged towards the enemy trenches. The Germans who had survived the artillery barrage fired into the advancing Italians. For the next four hours the Garibaldis bravely battled on but were unable to hold the newly gained trenches. At 10am they were ordered to retreat and move back to the road. At 7pm, under ineffective enemy artillery fire, they moved back to Le Claon.

The 1st and 3rd Battalions were tasked with the main assault. They marched in the early hours of 5 January to Lachalade and then into the forest to the camp at Sapiniere and were issued with wire-cutters. Two companies from each battalion would spearhead the attack. The plan was for the men to make their way under cover of darkness to the French front-line trenches at the Ravin des Courtes-Chaussés. Four passages would be blown through the wire for the 1st and 3rd to follow in the attack.

At 6:30am on 5 January four mines were blown simultaneously in the Ravin des Courtes-Chaussés, causing chaos among both the Germans and the Italians. The French 75mm guns pounded German support trenches and at 7.30am the signal to advance was given. The Garibaldis poured forward, sounding their bugles, to take the German front line. 'Viva I'ltalia', 'Viva la France', 'Viva Garibaldi', 'Viva Trente' and 'Viva Trieste' they shouted as the Red-Shirts rushed across the sixteen bridges that had been improvised over the French trenches to assist their onward rush.

Again Peppino urged the Garibaldis to use the bayonet. The first-line trench fell quickly but by the time the Garibaldis were moving on to the support trenches, the Germans had regrouped and poured fire into the advancing men. Like the attack of 26 December, the battle ebbed to and fro, but the Germans were too well organised in defence. Despite heavy losses, the Garibaldis fought bravely. At 11am the regiment was ordered to move back to Sapinière, as without support it couldn't hold the territory taken. Another hour passed and they were again ordered back; this time they left with the French occupying the ground taken. During the battle another Garibaldi brother, Costante, was killed. Corporal Salgemma, who had recovered Bruno's body, was also reported killed, but in fact was injured and captured by the Germans. At midday the regiments moved back and carried Costante to the church at Le Claon. Uncle Bob described the scene there:

> In the engagement I referred to I was sorry to pass the dead body of another son of Garibaldi [Costante]. What a brave family they are! War makes one very hard hearted, and in the end one gets used to seeing the dead and wounded that one takes no heed. I was just in a church (Le Claon) which has dead waiting to be buried. Tomorrow they will be put in a grave together, dressed as they fell; coffins are very exceptional.

On 7 January 1915 Bruno's funeral was held in Rome amid great pomp and ceremony. For six hours his body lay in state as thousands of mourners filed by. So packed were the crowds on the streets that his coffin, carried by former 'Red Shirts', did not arrive at the family vault at Campo Verano until nightfall. At this point a telegram was delivered to the old General Ricciotti and his wife, saying that Costante had been killed. General Ricciotti pledged 'Italy will avenge you', as Bruno's coffin was lowered into the vault. Outside the angry crowd demanded vengeance: 'Down with Austria, Down with Germany, War! War!'

*   *   *

In the Argonne on the evening of 6 January 1915 General Gouraud warned Peppino that the Garibaldis were now the main reserve unit and must be ready to move back into the forest at Maison Forestière. An assault was expected by the Germans near Abri de l'Ètoile on the Bois de Bolante. On 7 January the 1st and 2nd Battalions left early for Maison Forestière, leaving the 3rd in reserve at Le Claon. They arrived at 4pm and camped, waiting further orders. In the event, the expected German attack on that day materialised in the Haute Chevauchée sector. Touring the front line, General Gouraud was shot in the shoulder at Fille Mort and evacuated.

At 8am on 8 January the 1st and 2nd Battalions were sent to Pierre Croissée ready to support the front line. The 2nd Battalion was split and moved forward to join in a counter-attack at Côte 285 and Ravin des Meurrissons. At last they had a chance to avenge their dead comrades. Undoing their coats to reveal their red shirts to the Germans, they fell on them with bayonets and trenching tools in bitter hand-to-hand fighting that continued all day along the front. They were relieved by a French unit at nightfall.

The troops of the 3rd Battalion were called forward at 10am from Le Claon to Maison Forestière, from where they marched up to Pierre Croissée. Two companies then moved forward to support the battle raging around Côte 285. The other two companies under Peppino remained at Pierre Croissée as reinforcements.

By the end of the day all the Garibaldis were relieved and marched back to Le Claon and Le Neufour. Unknown to them, they had fought their final battle, their valiant endeavours securing their place in the history of the Battle of the Argonne. Perhaps the saddest event of the day was the death of 13-year-old Gaston Huet, the 2nd Battalion mascot. He was buried in the cemetery at Maison Forestière. Costante's body, like Bruno's, was given special permission to leave the front and was taken by train from St Ménéhould to Rome for interment in the Garibaldi family vault.

A few days later the Garibaldis were moved to Grange le Courte farm, near Clermont en Argonne. On 21 January the three battalions paraded and General Micheler awarded Colonel Peppino the French *Legion d'Honneur*. They were to take no further part in the war (at least, not until Italy joined the Allies later in 1915). Political pressure from Italy, still then neutral, brought an end to their gallant exploits in the Argonne campaign.

Of the 2,400 Garibaldis who served in the Argonne Forest campaign, 93 were known to have been killed, with a further 337 injured and

136 posted missing. A total of 75 Garibaldis were decorated for bravery. The eventual number of Garibaldis killed was given at over 500.

* * *

By January 1915 St Ménéhould, well out of artillery range, had become one vast hospital, with all public and large private buildings requisitioned by the state to provide bed space for the vast numbers of casualties.

In early January 1915 the former French journalist and man of letters Raymond Recouly, now an officer in the Moroccan Division, arrived in the forest. He would go on to write many stirring wartime accounts of life in the trenches under various names, including Captain X and Jean-Léry. He first visited General Gouraud, whom he knew from his time in Morocco and Paris. He found him in bed at Lachalade with a slight fever but otherwise in good spirits, considering he had just been shot in the shoulder. He described his 'handsome look, full of clarity and male energy, with a marvellous head of a soldier ... Looking at him alone men became brave. Fortune had smiled on him, the marvellous luck of those touched by Lady Fortune which marked him for higher destiny.'

On arrival in the front line in Bois de la Gruerie, Recouly described the trench line as like the teeth of a saw, with all the interruptions of nature and the enemy. The trees and shrubs were slowly being chopped down by machine-gun fire and artillery. Away from the front line, and the paths leading to it, the forest was dark, thick, forbidding and impenetrable. The Germans attacked a section of front every few days, always in a methodical and extremely violent manner. First came grenades, then a rush with hand weapons, as the trenches were too narrow for rifles to be used effectively. The lack of German artillery support with these attacks always worried the French as they feared it was being saved for a massive assault somewhere along the front line. Every French trench seemed to be overlooked by a machine gun, which opened fire as soon as any movement was seen. In the rain and appalling mud, men spent their whole day just emptying water from the trench with whatever came to hand – plates, cups, trenching tools, anything would serve.

Captured German prisoners revealed their amazement that the French had not capitulated and offered such stiff resistance. Recouly claimed, just as the Germans did of the French, that many of the attackers were under the influence of strong drink. Such was the close proximity of the trenches in the Bois de la Gruerie that even the most experienced men feared accidentally wandering into the opposition trenches by taking a wrong turn. The few lucky ones would be taken prisoner, but most were shot as soon as they were spotted.

A few days later Recouly bumped into General Gouraud again; he was inspecting a unit, with his arm in a sling. Recouly noted how the general questioned the men in detail about their food.

Recouly was impressed by the resoluteness and courage shown by the ordinary *Poilu*s and their officers despite the appalling conditions and the likelihood of a violent death. He reserved a special mention for the miners. In the spirit of the famous army engineer officer Sébastien le Prestre de Vauban (1633–1707), who had successfully laid siege to St Ménéhould and Clermont and brought about their surrender 250 years earlier, Recouly claimed it was a French Army engineer officer who dug the first mine in the Argonne in 1914 and blew it. This officer had noted that all attempts to capture a prominent German position in the autumn of 1914 had failed, with little to show except many lost lives. He said he could dig underneath and blow it up. So mining on the front line was born. Away from the front line, a shaft was dug down and then galleries driven towards the enemy strongpoints. It was slow, painstaking work, with each bag of spoil from the tunnels being passed back by hand and pulled up the shaft, then sprinkled in the forest out of sight of German balloons and planes. Recouly noted the miners' absolute loyalty to each other and the whole squad, and their mutual dependence. If a tunnel collapsed, the men dug with bare hands to rescue their lost colleagues. None of them showed any fear; all miners had to be clear-headed and not daunted by danger. One trapped miner, buried alive, waited twenty-six hours to be rescued, confident that his mates would find him. When a man died, they all took him to the rear for burial, and graves were tended every time the men were away from their digging duties.

The Germans soon followed suit and a vicious underground war broke out as men mined and countermined, blowing up trenches and strongpoints. Men set ambushes and broke into enemy tunnels and vicious fights with pistol, grenades and knives took place underground. On the front line the French cheered as a mine blew and German soldiers flew into the air and body parts came to rest in trees and bushes.

During a period away from the front Recouly noted the appearance of woodcutters from Morvan, who made the first real log cabins for the men to rest in. Men from Africa made wooden villages that resembled those they had left behind. English Quakers also appeared and helped the remaining locals to rebuild their homes in villages behind the lines.

In mid-January Uncle Bob wrote his last known note from the Argonne:

I have had a very hard time since I last wrote you. I will go through one day as a sample.

I left HQ with the General at 4.30am for the Poste de Commandement. At daybreak we sent 1,400 shells in a few minutes, 100 each from 14 batteries, of 4 guns each, and all the shells passed over our heads – you can imagine all the commotion and noise that occurred. Brock's benefit at the Crystal Palace was a simple wax match in comparison.

After this we sent a lot of *boches* into the air by the explosion of mines under their trenches, and in the panic caused by the shells and mines we took three German trenches and 116 prisoners with five machine guns. You should see the crowd leaving the field after an attack of this kind, which are almost a daily occurrence, wounded able to walk, wounded and dead on stretchers, prisoners with their guards.

It is not exactly a football crowd leaving after the game is over. I am shocked to read in the English papers that so many young fellows are still in football crowds at home, instead of helping their country and civilisation out here. No football should be allowed at present, but I will come back to the war.

It is incomprehensible the positions that one finds the dead in, and often one cannot believe one's eyes. One would not think an officer was dead if one saw him with a field glass to his eyes, but that is an instance of what I mean. One gets used to anything in the war.

We recognise the different kinds of bullets and shells by the different noises they make. We know that when we hear them we are all right, they kill or injure you before you hear them coming. You hear a shell but often it has already passed and exploded some yards behind you before you hear it.

Yesterday a Jack Johnson [a black German 15cm shell] or as the French call it Big Saucepan exploded 5 yards from where I was standing; as I saw it explode, I knew I was missed again and still alive. When will this war finish?

If we have to take it trench by trench, in the end there will be more trenches than men. No! some other way or cause will give us victory, which is difficult to guess yet. The French think a lot of our fellows and wish we would send a few millions more. From what I have seen, I would prefer to command a thousand volunteers against three thousand forced soldiers. You can easily understand that amongst the latter many do more harm than good, as their only thought is their own safety, which often leads to the death of others. The trouble is to get enough volunteers when it does come to a pinch and numbers will tell. One volunteer is worth three of the other sort.

I have just heard that the trench taken by us from the *boches* has been blown up by them and some of our men with it. America and Italy should join in to stop this slaughter a little sooner. I have now received the sad news that General Gouraud is wounded, while I have been writing this letter awaiting his return to the car. A bullet passed through his shoulder.

Since writing to you yesterday, when I told you my General had been shot through the shoulder, his wound has been examined and I'm glad to say, it has not been found serious. He is, however, forbidden to use the car for some time yet, and is carrying on his work from his bed in hospital. Accordingly, I'm now resting, which I assure you I need very badly, and I shall continue to rest until he is about again. I hope to go right through the war with him and my Mors.

Since writing to you, General Gouraud has been doing well, and his wound has not prevented him from keeping his command. He is too active and courageous to give way, and has been more than rewarded by results of his fine example.

I was driving him again three days after he was wounded, and as a road we passed was being shelled he asked me if the shelling affected my driving, but as the road was clay and in very dangerous condition, I told him I was more afraid of a side-slip than a shell at that moment, much to his amusement.

I must tell you one or two more anecdotes of the war, all the war news just now is the same. I had been out all day with the General and through some mistake the food he ordered to be given to me miscarried, and never reached me. When he heard of this and referred to me on the matter, I said it was a small moment as the war had taught me that I could go comfortably twenty-four hours without food. A few days after I experienced twenty-four hours without food, and told him my boast had been accomplished. He replied: 'Ah! No, Merry, you said forty-eight hours.'

Here is another, still about food. It was five o'clock in the morning, and we had been hard at it all night, and [were] quite ready for breakfast, but we had no right to have any breakfast where we were without special permission. The officer in charge asked this permission of the

General and was cut very short with 'Permission? I order you! Feed my men at once.'

I was on the bridge at midnight; no, it was a bridge that was being bombarded. An angry Colonel of the Artillery asked what the **** I was doing there? I told him that I had an appointment with General Gouraud, and I was kindly asked to wait elsewhere.

Another, I had to take an order to a town away from the front, and as I had been near the trenches that morning I was a little muddy. The lady of the house where I had to stay had been no nearer the front than the mud on my boots and tried to prevent me entering the house as she said in such a state you cannot enter the house with those boots. I said if it pleased me I should sleep in one of her beds with them on. She fainted and I took my boots off to go to bed as it makes a change after all. Talking of mud I have just been told my car is the dirtiest in the army. I am quite proud of it and should like to drive it down Regent Street. By way of compensation I have just had a bath and a shave.

On 24 January 1915 General Gouraud was promoted to command the 1st Colonial Corps on the Champagne Front. Uncle Bob remained with Gouraud for a further three months on that front. In April Gouraud was given command of the French Expeditionary Corps to the Dardanelles, at which point Uncle Bob was released by the French Foreign Legion and returned to London to enlist as an officer in the Army Service Corps. He returned to the front later in 1915 as a driver's mate. He couldn't be a translator, as he wasn't French!

By the end of January 1915 the Germans began in earnest their systematic siege campaign in what became known as East and West Argonne. West Argonne was primarily the Bois de la Gruerie, which was dominated by French redoubts running along the high ground. The front line ran east along the Vallée Moreau across the Binarville–Vienne-Le-Chateau road, up to the ridge line running east, along which stood the Martin, Labordère, Central 1&2 and Cimetière Redoubts. Then came the main defensive position at Bagatelle Pavilion, a former hunting lodge. From there the trenches ran south-westwards around a bulge known as the Donkey's Nose. A deep ravine pushed the line back northwards to the redoubts of Storks Nest, Rheinbaben Höhe and St Hubert Pavilion, another former hunting lodge. The front line then followed the ridge line south-westwards, crossing the Varennes–Four de Paris road before dropping down into the Vallée des Meurissons and back up to Bolante, climbing back northwards across the road at Barricade Pavilion, another former hunting lodge.

Now in East Argonne, the line swung southwards over the Varennes–Four de Paris road up to Fille Morte before swinging north again back to the same road. Sitting behind here were the two main French defensive positions on the highest points in the forest, Côte 285 and Côte 263. Behind this formidable 10-mile long defensive line sat the French.

*   *   *

Dogs were frequently used in the Argonne. The French trained 1,500 dogs for the medical section (*Société Nationale du Chien Sanitaire*) alone. These dogs located injured men in no man's land or buried in shell holes, under rubble or in dark forests. They would then go back carrying the soldier's kepi or other item and bring the *brancardiers* to help the wounded. Sometimes dogs carried out medical supplies to the injured and in some cases larger dogs pulled casualties back from no man's land. These larger dogs were also used to pull carts carrying ammunition and other supplies to the front. Others were trained as guard dogs to help in the lonely out-posts where Germans were liable to creep up in the dead of night. Another group were trained to carry messages from post to post. Others were adopted by *Poilus* just as companions or as faithful friends at the front.

One such *brancardier* was a local man, Lucien Jacques, who would later find fame as a poet, dancer, wood engraver and artist. He was born in Varennes-en-Argonne in 1891, moving to Paris as a child with his family. Every summer they returned to stay with his grandmother so he spent his formative years in the forest and villages surrounding Varennes, forming a lifelong attachment to the Argonne landscape and nature. Lucien was called up in 1912 and the war started just as his two years' conscription was up in the summer of 1914. He was retained in the army. As a man who did not wish to carry arms, he had been in his unit's band and at the outset of war he became a *brancardier* in his regiment, the 161st Infantry. They arrived at Bois de la Gruerie in January 1915, just as the campaign there entered a violent and awful stage.

On an almost daily basis Lucien Jacques risked his life carrying injured men back to the first aid posts. He noted in his letters that 'The once beautiful Argonne landscape of his childhood had become disfigured by man's stupidity'. He observed the walls of corpses; men standing thigh deep in muddy trenches, covered in greenish mud, a mixture of mud and body parts; the living and the dead were often difficult to distinguish. A drowned German soldier was pulled from the River Meuse, and Lucien wondered at the anguish of the man's family back home, when the news was received. He looked instead for small joys, taking pleasure in the carvings in the few remaining churches, in the spring, in the blue sky and cloud formations, and in the small groups of violets that somehow survived and grew despite the death and destruction all around. Early in the summer of 1915 Lucien contracted typhoid and was admitted into hospital, not returning to the Argonne until after the war.

*   *   *

In mid-January 1915 Erwin Rommel, back from injury and now acting as a company commander, was near Vallée Moreau and Bois de la Gruerie with his men. They were all bearded, for they lived a troglodyte existence amid trenches and bunkers; the war was no longer the mobile one he had left back in September 1914. It was now *Stellungskrieg* ('positional warfare'). The reality of this new phase of warfare was quickly brought home to Rommel when he and his squad were all but buried alive by a bunker collapsing on them, brought down by heavy rain.

On 29 January Rommel found himself in one of General Mudra's localised siege warfare attacks. The Germans blew four mines under the French front line in the vicinity of the Vallée Moreau and Bois de la Gruerie before the infantry, with no artillery support, dashed across the frozen front. Soon Rommel and his men found themselves pinned down under heavy fire. Once more Rommel seized the initiative and mounted a bayonet charge straight into the French front line. He later claimed there were signs of women in the trenches. Crossing through an open section of wire, he and his men pressed on to the French redoubt at Labordère, which they found partially unoccupied. They set about occupying and defending the redoubt from counter-attack. Anticipating a French counter-attack at any moment, and already short of ammunition, food, water and men, Rommel sent a runner back to bring supplies and more men forward. The main German line had advanced 1,200 metres during the attack, an unprecedented advance at that time. Rommel himself was a further 800 metres forward at Labordère, but his position was unsupportable and he was ordered to retreat to the new front line. With the French already surrounding the redoubt, his escape route lay back through the gap in the wire to the north. The retreat was to prove as death-defying as the attack had been. Once more Rommel and his men mounted a bayonet charge directly at the French and managed to force their way back through the gap. For this action Rommel was awarded an Iron Cross, First Class.

A French trench map captured at about this time showed the Germans for the first time the extent of the French line and the names of its principal strongholds. In future they used the same names to avoid any confusion.

There would be months of bitter fighting before the Germans reached Labordère again. Rommel and his men now moved to the east and were repositioned near the French redoubt at Bagatelle. Here life was more agreeable; the position was better built and gave a degree of comfort and safety. Life now settled into a routine, with ten days on the front line and then ten days in the rest and reserve trenches. Among the German troops an 'Argonne spirit' now developed, exemplified by Hermann Albert Gordon's poem and song, composed in 1914 or 1915, which soon spread all along the German front:

Argonnerwald um Mitternacht [Argonne at Midnight]

Argonne Forest, at midnight,
A sapper stands on guard.
A star shines high up in the sky,
Bringing greetings from a distant homeland.

And with a spade in his hand,
He waits forward in the sap-trench.
He thinks with longing on his love,
Wondering if he will ever see her again.

The artillery roars like thunder,
While we wait in front of the infantry,
With shells crashing all around.
The Frenchies want to take our position.

He did not ask why and not how,
Did his duty, as all of them,
In no song was it heard,
Whether he stayed or returned home.

Should the enemy threaten us even more,
We Germans fear him no more.
And should he be so strong,
He will not take our position.

The storm breaks! The mortar crashes!
The sapper begins his advance.
Forward to the enemy trenches,
There he pulls the pin on a grenade.

The infantry stand in wait,
Until the hand grenade explodes.
Then forward with the assault against the enemy,
And with a shout, break into their position.

The Frenchman calls: Pardon Monsieur!
Raises both hands into the air,
He implores us then for mercy,
We Germans, we grant it him.

During this storm a lot of blood also flowed,
Many a young life has ceased,
We did it, however, for Germany,
For the beloved, dear fatherland.

Argonne Forest, Argonne Forest,
Soon thou will be a quiet cemetery.
In thy cool earth rests
Much gallant soldiers' blood.

And I come once to the door of heaven,
An angel of God stands for this,
Argonnerkämpfer, enter,
Here for you is eternal peace.

*   *   *

Edith Wharton was a wealthy and well educated American divorcée, who spoke French fluently. With her position in society and wealthy background, she was able to gain access and make contacts at the highest level on both sides of the Atlantic. Following her divorce, she moved permanently to Paris. She had fallen out of love with what she saw as the newer, brasher and more vulgar America by then. When war was declared, unlike many Americans who left for home, Edith decided to stay. Using her contacts at the highest level in France, she set about offering support for the war, initially helping homeless women but, with the influx of Belgian refugees to Paris, she opened hostels for them too. In February 1915, along with Walter Berry, another committed American Francophile and head of the American Chamber of Commerce, she was given unique access to French army hospitals and the crushed villages behind the French sector of the front. Mindful of the French dependence on American loans to maintain the war effort, the prospect of favourable coverage – one might almost say propaganda – from Edith's pen would no doubt have been behind the unusual permission being granted. Her essays were first published in *Scribner's Magazine* in the USA in 1915. Although considered by some to be propaganda, her unique style did provide some of the first contemporaneous accounts of the destruction at the front:

> The country between the Marne and the Meuse is one of the regions on which the German fury spent itself most bestially during the abominable September days. Halfway between Châlons and Sainte Ménéhould, we came to the first evidence of the invasion: the lamentable ruins of the village of Auve.
>
> The pleasant villages of the Aisne, with one long street, their half-timbered houses and high-profile granaries with espaliered gable-ends, are all much of one pattern, and one can easily picture [how] Auve must have looked out in the blue September weather, above the ripening pears of its gardens, to the crops in the valley and the landscape beyond. Now it's a mere waste of rubble and cinders, not one threshold distinguishable from another. We saw many ruined villages after Auve, but this was the first, and perhaps for that reason one had there, most hauntingly, the vision of all the separate terrors, anguishes, uprootings and rendings apart involved in the destruction of the obscurest human communities.
>
> The photographs on the walls, the twigs of withered box above crucifixes, the old wedding dresses in brass clamped trunks, the bundles of letters laboriously written and painfully deciphered, all the thousand and one bits of the past that give meaning and continuity to the present – of all accumulated warmth nothing was left but a brick-heap and some twisted stove pipes.
>
> ... and below and beyond us lay a long stretch of ruins: the calcined remains of Clermont en Argonne, destroyed by the Germans on the 4th September. The free and lofty situation of the little town – for it was really a good deal more than a village – makes the present state the more lamentable. One can see from so far off, and through the torn traceries of its ruined church the eye travels over so lovely a stretch of country! ... the beauty enriched the joy of wrecking it.
>
> At the far end of what was once the main street another small knot of houses has survived. Chief among them is the hospice for old men, where Sister Gabrielle Rosnet, when the authorities of Clermont took to their heels, stayed behind to defend her charges, and where, ever since, she has nursed an undiminishing stream of wounded from the Eastern Front.

We found *Soeur* Rosnet, with her sisters, preparing a midday meal for her patients in the little kitchen of the Hospice: the kitchen which is also her dining room and private office. She insisted on our finding time to share the filet and fried potatoes that were just taken off the stove; while we lunched she told us the story of the invasion – of the Hospice doors broken down '*a coups de crosse*' and the grey officers bursting in with revolvers, finding her there before them, in a big vaulted vestibule, 'alone with my old men and my Sisters'.

Soeur Gabrielle Rosnet is a small round active woman, with a shrewd and ruddy face of the type that looks out calmly from the dark background of certain Flemish pictures. Her blue eyes are full of warmth and humour, and she puts as much gaiety as wrath in her tale. She does not spare the epithets in talking of '*ces satanes Allemands*' [sic] – these sisters and nurses of the front have seen sights to dry up the last drop of sentimental pity – but through all the horror of those September days, with Clermont blazing about her and helpless remnant of its inhabitants under perpetual threat of massacre, she retained her sense of the little inevitable absurdities of life, such as her not knowing how to address the officer in command 'because he was so tall that I couldn't see up to his shoulder straps' – '*Et ils etaient tous comme ca*' she added, a sort of reluctant admiration in her eyes.

... that if we liked we could see the fighting from a garden over the way. It did not take long to reach the garden! *Soeur* Gabrielle showed the way, bouncing up the stairs of a house across the street; flying at her heels we came out on a grassy terrace full of soldiers. The cannon were booming without a pause, and seemingly so near that it was bewildering to look out across empty fields at a hillside that seemed like any other.

But luckily someone had a field glass, and with its help a little corner of the Battle of Vauquois was suddenly brought close to us – the rush of French infantry up the slopes, the feathery drift of French gun smoke lower down, and, high up, on the wooded crest along the sky, the red lightnings and white puffs of the German artillery. Rap, rap, rap went the answering guns, as the troops swept up and disappeared into the fire-tongued wood: and we stood there dumbfounded at the accident of having stumbled on this visible episode of the great subterranean struggle.

Though *Soeur* Gabrielle had seen too many such sights to be much moved, she was full of lively curiosity and stood behind us, squarely planted in the mud, holding the field glass to her eyes, or passing it laughingly about among the soldiers. But as we turned she said, 'They've sent us word to be ready for another four hundred tonight', and the twinkle died out from her eyes.

Edith Wharton returned to Paris from her travels along the front later in 1915 and continued for the remainder of the war to help both France and Belgium with valuable charity work. She was no armchair helper either: nineteen-hour days were the norm and it's claimed her health never fully recovered from her war work. She was decorated with the *Legion d'Honneur* by France in 1916.

* * *

In March, April and early May 1915 Rommel and his men worked on saps, pushing them towards the French redoubts known as Central 1 and 2. During this time they were under constant shellfire, which added to the casualties and frayed men's nerves. At the end of May Rommel moved back to Bagatelle, where the trenches were now so close together that constant grenade battles took place. With the appearance of spring and warmer weather, the trenches and no man's land began to emit the vile odours of the dead.

The dead were now a recurring problem all along the front line. Joffre's order of November 1914 had forbidden the removal of the dead from the front. Despite this, some dead British officers had still been removed to Britain, possibly even a Canadian. Worse, Joffre's order did not even begin to solve the real problem, which was what to do with the dead. Notionally at least, since the men had fallen in France, all of them – French and British – were now the responsibility of the French government. The scale of the task was overwhelming and chaos reigned on all sides of the front. Into the maelstrom stepped an unlikely hero: Fabian Ware, a British volunteer and fluent French speaker. He had arrived at the front in 1914 as commander of a civilian Red Cross ambulance section.

While moving the injured around the front, Ware had started to map and collate the graves of British servicemen he or his men had seen as they drove around. Almost single-handedly, Ware would shape the treatment of the British, French and later American dead along the whole front for the duration of the war. Early in 1915 one of his earliest pieces of lobbying resulted in a ban on the exhumation of bodies for repatriation to Britain. He also stopped the proliferation of family memorials to the British dead, already littering the front. These, the French were beginning to resent.

Soon Ware was to leave his civilian status behind and assume the rank of major in the army as commander of the newly formed Graves Registration Service (GRS). One obstacle he encountered during the spring and summer of 1915, as the numbers of dead continued to mount, was a French proposal to cremate the dead. They had planned it down to the last detail: huge pyres, sites adjacent to wood sources, woodcutters, petrol or tar to ignite the pyres. No detail was missed in what was seen as a hygienic and space-saving answer to an increasing problem. Ware lobbied both the French and the British against this measure. Given the French attachment to needing a body to mourn, it was hardly surprising that the proposal to cremate the remains never gathered any popular support in France.

This suggestion as a means of body disposal was probably not helped by the circulation in Belgium in the summer and autumn of 1914 of the story that Germany was rendering down its dead and turning them into soap. The German corpse factory (*Kadaververwertungsanstalt*) was a fabrication and probably one of the worst German atrocity propaganda stories to enter public circulation. Its origin was possibly the work of Captain John Charteris, Haig's chosen intelligence guru. Part of his brief was to disseminate rumours and false information. Charteris was also rumoured to be behind reports of the 'Angel of Mons'. Public and newspaper outrage followed the 'soap' story, even in Germany, and effectively put paid to trials the Germans had undertaken in early 1915 with mobile cremation units.

For the remainder of the war men were now buried, either singly or in mass graves, in burial grounds set back from the front line, on land designated for the purpose. All the armies broadly observed this procedure for the duration of the war.

*   *   *

Back at the Argonne front, during the period from February to May 1915 the Germans continued to chip away at the defences around Bagatelle, gaining vital footholds. Once in sight of Bagatelle, the attacks switched to mining, with the French counter-mining. The 'war of mines', as it became known, was fought in two ways. Mines were dug under enemy positions, and the craters formed when they were blown were occupied by advancing troops, while counter-mining saw each side trying to locate the other's mines and then dig into them in order to blow them prematurely.

A German offensive was launched in the west, in the Bois de la Gruerie area, which became known as *Hexenkessel* ('Witches' Cauldron') to the

Germans. To the French, it would become the *Bois de la Tuerie* ('wood of slaughter'). An anonymous eyewitness in Bois de la Gruerie recalled:

> On the right, stand the heights. They are naked, unobstructed! Not a trunk, not a leaf. The trees are crushed, charred, shredded, the undergrowth completely disappeared. The earth is turned, a thousand times mined and torn, full of debris and dust. Craters are like extinct volcanoes. Here are trenches and saps, and during the long months of fighting, everything that grew green disappeared. A machine gun crackles, the projectiles explode. Without a moment's respite, the heights are conquered. A heavy cannon fires. It detonates like a thunderclap and the echo spreads the din in the ravines. Breathe the air, do not you feel anything? It smells like in the corridors of a hospital. It smells of chlorine and other things. This smell is felt if one approaches the Forest of Argonne. The whole forest, full of moisture, has permeated this odour. It comes from gas shells and trenches filled with chlorate of lime. Creepy ...

On the eastern Argonne front the Germans sought to gain a toe-hold on Fille Morte–Côte 285 line, with limited success. Objectives on both forest sector fronts for the most part were localised and tactical: perhaps to straighten a line, shorten a frontage, remove an overlooking machine-gun post or mortar position, obtain better observation of the enemy or remove enemy observation. For each month that this piecemeal campaign was fought through the winter of 1914/15, casualties ran at around 3,000 men killed, injured and posted missing on each side.

Given the Germans' extended lines of communication and supply, it was a marvel of engineering and improvisation that kept the army in the field. Reserve Railway Construction Company 7 laid down an entire network of narrow gauge railways (600mm) and field tramways right up to the off-loading points behind the front guns. The *Argonnenbahn* was a triumph of engineering expertise. By the time of the major attacks in the summer of 1915, steam engines were operating on the section between Lançon and Charleveaux Mill, and from there forward petrol-driven locomotives or horses were used to deliver men and materials to the battle front.

The French ran a similar railway system to support their forest front line. It was known as the *Decauville* system, named after its inventor Paul Decauville. The 600mm narrow gauge railway was used to move ammunition and supplies from the rail head at Les Islettes to the front. The initial railway across the forest was a system used for transporting the local field crop, beetroot, but this was cannibalised for the Decauville system.

A line was pushed from Le Claon north to Maison Forestière, in order to increase the capacity of stores moved to the front. This was further extended to the Ravin du Génie, allowing 40 tons per day of food and ammunition to be moved, along with rocks to keep the main forest road usable. Like the German rail system, it required constant maintenance to keep it operational, as lines sank, embankments and cuttings caved in and shells damaged the tracks.

In the spring, with better weather and more daylight, Mudra planned a major offensive that was scheduled to start on 10 May, but Mudra's plan was thrown into confusion by the French 10th Army offensive further north in the Artois region, which started on 9 May. Non-essential operations along the entire German Western Front were halted, with all available heavy artillery and ammunition being diverted north to support the German lines.

Life behind the front line was not all that easy. Much time was taken up with burying the dead; casualty numbers continued to mount as French artillery fire rained down on the trenches. There was no let-up in the German casualty rates in the Argonne, even on the defensive. Mudra was convinced that the fight still had to be taken to the French. Falkenhayn at OHL had previously cast doubt on the viability of continuing to press in the Argonne Forest. Mudra, with the support of Crown Prince Wilhelm, commander of the Fifth Army, travelled to the now more advanced OHL at Charleville-Mézières to make his case in person. Mudra pointed out that the suspension of offensive operations had not led to any diminution in casualties because of the incessant French gunfire, and that withdrawal was out of the question. Therefore, the only way to move out of the unfavourably placed positions was to go on the offensive, but with adequate quantities of artillery and ammunition in support. Falkenhayn accepted the argument, and agreed that once the pressure in Artois had been relieved, Mudra could have the artillery and ammunition he needed.

By 9 June heavy artillery had arrived on the Argonne front, capable of delivering the latest weapon to disable and dislodge soldiers: gas. All the First World War belligerents in 1914 had been party to the signing of both the Hague Conventions of 1899, which prohibited the use of asphyxiating/poisonous gases delivered by projectile. This was followed up in 1907 with the convention on land warfare that prohibited the use of 'poison or poisoned weapons' in warfare.

The use of gas therefore had a faltering start in the war, with each side accusing the other of being the first to use it. In order to try to stop the German advance in Belgium during the summer of 1914, the French had used tear gas but to no great effect; apparently the Germans failed to notice it. Next it was the Germans who used it in October 1914 at Neuve Chapelle, firing an irritant at French and Indian troops, again with no noticeable effect.

The Germans then tried to disperse tear gas from their artillery on the Russian front in January 1915. A combination of the cold weather and lack of wind made the gas dispersal all but impossible. At around this point Fritz Haber joined the German Army. A physicist, he began work on the discharge of chlorine gas from pressurised containers, which OHL felt was not in direct contravention of the Hague Convention, as although asphyxiating, it was not delivered from a projectile.

During the Second Battle of Ypres in April 1915 the Germans used chlorine gas delivered from pressurised containers against the French. As a bluish-white mist enveloped the Algerian lines, men panicked and fled. Others lay on the ground frothing at the mouth, dying. The Germans advanced in their newly issued gas masks across yellow ground and found 5,000 of the enemy either dead or dying; another 10,000 had fled. For reasons that remain unclear, the Germans, despite having secured such a major breakthrough with their new weapon, failed to capitalise on it. Within days the French, Canadians and British had issued an early version of a gas mask.

*   *   *

In early June Rommel was back at Central, where the saps had been driven far enough forward for the German soldiers to again be engaged in constant grenade battles with the French. Rommel and his men now prepared to take part in the impending German offensive. The French brought extra troops into the Argonne and they watched, skirmished and waited for the expected German onslaught. At 5.15am on 20 June a deafening barrage fell over the forest as over a hundred pieces of artillery and trench mortars opened up on the French front-line trenches and bunkers. It was then the turn of the rear echelons and counter-battery fire. Behind this barrage were the heavy howitzers firing, for the first time, gas shells. Their arsenal also now included another new weapon, the flame-thrower, to strike terror into the heart of the French.

The main axis of the southerly advance was in the Western Argonne and was intended to push the French from their positions in Bois de la Gruerie and along the Binarville–Vienne-le-Château road. The fighting was intense and at close quarters. As the Germans penetrated the French lines they became disorientated in the trench network. Here the French were able, on familiar territory, to quickly mount counter-attacks and lure the Germans towards machine-gun posts. The French soldiers' tenacity and sacrifice in defence were extraordinary, but the momentum was now firmly with the Germans and by nightfall most of the defences on either side of the Binarville–Vienne-le-Château road were in German hands, as was the ground around the Labordère redoubt. With key elements of their defensive positions already in German hands, the French repeatedly counter-attacked from 21 to 29 June with artillery and mortar fire raining down on their former positions. The Germans threw back all the French ground assaults.

On 30 June the Germans went back on the offensive. After so much fighting and artillery fire, much of the front was now devoid of forest and scrub so that each side had a clear view of the other. The Germans managed to dismantle two artillery pieces and move them to within 150 metres of the French lines and fire directly at the gaps. The minor French redoubts fell quickly, as did the major defensive position at Bagatelle Pavilion later that day. Rommel and his men successfully stormed and captured the Central 1 and 2 redoubts. Rommel remarked that he had never seen such devastated land before. Bois de la Gruerie was now a mass of smashed trenches; splintered tree stumps, shell craters full of water and bodies, mangled metal, wire and men lay everywhere. Now they stood in front of the second line of defence, the Green Trench or *Grünen Graben*. German attacks also came in from the east of Bois de la Gruerie from the direction of St Hubert Pavilion. With Green Trench under attack from all sides, it too fell on the evening of 2 July, as did all the French redoubts in Bois de la Gruerie, except St Hubert. The Germans advanced south to new high ground, uncontested.

It was a formidable victory and one unsurpassed at that time along the entire front line: they had seized an entire French trench network. A much-anticipated French counter-attack on their new positions failed to materialise. The Germans who had borne the brunt of the fighting were rewarded with relief and a medal ceremony away from the line. To those who were left on the front line fell the grisly task of removing and burying in mass graves the French dead – over 1,500 men. Prisoner interrogation also revealed that as a result of the German offensive, valuable troops needed elsewhere were now tied up in the forest. It also revealed that General Sarrail planned a major offensive along the whole Argonne front with close to 100,000 men on 11 July.

Mudra now began to plan his second offensive, to attack the eastern Argonne and finally capture St Hubert Pavilion and Barricade and the high ground along a southerly arc from Fille Morte to Côte 285 and 263. Minor operations continued along the front line while the offensive was prepared. A Polish deserter crossed the French line during the night of 12/13 July and informed them of the impending German offensive. The French had already postponed their 11 July offensive until 14 July, Bastille Day. Mudra now planned his assault to begin on 13 July.

Surprise was still with Mudra though, and as with the previous offensive over a hundred artillery and mortar pieces poured death, destruction and gas onto the French lines, support trenches and known artillery positions. Although the French had anticipated an offensive, such was the German morale now that once again their attack quickly assumed an unstoppable momentum.

The initial German advance was toward Côte 263, with the main advance directed at Fille Morte and Côte 285. As with the previous offensive, the fighting was close quarter and hand-to-hand. Each French trench and bunker had to be taken, sometimes at great cost to the Germans. The French defended in many cases to the last man, and ground was not given up easily. The Germans gained positions on the higher ground of Côte 285 and 263 and on Fille Morte in the early afternoon, leaving the French clinging tenaciously to the southern slopes. St Hubert and Barricade Redoubts fell as well, but at great cost to the Germans. The French then counter-attacked and threw the Germans off the top of Côte 285, leaving each side clinging desperately to the lower slopes.

The French press reported a successful counter-attack across the front on 14 July, but the reality was very different. With most of their ammunition used the previous day, some modest advances were made, but the captured southerly forest hilltops remained firmly in German hands. The loss of so much ground was paid for by the removal of General Sarrail as Third Army commander. Never popular with Joffre, he was seen as a political appointment to appease the French left wing, given his socialist views. Political pressure, however, saw him re-emerge with the rather grand Napoleonic title of Commander of the 'Army of the Orient', a title dreamed up by Sarrail himself. He was replaced in the Argonne campaign by General Georges Humbert.

Throughout the remainder of the summer of 1915 each side continued to seek local tactical advantage. On 2 August Rommel and his men were back in action again, this time attacking the redoubt at Martin. Rommel's final action was an attack in the Vallée Moreau area between 5 and 8 September 1915. His personal bravery and attacking zeal had been noted and he was promoted and moved away from the Argonne.

* * *

St Pierre Croix, just off the *Haute Chevauchée* in the Argonne Forest, was an ancient roadside cross, restored in 1848. It was out of artillery range and now served as a storage depot for the front. *Poilus* passing on their way to the front stopped here and crossed themselves. Sergeant Hardouin of the 46th Infantry Regiment saw something more ominous though. 'It's like a vision of entering a cemetery at night. Down there, the gateway: the stone cross on its pedestal, the avenue of disproportionately tall cypresses, and beyond that, the field of death, the trenches.'

In reality, the defences were becoming more impregnable. Each side was now able to see the other along the barren front line. Tunnels were dug to enable troops to enter and leave their front lines, out of sight and in safety. By the autumn of 1915 the Germans had secured their newly won front line running east to west across the forest. On average, the line had advanced about 1,500 metres and now assumed a more linear appearance with most of the previous bulges removed.

The French, though, had stubbornly defended the line, preventing a wholesale German advance through the forest and saving Verdun from being cut off, even though the loss of the strategic high ground at the north-eastern end of the forest now limited French rail support for the town. With the Germans also holding the heights further east at Vauquois and Montfaucon, the rail links after Aubréville from either, St Ménéhould or Vaux Marie were increasingly unable to supply Verdun. The war in the Argonne continued but now it became mainly one of mining and counter-mining, with casualties continuing to mount on both sides.

At the Chantilly Conference held on 6–8 December 1915 the four major Allied powers – France, Russia, Britain and Italy, the Italians having joined the war on 23 May 1915 – agreed to coordinate their offensives in the summer of 1916. The aim was to tie down the German and Austro-Hungarian Army and prevent reserves/reinforcements being moved to support other fronts.

As 1915 came to an end, Fabian Ware pulled off his master-stroke. On 29 December 1915 it passed into French law that the French would purchase, at their own cost, the necessary land (and access to it) for all Allied war cemeteries. It also finally stopped the exhumation of French bodies from the front. The French dead would now remain where they had fallen,

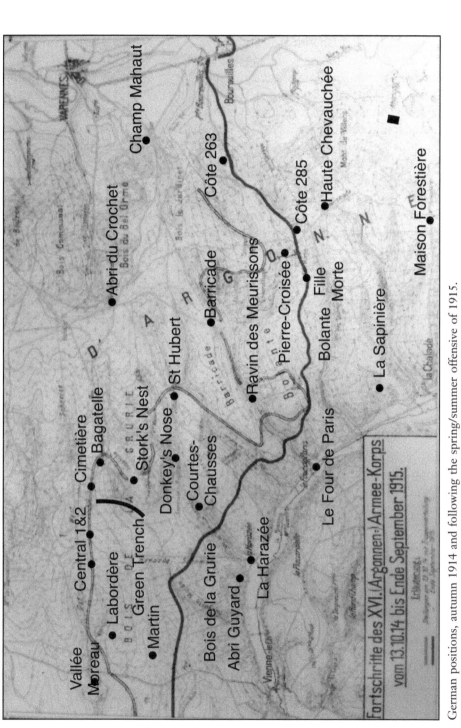

German positions, autumn 1914 and following the spring/summer offensive of 1915.

as would the British and Empire troops. They would also be entitled to individual burial plots. Ware's masterstroke was to have included into the legislation that Britain and the Empire, at their own cost, would build and maintain their own cemeteries. This would later irrevocably change the postwar landscape of large parts of northern France.

At around this time, with deaths on a scale unseen in Europe before and most people left with no body to mourn, a phenomenon reappeared. Spiritualism had been formalised by a French author writing under the name of Allan Kardec in 1857, and it achieved more widespread acceptance during the American Civil War. Then, as now, grief-stricken and bereaved parents, wives and children sought communication with their lost loved ones through mystics, clairvoyants and fortune-tellers. The providers of these services ranged from helpful believers to unscrupulous opportunists. The frauds used a variety of ruses to suggest communication with the afterlife, with no other purpose than making money from distraught relatives. In Britain no less a figure than Sir Arthur Conan Doyle, a pre-war believer in spiritualism, added credence to the growing phenomenon. Its chief exponent, though, was to become Sir Oliver Lodge, a famous radio pioneer, who had published a pre-war book on life after death. After the death of his youngest son at the front in 1915, the following year he wrote a book, *Raymond Life or Death*, about his communications with his son at séances.

*   *   *

On New Year's Eve 1915 men on both sides of the Argonne front line no doubt assumed that once spring came, offensive operations would begin again, just as they had done the previous year in the Argonne Forest.

Chapter 3

1916–17

1916

Instead of a renewed push southwards through the Argonne Forest in 1916, the soldiers of the Crown Prince's Fifth Army found themselves fighting 20 miles further to the east. They were now part of General Erich von Falkenhayn's new plan, Operation Judgement, to attack the heights above the fortress city of Verdun, east of the River Meuse. In the early hours of 21 February 1916 tens of thousands of German artillery rounds landed around the heights.

One of the earliest casualties was Colonel Émile Driant, who commanded the 1,200 men of the 56th and 59th Chasseurs. It was Driant, using his position as a Deputy in the French Parliament, who had criticised Joffre's denuding of Verdun's defences in December 1915, only for Joffre to deny that an attack was likely in the vicinity of Verdun. For almost two days Driant and his men defended doggedly, against overwhelming odds, buying valuable time for the French High Command to reorganise their defences and bring up reinforcements. Late on 22 February they were overwhelmed by the Germans, and Driant was finally killed while ordering the retreat of only a handful of survivors.

* * *

At about this time, Dr Nicole Girard-Mangin was working in an infectious diseases hospital at Glorieux in the suburbs of Verdun. Originally Argonnaise, she was born Nicole Mangin in October 1878 in Paris, and her family lived in Varennes. Their summer holidays were spent in Very, Argonne, staying with her grandparents. By 1914 Nicole was divorced, which had cost her custody of her son, but she was now a qualified doctor, an achievement she had always aspired to. She had hyphenated her name, retaining both her maiden and married names. Fate now played its hand; a clerical error and her hyphenated name saw mobilisation papers sent out to a 'Dr Gerard Mangin' on 2 August 1914. Ignoring the fact that women in France were not permitted to serve in the Army, and wishing to do her bit, she reported to the oldest military thermal hospital in France at Bourbonnes-les-Bains in the Vosges. The medical director there sought to have her removed immediately, but bureaucracy, having made an error, was in no mood to change its mind and anyway they were short of doctors. Nicole was duly enlisted on 5 *sous* a day and given a daily tobacco allowance. There were no women's French Army uniforms, so she was issued a British one instead, comprising a four-patch pocket jacket with belt, an ankle-length skirt and a British Army field cap in lieu of a kepi, to hide her hair underneath.

From Vosges she moved north to help on the casualty trains ferrying the injured from the Champagne Front to Rheims. The army, though, was still in no mood to see her assume the front-line medical duties she aspired to. Early in 1915 she was posted to the quiet Third Army sector around Verdun and for the remainder of the year she continued to work in a number of field hospitals behind the lines between Clermont en Argonne and Verdun. At Baleycourt field hospital she was not allowed for weeks even to enter the tents where patients were being dealt with, and she wrote that she was treated worse than a plague victim. The more she insisted that she wanted to treat battlefield patients, the further from the front they moved her. At the start of 1916 she was posted to Hospital No. 13 at Glorieux, in the western suburbs of Verdun, tasked with looking after typhus patients. Presumably the army assumed that here she was out of sight and out of harm's way.

Soon, however, streams of injured men from the Meuse Heights were entering the hospital, despite the 'Contagious Hospital' signs posted outside. The chief doctor was bed-ridden with a broken leg and was reduced to issuing orders from his bed. Nicole found herself unable to turn away the injured men, some of whom were labelled with specific injuries, while others were simply shell-shocked survivors of the huge German artillery bombardments. Many of them also had burns as a result of the fires sweeping through Verdun. One local French artillery commander came to her hospital just to use the phone as everything had been destroyed at his location.

Outside shells fell all round the hospital, as the injured men told of the brave stand by Colonel Driant and his Chasseurs. On 25 February, with no electrical power, Dr Michaud, Nicole's immediate superior, ordered the evacuation of all patients and hospital staff from the Verdun military hospitals, including Glorieux and its 178 patients. Nicole requested that she be allowed to remain with her patients, but the Chief Medical Officer,

Dr Martin, refused, fearing Mangin would lose contact with Michaud. However, Dr Michaud was luckily passing by and agreed with her request and Nicole and two nurses were allowed to remain with their patients.

Michaud, with tears in his eyes, came to say goodbye and wish her luck, knowing he was leaving her in great danger. The last train had already left the city, leaving her with only one ambulance to move patients. All around them shells fell in a terrifying crescendo and the city burned, illuminating the night sky, silhouetting German observation and bomber planes dropping their loads on the defenders and reinforcements. On the eastern heights above the city, the battle for Verdun raged on.

Nicole and her nurses were only able to treat the steady stream of patients by the headlights of her remaining ambulance. Slowly but surely, over the next few days, the remaining ambulance evacuated the sick towards Bar-le-Duc, until Nicole was finally left with just nine patients. On the morning of 26 February an ambulance arrived at the hospital and took five men to Baleycourt. With the remaining four patients, Dun (her Alsatian dog) and her faithful driver Fouquet, Nicole now decided to try to make her own way with them to Clermont en Argonne, in a car. As soon as it was dark they set off, often coming under shellfire, along the pitch black, cratered road. At some point Nicole was injured by a small piece of flying glass after the windscreen shattered when a shell landed nearby. They drove through Sivry-la-Perche, Dombasle and onto Parois. There she saw a locomotive three-quarters buried in a large shell hole, with only its rear wheels showing. The main train supply route to Verdun from the west was now cut.

Late in the evening the little group arrived at the hospital of Sister Gabrielle in Clermont. From here, due to the large influx of wounded and the contagious nature of Nicole's patients, she was redirected 8km further south to Froidos. The road was full of troops moving up to the front and Nicole's driver had to weave in and out of them in the dark, each shouting profanities at the other. At Froidos, apart from the sound of distant artillery, they were still unaware of the scale of the crucial battle now being fought at Verdun. Nicole was now finally able to leave her patients safely in a large country house. After a hot meal, she and Fouquet set off back to Bar-le-Duc by car, where they arrived in the early hours of the morning. Here she reported to the General Inspector and was given a mattress to sleep on on the floor. The following day she was assigned to Hospital No. 12 at Vadelaincourt, between Clermont and Verdun. On her way there, she picked up two injured men.

Male colleagues were still sceptical of her, but due to the unending sea of casualties she was at last able to really utilise her skills. Shortly after her arrival, she saw the first cases of trench foot and frost-bite, caused by the men standing for days on end in waterlogged trenches. Initially she worked on patient assessment, first aid treatment and suturing, but as the campaign intensified, she was finally allowed to operate, initially minor procedures but later also performing amputations. Between February and June 1916 some 10,800 injured men passed through the hospital. Gas gangrene appeared in the wards as they struggled to deal with the unending tide of misery. Nicole wrote home, noting how the French soldiers called for God's help and the Zouaves and Tirailleurs called out for Allah's help. It was also claimed that during this period she was regularly driven out at night in a vehicle donated by a grateful patient, looking for injured men. In the autumn of 1916, as the Verdun campaign tailed off, she was transferred for a much-needed rest to a hospital in the Pas de Calais region, dealing with tuberculosis patients. Although the medical establishment still struggled to acknowledge her work, her patients did not forget her and presented her with a copper plaque for her service at the hospitals at Glorieux and Vadelaincourt. On it were inscribed Kipling's words from 'Some Aspects of Travel' (1914): 'It is one of the mysteries of personality that virtue should go out of some men to uphold – literally to ennoble – their companions even while their own nerves are like live wire, and their mouths are full of the taste of fever and fatigue. There is no headmark by which we can recognise such men before they have proved themselves. Their secret is incommunicable.'

*   *   *

With Verdun effectively cut off on three sides, the main supply route to the city came via the southerly *Voie Sacrée* ('Sacred Way'), 50 miles of road from Bar le Duc. The architect of this crucial supply route was Captain Joseph Doumenc, deputy to the director of the automobile section for the region. Throughout the Verdun campaign the route transported 90,000 men and 50,000 tons of equipment every week, using 2,000 vehicles a day. With a strict convoy procedure in place, it took a nimble driver and vehicle to move between the streams of men and vehicles moving in both directions.

This was the same Captain Doumenc who a year earlier had first agreed to let a group of young American volunteers help the French injured. The *brancardiers* brought the wounded into the Aid Posts for initial assessment and treatment, after which they faced an uncertain, uncomfortable and at times long journey by covered horse-drawn wagon to the hospitals further back. The American Ambulance Field Service (AFS) had been set up earlier in the war by A. Piatt Andrew to help the American Hospital in Paris. Bored with what was known as 'Jitney' work, he looked for more interesting and exciting work for his young volunteers. Doumenc agreed to give them a trial in the Alsace sector and so was born the *Section Sanitaire Americaine* (SSU), under command of a French liaison officer. All the other personnel were American.

The Ivy League College 'Gentlemen Volunteers' who signed up for a six-month period of service in France not only had to pay their way to France but buy their own uniforms as well. They received the same wages (5 *sous* a day) and rations as the *Poilus*, provided by the French. They were subject to the same regulations and discipline as regular French service-men but were not allowed to carry arms or become combatants. Although their work along the front the previous year had won support and favour amongst the *Poilus*, it was at Verdun that they won their spurs, weaving in and out of the traffic on the *Voie Sacrée* and saving hundreds, if not thousands, of lives by getting the wounded quickly to the *ambulance* (field hospital). Articles written by the Gentlemen Volunteers appeared syndicated all over the USA.

Their vehicle of choice, which enabled them to weave in and out of the specified gap of 20 metres between vehicles on the road, or to divert across the adjacent fields, to and from Verdun, was the Ford Model T Truck (known as Flivvers). These were bought from fund-raising in America and shipped as just chassis and engines to France, to save on shipping costs. Henry Ford offered no discount, despite the numbers ordered, which ran into hundreds. The Flivvers were chosen for their engineering simplicity, lightweight construction, ease of manoeuvre on the narrow French roads, mechanical durability, tight turning circle, their ability to be righted quickly if they turned over or to be pushed out of a shell hole or mud, but above all else, the ability to change parts from one vehicle to another. The earlier experiences of both the French and British Armies and ambulance services with a variety of vehicles had demonstrated the problem of not being able to cannibalise unserviceable vehicles and use the parts on other serviceable vehicles.

Once in France the Flivvers were reassembled, with extended upper bodywork to enable French army stretchers to be slid inside. The vehicles provided for three *couchés* (stretcher cases) or four *assis* (sitting), plus room for two or three more (in an emergency) sitting at the front with the driver. The windscreens were made of rolled canvas, as glass was considered too dangerous. The trucks were initially covered in canvas, later replaced by wood, which provided better protection from shrapnel. They were painted slate grey to distinguish them as non-combatants, with a Red Cross painted on the roof and sides. The unit number was also stencilled on the sides, along with the unit logos, the most famous being Section 1's Indian Chief's head.

Clarence J. Griffin of SSU 12 recalled:

> The 'ambulanciers' are the gypsies of the war. Wherever you go you will see the familiar Ford, either still or moving along, its destination figured in advance. The Ford is a welcome sight to a *Poilu*, he detects the well-known rattling cough of its motor at long distances when all is still o'nights. It often happens that this little tin car is his home when he knows that it will get him to some haven of rest. If not badly hit, he immediately falls asleep when he is put in the Ford. His responsibility is over. Never a word of reproach does he utter if the unlucky driver loses his way or an untimely accident delays his passage for several hours.

Likewise, Henry Shearan of SSU 2 recalled events during the Verdun period:

> During the first week our cars averaged runs of two hundred miles a day, over roads chewed to pieces, and through very difficult traffic. In several of the villages there were unusually formidable shell gauntlets to be run ...
>
> Bois de la Mort, the wood of 100,000 dead, and side by side the living, the soldiers of the army of France, holding through bitter cold and a ceaseless shower of iron and hell, the far-stretching lines. If there is anything I'm proud of, it is having been with the French Army, the most devoted and heroic of the war.

*   *   *

The year 1916 offered no abatement in the trials and tribulations of the dead. The French government set up its answer to the British Graves Registration Service, the *Service Général des Pensions*, within the War Ministry. Its staff had two principal roles: firstly, to help with pensions for the disabled and widowed, and secondly, to act as a coordination service for identifying and burying the dead and recording the location of graves and cemeteries. They were also responsible for maintaining central records of the deceased.

It was the French public, though, who were asked to provide a more basic but vital service. In early 1916 the French President Poincaré helped launch a new initiative encouraging members of the public and relatives of the deceased to purchase a *'Cocarde de Souvenir'*. This was a small metal tricolour cockade in the style worn during the French Revolution, on which was inscribed the name and date of death of the soldier. These metal cockades were more robust than the current haphazard grave-markers, which were quickly falling into disrepair. The cockades would serve as much hardier grave markers until such time as permanent cemeteries, graves and headstones became available.

The initiative came from *Souvenir Français* whose roots lay back in the 1870–1 Franco-Prussian War. In order to commemorate their war dead in the now-annexed Alsace, the graves of French soldiers were given a *cocarde* by girls dressed in traditional clothing on All Saints Day (1 November) each year, reminding people that although Alsace had been annexed by Germany, it was still part of France. One of the movement's founding members was expelled from Alsace and moved back to France, where he established a national *Souvenir Français* in 1888 to take on the responsibility for maintaining the graves and memorials of the 1870–1 French war dead, along with other battle sites, such as Waterloo. At that time there was no official body responsible for this task. In 1913 the Alsace *Souvenir Français* movement was brutally put down by the Germans, who either exiled or arrested its members. In 1915 the main French *Souvenir Français* started to work with the French authorities to manage the new cemeteries and memorials springing up along the front, a task that it continues with to this day.

The French government maintained its strict no exhumation policy at the front (*Zone de l'Armée*) but this policy had a major weakness. In the areas further to the rear were aid stations where many men died from their wounds. Others died in hospitals set up in civilian areas hundreds of miles away from the front. Different rules applied here and French families were still at liberty to arrange the transfer home of their dead loved ones.

With two such different policies effectively up and running concurrently, families determined to be reunited with a dead loved one buried at the front sought other ways to get round the ban. A macabre grave-robbing service came into being. How many bodies were illegally dug up is uncertain, but the number is thought to be many hundreds or even thousands. The conveyors of the battlefield cadavers were sometimes well intended, but others were more unscrupulous, simply exploiting a family's grief. In many cases they brought back no more than a partial body, or the wrong body, or sometimes no body at all, just a coffin of an appropriate weight. Such was the family's grief, though, that having something to mourn was better than nothing. Paperwork was still needed, and therefore a degree of official complicity was also apparent. Prosecutions were few and far between, and in any case the family's grief was so great that no one was going to be sent to gaol.

At least identifying the dead had become easier in 1916. Now French and British (thanks to Fabian Ware) soldiers came to the front with two ID disks, one of which was left with the body when it was buried while the other was sent to the rear with the paperwork. The Germans were issued with an ID disk with their details on both halves. When a soldier died, his disk was snapped in half, and one half remained with the body while the other was sent to the rear with the paperwork. German burial sites initially looked like those of the Allies, with single and mass graves on both small and large sites, scattered across private and public land. For them there were no French laws banning exhumation, but it appears there was little public agitation to return the dead home. Their cemeteries began to acquire an air of permanence that was absent from the temporary-looking French and British cemeteries. They acquired fences, in some cases made from concrete, and had metal gates. Inside, usually in the centre, stood obelisks of varying design and form, often with the names of the missing inscribed on them. As the new German border, in their view, was now here near the front, why should the cemeteries here not look like those at home?

One of the war's more famous poems was written in 1916 by Alan Seeger (1886–1916), an American Volunteer in the French Foreign Legion:

I Have a Rendezvous With Death

I have a rendezvous with Death
At some disputed barricade
When Spring comes back with rustling shade
And apple-blossoms fill the air.
I have a rendezvous with Death
When Spring brings back blue days and fair.
It may be he shall take my hand
And lead me into his dark land
And close my eyes and quench my breath
It may be I shall pass him still.
I have a rendezvous with Death
On some scarred slope of a battered hill,

When Spring comes round again this year
And first meadow-flowers appear.
God knows 'twere better to be deep
Pillowed in silk and scented down,
Where Love throbs out in blissful sleep,
Pulse nigh to pulse, and breath to breath,
Where hushed awakenings are dear ...
But I've a rendezvous with Death
At midnight in some flaming town,
When Spring trips north again this year,
And I to my pledged word am true,
I shall not fail that rendezvous.

Seeger died in 1916 (ironically on 4 July) in the attack on Belloy-en-Santerre, where he was shot in the stomach. Following his death, the French military authorities awarded him the *Croix de Guerre* and a *Médaille Miltaire*. He was buried in a mass grave.

By 1916 Fabian Ware had realised he was now fighting a political battle to ensure the men at the front would be buried decently at the war's end, and so moved to London.

* * *

Technically the villages in the Argonne lay within the *Zone de l'Armée*. Most of them had been evacuated of civilians in 1914, when the first Germans advanced, but some people had chosen to remain. After the German retreat, many more villagers returned with their children, despite not being legally permitted to live in their old houses. Various attempts were made to force them out, but soon they were providing a variety of services that made them indispensable to the army. They offered their houses as accommodation for resting soldiers, they washed and mended clothes, grew food and provided cafés, which ranged from law-abiding establishments to ones that were little more than brothels and sold absinthe, banned owing to its high alcoholic and psychoactive content.

In St Ménéhould, the region's major town, photographers found business booming. They took studio portraits of soldiers bound for or resting from the front, and visited the front themselves to take pictures. The French had none of the British reservation about photographs from the front.

On 2 March Sister Gabrielle and her redoubtable Sisters of St Vincent de Paul were finally ordered from the Clermont hospital, owing to the dangers of German artillery fire. The Verdun offensive was now happening on the western side of the Meuse as well. The new longer-range heavy artillery weapons had now brought Clermont within range. Gabrielle and her Sisters initially went to work at the *Ambulance* 3 at Froidos and then to *Ambulance* 5 at Benoite-Vaux, where they remained until the end of the war. The army units remaining in Clermont now dug caves under the hill of St Anne to provide protection from the regular shelling of the village.

*   *   *

The proliferation of questionable French cafés and bars along the French sector of the front brought to a head the growing concerns in the French High Command about alcoholism and venereal diseases among their troops. In response to this, Marshal Joffre the French Army commander, authorised the expansion of the *Foyer du Soldat* (YMCA).

George Williams, a London draper, had founded the Young Men's Christian Association (YMCA) in 1844. As Britain industrialised and men came from the countryside to work in the cities, there was growing concern among Christians that men were falling under the evil influences of drink and prostitution. Williams founded the organisation to offer a healthy mind, body and spirit. These three virtues were represented in the YMCA's red triangle logo. The virtuous ethos meant the YMCA soon reached the USA, where it underwent a rapid expansion during the American Civil War, when volunteers helped with medical work, running 'Ys' (as the YMCA tents and buildings were known) and improving literacy.

The YMCA had enjoyed early support in France and was widespread in French cities. In 1905 the French government brought in the Law on the Separation of the Churches and State. This allowed people to freely choose their religion and practise it. For the YMCA, though, the most far-reaching change was that the state would not recognise, pay or subsidise any religious group. Their brand of muscular Christianity could continue, but the state would not support it. It was therefore not surprising that in 1914 there were only two *Foyer du Soldat* (YMCAs), both operating well behind the lines in the French sector. They provided a home from home for soldiers resting away from the front, but with no religious teaching. American money started to arrive to support the *Foyers*, which steadily expanded during 1915. It was not until later in 1916, and Joffre's order, that they received their first official recognition. This increased the number of *Foyer du Soldat* to seventy-eight, on the proviso that they concentrated on the 'moral' aspect of YMCA principles, not on religion.

Although there were probably several *Foyers* in the Argonne region, the only one in the official records was at St Ménéhould.

* * *

The American presidential election took place in November 1916. The incumbent, Democrat President Woodrow Wilson, was up against the Republican Supreme Court Justice Charles Evans Hughes. Hughes lambasted Wilson for not making the 'necessary preparations' for a war in Europe. American neutrality had already been badly shaken on 7 May 1915 when a German U-boat sank the RMS *Lusitania* off the coast of Ireland. Nearly 1,200 lives were lost, including 128 American citizens.

But Wall Street continued to prosper on the back of war loans to Britain and France. American farmers sold horses, mules and feed to France and Britain. American manufacturers sold their goods to countries that Britain and France could no longer trade with. Wilson fought on the ticket of maintenance of the 'Munroe Doctrine'. He also reassured mothers that their sons would not have to grow up to be soldiers, a line taken from a current popular song. It was therefore hardly surprising that Wilson was duly re-elected President on 7 November 1916 with an increased majority.

* * *

Back in the Argonne, two powerful mine blasts shook the French front line during December 1916, as the Argonne mining war continued. On 10 December a huge explosion took place on Fille Mort. An even bigger one happened two days later, on 12 December, when over 50 tons of high explosive left a huge crater that is still visible today on Côte 285, adjacent to the *Haute Chevauchée*. The Germans were still trying to dislodge the French from their remaining positions on the lower slopes.

* * *

Howard Burchard 'Rainy' Lines, born in New York in 1891, was an AFS volunteer. As a child, he moved to Paris with his parents, who were ardent Francophiles. He qualified with a Baccalaureate in Paris before attending the Ivy League Dartmouth College in the USA. His mother Elizabeth and sister Mary sailed from Southampton on the ill-fated RMS *Titanic* to watch Howard graduate from Dartmouth in 1912. Both survived the sinking by managing to get on board a lifeboat, and were subsequently rescued by the RMS *Carpathia*.

Howard went on to Harvard Law School but on 8 September 1915 he joined the AFS. On 16 September he was sent to Section 1, working in the

Dunkirk area for the French Army between the British and Belgian sectors. In December Section 1 was posted further south and Lines was given six months' leave in order to complete his studies at Harvard. After graduating, he returned to France to rejoin the AFS in the summer of 1916, but became unwell with appendicitis. After recovering, he joined Section 8 at the end of September, stationed near Verdun. A few weeks later, on 11 October, he was reclaimed by Section 1, now based in the Argonne sector at Grange aux Bois.

Howard's experience and calm, steady manner were soon recognised and he was set for promotion, but just before Christmas 1916 he was taken ill, initially with a cold, which developed into pneumonia and finally meningitis. He died on 23 December 1916. Only the day before he had written to a friend in the USA asking for his help to raise funds for a bed in the American Hospital in Paris, on which would be a brass plaque recognising Dartmouth's sponsorship. On Christmas Day 1916 four of Howard's comrades from Section 1 carried his coffin from the accommodation in La Grange-aux-Bois to the nearby military cemetery. He was buried with full military honours, with a *Poilu* guard of honour. A. Piatt Andrew, Robert Bacon and Rainy's parents and sister, who still lived in Paris, were given special permission to travel to the front in order to attend. He was awarded a posthumous *Croix de Guerre* for his work. His friends in America soon raised the funds to sponsor the bed and it had on it a brass plaque inscribed with the words: 'Howard Burchard Lines, son of Dartmouth, a sympathetic, loyal, generous friend, whose death befitted his life and who needs no words to pay him honor.'

*   *   *

At the end of 1916 Joffre was promoted to Marshal of France, effectively removing him from the day-to-day command of the French Army on the Western Front. Although still popular with the public, he was not so highly thought of by the politicians. After huge French losses at Verdun and on the Somme, with over 400,000 killed and a similar number injured, and not a lot to show for it, the politicians had had enough. The failures at Verdun, the successful British and French attacks on the Somme and the losses during the Brusilov offensive on the Eastern Front had also cost Erich von Falkenhayn his job as Chief of Staff in the summer of 1916. He was replaced by General Paul von Hindenburg for the remainder of the war.

Russia had suffered catastrophic losses on the Eastern Front by the end of 1916. Between 1.6 million and 1.8 million soldiers had been killed or injured, with an additional 2 million taken prisoner and a million posted missing. Tsar Nicholas's attempts to put down strikes in March 1917 overplayed his hand and he was forced to abdicate.

1917

In January 1917 AFS Section 2 moved from Verdun to a well-earned rest in the now quiet Argonne sector, taking over from Section 1, based in the village of La Grange-aux-Bois. John E. Bott recalled in *Work in the Argonne*:

> From this time on our life was an easy one. We had only two main *postes*, one up in the woods *Sept Fontaines* (now Chardon), the other in a beautiful valley at the *Abbaye de Chalade*. For the last few days we have worked at another poste, *Le Chalet*, nearer the lines, but the Germans as usual became unpleasant and nearly 'finished off' several of our cars as well as several of our drivers. As there was practically no work here, it was decided to send cars only on call from Lachalade, with the immediate result there were no more 'close squeaks', at least not for some time. The *boches* picked a quarrel with Lachalade and shelled the district intermittently, but beyond planting a few shells in the buildings and peppering one car with *éclats*, succeeded in doing no damage.
>
> During the five months' rest cure in the Argonne, the only casualty suffered by the section occurred on the afternoon of 25 April, when Raymond Whitney was bitten in an unmentionable part of his anatomy by a large black dog. This severe wound was cauterised at the hospital amid the cheers of the assembled drivers.

In early 1917 events took a dramatic and unexpected turn in Britain and France's favour. In January the Germans announced they would sink any shipping as part of their 'unrestricted submarine warfare' policy. President Wilson had already become concerned that American ships were being targeted and sunk, and had sent notes to the German government warning that future sinkings would be regarded as 'deliberately unfriendly'. Hot on the tail of the German declaration came a major intelligence coup for Britain, when agents intercepted and broke the code of a signal from the German Foreign Ministry to the Mexican government. It was known as the Zimmermann telegram after the German Foreign Secretary, and in it Arthur Zimmermann had proposed a military alliance between Mexico and Germany in the event of America entering the war in Europe. In exchange, Mexico would get back Texas, Arizona and New Mexico.

In March 1917, after much denial, the German Foreign Secretary Arthur Zimmerman finally admitted the telegram was indeed genuine. This enraged American public opinion and on 2 April 1917 Wilson asked Congress to declare war against Germany. It did so on 6 April.

One AFS member, Croom W. Walker from Section 12, noted:

> Then we woke up one morning, about 6th April 1917, and learned that the United States had declared war on Germany. Never were we happier and never were we treated better or welcomed with more enthusiasm than when we carried the news to the front. Bottles of wine were unearthed, and we were patted on the back until we felt as if we ourselves had been responsible for this declaration.

Once war was declared, a British Mission led by Foreign Secretary Arthur Balfour arrived in America. Balfour's first request was for medical assistance in the form of six base hospitals and 116 medical officers. Britain had lost over 400 surgeons killed or wounded during the Somme offensive of 1916. Given Britain's already depleted medical force, American medical support was urgently needed, as an offensive in the area of Passchendaele was planned for the summer of 1917.

The American troopship SS *Mongolia* sailed from New York in May carrying the first medical staff. On 20 May they had assembled on deck to watch the newly installed 6-inch anti-U-boat guns practise when two nurses were killed and another injured by flying shell casing. Clara Ayres and Helen Burnett Wood became the first American casualties of the war, albeit they were still in American waters. Their bodies were transferred to another returning ship and the SS *Mongolia* continued across the Atlantic. It became the first American ship to engage and possibly sink a German U-boat in an encounter in the English Channel.

Once ashore, the medical staff were active almost from their first day as they quickly took over six British field hospitals. It wasn't long before the grim reality of trench warfare became apparent to them as their medical units moved up to support the British casualty clearing stations at Passchendaele in late July 1917.

* * *

Meanwhile, discontent in the French Army seemed about to change the battlefield landscape. The fighting on the Chemin des Dames during April and May 1917 again saw limited gains despite heavy French losses. The soldiers' discontent with the seemingly endless slaughter now came to a head, exacerbated by rumours of the Russian Revolution and the failure of large numbers of American troops to appear in France. In early May the French 2nd Division refused to attack and the mutiny quickly spread through the French Army. In St Ménéhould it was reported that two regiments had mutinied and seized their barracks on 4 June, demanding home leave. They were heard to shout 'Peace or Revolution' and sing the *Internationale*. Soon over 40 per cent of the French infantry was in some way participating in the mutiny. In early June decisive action was taken by the authorities, with mass arrests and courts martial. More than 600 men were sentenced to death, although only forty-three men were executed. Four of them, from the 129th Infantry Regiment stationed at Rarécourt, were laid to rest in the military cemetery at Les Islettes. Tried for 'abandoning their post and refusing to obey orders in front of the enemy', they were sentenced to death and executed on 28 June 1917. The battalion lost its colours and was dissolved on 29 June.

To end the indiscipline, a new French Army commander, General Henri Pétain, the hero of Verdun, was brought in to replace General Robert Nivelle, Joffre's replacement and the architect of the *Chemin des Dames* débâcle. He immediately halted any more suicidal attacks, gave the men more home leave and softened up the harsh military disciplinary system. Despite the scale of the insurrection, news of it was kept from the French public in order not to lower their morale, but more importantly to keep the news from the Germans.

In August Pétain signed an accord with the YMCA to expand the *Foyer du Soldat* as part of the need to implement broader improvements for the *Poilus*. In order not to break the law, the *Foyer* expansion would be administered by a new organisation, the Franco-American Union, working with the government. The Union brought in other welfare organisations such as the Red Cross and the Salvation Army, which were also supporting the French Army. The Union was specifically tasked with the 'moral welfare' of the troops.

* * *

Despite the horrors of the American Civil War (1861–5), which had seen awful battles and over 600,000 deaths, America was totally unprepared for a European war. Its sole participation in the war in Europe to date had been through medical support and Americans joining either the French Foreign Legion or *La Fayette Escadrille* (a flying unit made up of American volunteer pilots flying under French leadership). Its professional army was only around 140,000 strong, a large proportion of which was stationed on the Mexican border, with a further 100,000 or so men in the National Guard. The National Guard was localised and historically based along militia lines, which until 1916 couldn't serve overseas. Its officer corps included some quite elderly men, some of whom it was claimed were Civil War veterans. In summary, its army was not a modern one, and it had too few men equipped for the type of total warfare now going on along the Western Front.

The army's most recent military experience had come in low-intensity fighting against competent guerrilla armies such as the Indians of the West, and Mexican, Cuban and Philippine insurgents. America had long been involved in a border war with Mexico, during which the bandit Pancho Villa had crossed into America and attacked the town of Columbus in New Mexico. In response, America had sent a military force into Mexico under 'Black Jack' Pershing, which unsuccessfully tried to track down Villa. Despite returning without him, the press had latched onto Pershing and his exploits, and he had become something of a media celebrity with a catchy name, Black Jack, which people could remember.

'Black Jack' Pershing was summoned to Washington from the Mexican border in late April 1917. He assumed he was to be given command of a division in the American Expeditionary Forces (AEF), but instead he found he was to be given command of the entire AEF. John J. Pershing's rise to such a prominent position was both meteoric and marred by great personal tragedy. After joining the army, he looked to be destined for a modest career. He had only just scraped into West Point and had been an average student. He did not initially benefit from either family or political connections that usually ensured military advancement to more senior command positions. He did, though, adapt well to soldiering and saw active service in the last campaign against the Indians and later served with Black soldiers on the Western Frontier, thus earning the nickname, 'Black Jack'. He also saw service in the Cuban and Philippine campaigns. Now his star really began to shine as his field experience and competent staff skills marked him out above his contemporaries. Back in Washington, he was appointed to the army general staff and befriended the powerful Senator Warren, Chair of the Senate Military Affairs Committee. Warren had a 24-year-old daughter called Frankie, who caught Pershing's eye despite him being nearly old enough to be her father. The senator approved of the relationship and they were married in 1905, with President Theodore Roosevelt in attendance. By 1911 they had four children, three girls and a boy. Political patronage now saw Pershing promoted to brigadier general ahead of hundreds of more senior and time-served officers.

On 27 August 1915 Pershing was commanding the American forces in Texas, keeping the peace along the lawless Mexican border. His wife and four children were in army quarters in the Presideo army base in San Francisco. They were due to join him the next day in a house he was making ready for their arrival in Fort Bliss. A phone call from a newspaper man, who assumed he was speaking to Pershing's aide, informed him that there had been a fire in the house in Presideo and Frankie and his three daughters had all perished. Pershing, grief-stricken, could barely believe what he had just heard. Back in San Francisco a few days later he stared in disbelief at the four caskets and the burnt-out ruin of his former house. The only consolation he had was that his son Warren had miraculously survived, as he had been out of the house at the time. Life was never the same for Pershing after the tragedy, though he continued to rise up the army chain of command. It was his late wife Frankie's father who summoned him to Washington in 1917.

Prior to his departure for France, Pershing met with Secretary of State for War Newton Baker, a political appointment rather than a man with any innate military knowledge or aspiration. He had, though, behind the scenes brought in a draft bill to enable the conscription of a 4 million-strong army in the event of war with Germany. As a result of his preparations, within a month of the declaration of war the Conscription Bill was passed and all male US citizens aged between 18 and 45 were required to register for service. In a country made up of young immigrants, nothing was straightforward. Those who were not yet citizens did not need to register, but could fast-track their application to become a citizen by volunteering, which over 500,000 had done by the end of the war. Others sought to dodge the draft, on the basis of their coming from a neutral country. These men were later barred from seeking citizenship. It did not end there; half a million Germans went home to fight for Germany and another 90,000 went back to Italy to fight there.

There was also an urgent need to find sufficient horses, donkeys, mules and feed to carry the men to war. The American Army now found itself competing with the already well established network of British and French buyers and their American contacts.

Pershing and Baker, surprisingly given their very different backgrounds, got on well. They went on to meet President Wilson, but Pershing's hope of enlightenment on his role and the army's general terms of reference in France were brushed aside by the President.

On 29 May 1917 Pershing, with only a rudimentary knowledge of French and a miscellaneous collection of 191 staff officers, a marching regiment and band, departed from America for Britain on the White Star Liner *Baltic*. He was now commander-in-chief of the AEF. He arrived to great pomp and ceremony in Liverpool on 8 June 1917. After an early skirmish with the British and American press, he sent a signal back to America to limit the amount of media in attendance with the AEF in France. Later the same day he and his entourage arrived in London and took up residence in the Savoy Hotel. The following day he met King George V at Buckingham Palace.

Away from America, the reality of war now became apparent to Pershing and his staff. There were night-time German air raids, endless widows dressed in black, women undertaking a multitude of tasks still done by men in America and, most shockingly, women smoking in public. Menus were bereft of any appetising food. Most worrying, though, were the losses of Allied shipping on the transatlantic route from German U-boat activity. Some 1.5 million tons had been lost during the past two months alone. Pershing began to worry whether there would be sufficient shipping left to bring his army over. He could also see how near Britain was to starvation. He was reassured to learn that Admiral Sims, with Prime Minister Lloyd George's backing, was instituting a convoy system, which almost immediately reduced transatlantic sinkings.

Although impressed by the realistic training methods of the British Army recruits, he and his staff couldn't help but notice the poor physical condition of the men destined for the front. Three years of war had taken its toll on Britain's best and fittest men. Pershing now found himself at odds with his new Allies. The British wanted to subsume Pershing's army into theirs, whereas he had in mind the Lorraine sector adjacent to the French. The issue of providing capacity on transatlantic shipping came up, with British hegemony over it; Pershing was going to struggle to bring his army over. The issue of shipping space was going to irritate Pershing for another year, with the British effectively trying to blackmail him into subsuming his army into the British Army in exchange for shipping capacity.

Pershing's time in London was brief, but the stopover had served a useful purpose, as each side had the chance to size the other up. The British public, long fed on a diet of losses and bad news from the front, had at last received a boost to their morale. Relationships that would be crucial over the next eighteen months had been formed, and Pershing and his staff were now under no illusion as to the nature of the war on the Western Front. He arrived with his retinue in Paris on 24 June 1917, again to great pomp and ceremony. He took offices in Rue Constantine and was lionised by a war-weary country.

Roger P. Stone of the AFS noted his arrival:

I was present tonight at one of the most wonderful demonstrations I ever hope to see. General Pershing and his staff arrived in Paris this evening, and the reception was wonderful. On all sides of the Place de l'Opera thousands and thousands of people were massed … All the women were tossing flowers of various kinds at the cars, and the girl I was with threw a whole bouquet of roses to General Pershing, who caught them and thanked her.

Pershing visited the tomb of the Marquis de Lafayette, the French general who had helped the Americans defeat the English at Yorktown during the War of Independence in 1781. His visit to the tomb at Picpus cemetery in Paris took place on 4 July, American Independence Day. A great throng gathered to hear him speak.

The French had assumed that a nation of America's stature must have a large army just waiting to enter the war. With the French Army mutiny in the process of being put down, French generals used the excuse that they were now waiting for the American Army before launching more attacks in order to help improve *Poilu* morale. Pershing had the relative safety of America in which to recruit and train an army of millions. But the men and their equipment then had to make a potentially hazardous 3,000-mile Atlantic crossing and then make their way to the front.

Sitting in Paris in the summer of 1917, Pershing looked at the French and British logistical situation and tried to work out how he could bring his army over. Each supported armies overseas, Britain in the Middle East and France in Salonika, but the overwhelming bulk of their armies were in France. Here France was able to use its short supply chains, while Britain's were slightly longer and required shipping. Britain's colonial troops from as far away as New Zealand and Canada were initially equipped in their home countries, but once in France fell under the British supply chain. Britain and France already had hegemony over much of the transatlantic shipping, to supply their own armies with horses and feed and food. Furthermore, the escort ships for the convoys would mainly have to come from Britain's Royal Navy.

Part of Pershing's advance party set off to tour the French ports, and what they reported back was not encouraging. Britain already controlled the Channel ports, and there was little room for extra capacity to be created. British mainland ports could be used, but again they were at near-capacity. There was capacity in the south of France and in Italy, but using these would add extra days on to the already long Atlantic crossing. This left the ports on the west coast of France: Brest, St Nazaire, La Pallice, Rochefort and Bordeaux. These had, to a degree, fallen into disrepair. They also had nowhere near the capacity needed to become the main reception ports for the AEF. Furthermore, the French rail system primarily ran north to south to support the Western Front. It was supporting and moving the huge French and British armies already in the field and had no spare capacity to support large cross-country rail moves from the western ports to the front.

Britain held thirty days' supply of food, ammunition, fuel, animal feed, medical supplies, etc., for the men at the front. Pershing made a dramatic decision; given the precarious state of the Atlantic route and the risk of disruption from submarines, he ordered that they hold ninety days' front line supplies in France. His point was emphasised on 5 February 1918 when the SS *Tuscania*, carrying over 2,000 American troops, plus a British crew, was sunk by a German U-boat while passing between Scotland and Northern Ireland en route to Liverpool. Although only 210 soldiers and crew died, it was the largest single day's casualties the USA had experienced to date and it sent shock-waves through the country. It also served as a timely reminder of the precariousness of the Atlantic supply route.

Pershing was also looking nervously at the situation unfolding in Russia. Instead of the half a million-strong army originally pencilled in for the AEF, he thought that at least 2 million men would need to be recruited and shipped to France to win the war. Each division would have to arrive with thirty days' supplies to support themselves, while the ninety days' reserve supplies would be sitting in France waiting to be moved to the front and constantly replenished.

A couple of months of Parisian distractions was enough for Pershing. He had to plan and build an army from nothing that would be ready to stand shoulder to shoulder with France and Britain, who were now both, in terms of experience and logistics, three years further down the road than America. He moved his HQ to Damrémont Barracks in Chaumont, near the Champagne region and home to France's glove industry. He occupied a local château, the walls of which were covered with stuffed animals of every description. Now work could at last begin in earnest.

The task of supporting this logistical behemoth fell to what was initially called Lines of Communication (LOC), which was reorganised and renamed the Service of Supply (SOS) in February 1918 and later won the accolade of 'America's Miracle in France'. Without it, it would be fair to say the AEF would never have entered the field of combat in France. The LOC was initially based with Pershing at Damrémont but later moved to Tours, to allow Pershing to concentrate on planning the fighting at Damrémont The LOC would have to create the AEF capacity itself.

Into the LOC came a new breed of soldier, mainly former civilians but with a can-do ethos. These were men who had pushed the railroads out west over inhospitable terrain, driven trains, built the country's ports and piloted harbour boats, built the underground railway systems, constructed infrastructure. Added to them were lawyers and accountants from across the country who were either drafted or volunteered to join the LOC and help bring the AEF to France and victory.

The whole process had to be done in reverse. First they scoured the east and west coasts of America and south America for ships suitable to cross the Atlantic, using cruise and passenger ships for troops and cargo vessels for cargo tonnage, tugs and dredgers. The western ports of France had to be dredged and piers built for ships to moor alongside. They built cranes to unload the ships, warehouses to store goods, and railways to carry stores from the pier heads to the warehouses. They also created accommodation for the men who would build all this, bakeries and ovens to cook their food, and refrigeration plants to keep meat and dairy produce fresh.

All this had to come from America, flat-packed to minimise space in the hold, and then be reassembled in workshops at the ports. Once these were built, troops could begin to arrive, but they too had to have barracks, hospitals and stores, not to mention transport. A railway network was built to cross France, again brought flat-packed from America and reassembled in workshops. Coal and timber have to come from America for winter fuel and for construction. Coal was particularly important as ships had to use all available space to bring cargo over, so had to be recoaled and watered for the return journey, adding days to a turnaround. The primary workers at the new ports unloading goods were African-Americans in labour units. 'Making the world safe for democracy', as President Wilson had put it on the declaration of war, seemed inaccurate to many of them. They had joined to fight but now found themselves working under white officers and NCOs in similar conditions to the plantation work they thought they had left behind.

* * *

Meanwhile, in the Argonne Forest the American volunteer ambulance men had sections stationed there on a regular basis, despite the sector's relative quiet. Section 19 took over from Section 12 in May and stayed until September 1917 at the barn in Grange-aux-Bois. Paul A. Rie recalled:

> In a large barn, with holes in the roof and walls, and a really dirty dirt floor, over which rats and fleas frolic nightly. In the middle of the place are a wooden table and benches, and here we eat our meals. The sanitary arrangements are the following: In the morning when we are up and partially dressed, we take our towels and other implements of toilet and wade through a yard full of manure and mud to another manure pile and mud heap, in another yard, where there is a well, from which can be extracted dark brown water, with which we 'ablute' our hands and faces, and, once in a while, our teeth.
>
> We have two postes, Lachalade and Chardon, two men being assigned to each poste, and relieved every 24 hours. Today I'm on poste duty at Lachalade, which is an old abbey partially destroyed by shellfire and located in a little open valley between wooded hills, with the ruins of a tiny village in the rear of it, towards the lines.
>
> The ground rises gradually from the abbey, and the crest of the slope must mark the front-line trenches, as the ground in the distance near the summit assumes that white, barren look one associates with the idea of no man's land, and the only trees which break the skyline are the torn and leafless trunks of what was, at one time, a flourishing forest. The building itself, except the chapel, which is partially destroyed, is used as a dressing station. Of the chapel, one side altar alone remains, and there mass is said every morning by one of the *brancardiers*, who is a priest. The main part of the abbey, which must have served originally as quarters for the monks and was later remodelled as a private home, is a large, barnlike construction. The interior is bare except for the cots and rough tables of the *brancardiers*.
>
> It is impossible to describe the charm and picturesqueness this old abbey has for us, but I'm wondering if perhaps it marks the scene of our first work at the front. For when the realisation comes that it is the dreamed-of moment, that one is actually serving in France, actually in the war at last, the surroundings of that moment, however ordinary, are forever after colored in romance.
>
> Today I go on duty to Chardon, and we drove up there this morning to learn the roads. Although the poste there is only a little distance from Lachalade, it is an entirely different sort of place. The

road to it leads up a steep hill through thick Argonne woods, and the poste itself is a little underground dugout with dirt and logs piled on top, the entrance alone being visible. We left our car before the door, descended a few steps, and passed through a passageway into a small, roughly furnished room which looked for all the world like the cabin of a ship.

On Decoration (Memorial) Day, May 1917, Charles Conrad Jatho AFS wrote: 'In the afternoon some of the section went up to the cemetery above La Grange-aux-Bois and decorated the grave of Howard Lines, who died of pneumonia in Section 1 last winter.' And on 10 June 1917, Paul A. Rie AFS recalled: 'Jimmy and I stopped to visit the military cemetery [St Ménéhould], where are over 4,000 little crosses, squeezed side by side with small tricolored cockades on them. It was the most depressing sight I've ever seen, because the majority of graves are quite bare, without a wreath or sign of remembrance on them.'

On Sunday, 22 July 1917 Charles Conrad Jatho AFS described the shelling: 'Lachalade, our outpost, has been bombarded. A number of 150s have been firing with ruinous effect upon the old monastery as well as playing havoc with the roads. There are no Sabbaths in wartime. Here the booming of the guns answers for a church bell, the trenches are the pews and the preacher is – hope.'

Death was ever-present. John 'Jack' Verplank Newlin, aged 19, was from Princeton University, where he had edited two magazines. With America now in the war, he had left Princeton before graduating and gone to France as a volunteer in the AFS. He arrived in France on 26 May 1917 and was posted to the newly formed Section 29 in early June. They left for the front from the AFS HQ in Paris on 30 June 1917, assigned to Ville-sur-Cousances near Clermont en Argonne. Their *poste des secours* was at Esnes, east of the Argonne, which covered the Mort Homme–Verdun sector, with a relay poste at Montzéville. The sector was a busy one and regularly under German shell-fire. On 3 August a German '77' landed near the AFS *abri* at Montzéville. It destroyed two Flivvers and injured Julian Allen in the knee and Newlin in the back. They were immediately removed to the hospital at Ville-sur-Cousances and from there, owing to the seriousness of their injuries, were taken back to the hospital at Fleury sur Aire. Newlin was well enough to undergo an operation on 4 August and was visited by the French section commander and several friends on 5th. He was presented with the *Croix de Guerre* and appeared to be recovering. That night he died of his wounds.

General Mordocq, commander of Newlin's section, read this address:

Comrades. One of our number has died this night from a severe wound which he received the day before yesterday in carrying out his noble errand of mercy for our wounded. He was decorated yesterday with the *Médaille Militaire* and *Croix de Guerre*. He was the first of our number to fall before the enemy as a soldier and with honour. May his sacrifice be a noble example to you, free sons of America, who have been sent for the defence of right and liberty against a most savage and unjustifiable of all aggressions. In the name of France, comrades, I return thanks to the brave Newlin for his sacrifice – to you all for the devotion which you have shown during the last days in accomplishing your noble service under the most perilous circumstances.

Others were taken with the beauty of the Argonne countryside. Henry G. Crosby of SSU 71 wrote:

It was a marvellous sunny day in the Argonne, one of those spring days that make you want to bask in the warm sun. We spent the afternoon dozing and daydreaming on the warm grass, or gazed at the German aviators, who flew over the village of Clermont for the greater part of the afternoon. They looked like tiny white specks against the clear blue sky. Circling high in glittering security, beyond reach of the anti-aircraft shells, they spun their wary course.

Towards dusk – as if tired by their day's tedious task – they turned back towards their own lines, dropping down the sky out of sight in the haze of early evening, leaving a pale star or two gleaming in their place.

*   *   *

With America now in the war, the AFS was able to form a new section. The French Army was now critically short of *camion* (truck) drivers and many of the current drivers were too old for the rigorous demands of convoy work. Commandant Doumenc, now head of the French Army Automobile Service, suggested that, in addition to volunteer ambulance drivers, America might help with transporting troops, munitions and other equipment to the front. He had initially supported Piatt Andrew's request to work at the front in ambulances back in 1915 and later masterminded the *Voie Sacrée* from Bar le Duc to Verdun. Piatt Andrew responded positively; he would find men. These came from the next batches of volunteer ambulance drivers to arrive in France in April and May 1917 and all the way through the summer, 800 in all. They joined what became known as Reserve Mallet, named after Commandant Mallet, its commander. These camion sections performed valuable work all through the spring and summer of 1917, mainly in the Chemin des Dames theatre.

However, it was not long before the American government cast its eye over the various American voluntary ambulance and camion services, which they wanted brought into the American military fold. Joffre himself travelled to America to seek their continuance, so deeply were the assorted services ingrained into the French Army. A compromise was reached; the units would be absorbed into the American Army, but immediately loaned back to the French. This was a solution many of the volunteers were happy to agree to as they had formed a strong attachment to their *Poilu*s.

Colonel Jefferson Kean arrived in Paris in late August 1917 to oversee the recruitment of the volunteers into the US Army Ambulance Service. The AFS and the Norton-Harjes sections were formally merged into the US Army Ambulance Corps on 30 August 1917. The transition was never going to be smooth, given the history of the volunteers and the ethos that had prevailed in the units. The Norton-Harjes sections (another ambulance volunteer group) never rose to the numbers that the AFS did, consisting at their height of 150 men in three sections with twenty-five vehicles. Although a few men agreed to be transferred from the Norton-Harjes sections, most didn't. Norton didn't either and resigned.

Not unsurprisingly, for Piatt Andrew American intervention could not come soon enough and he initially welcomed the militarisation of the AFS. With their independence gone, though, many chose to go home; those who remained transferred into the US Ambulance Corps. Some volunteers, along with men who had served already, now volunteered to join the American Army to take part in the fighting. But Piatt Andrew now had to swallow his pride as he saw the AFS absorbed into the US Army Ambulance Service. Regular officers took over command and Andrew's experience was ignored, even when he pointed out that French stretchers were longer than the new American ambulances. He kept his council, though, and sat on the sidelines for the remainder of the war, although he was promoted to lieutenant colonel in the US Army Ambulance Service.

By the end of 1917 about 50 per cent of the camion section drivers had transferred over and about 40 per cent of the ambulance drivers. The transfer was never going to be smooth; gone was the gentlemen's club atmosphere, now replaced with rigid American military discipline. There were no more quiet afternoons spent writing; it was all spit and polish now. Where they could, former volunteers let their old unit number and logos show through the new paintwork of their ambulances. Odd pieces of AFS uniform were worn, but the former spirit was lost with militarisation.

*   *   *

The LOC had two bywords, men and tonnage, and their main concern was how much of each could be put on a ship and brought over. Each service arm was given a tonnage per convoy; each then allocated space according to their priorities. Engines before wings or beds before hospitals?

Across France a duplicate telegraph and phone system was installed by America to convey all communications. In late 1917 a call went out in America for women volunteers to go to France. American men serving in the Signal Corps were not dextrous enough to deal with the high volume of phone calls, make the switchboard connections and speak to French female operators. The women volunteers from across America needed two skills: to operate a switchboard and speak French fluently. Eventually 223 women, known as the 'Hello Girls', worked on switchboards across France. Despite wearing a distinct blue uniform and being subject to military discipline, they were categorised as civilians, not receiving veteran status for another sixty years.

Across France the American railways were built under, over or around the existing French rail system. Train crews could be American or French under American supervision, in which case the supervisors needed a basic grasp of French. At each station stood a railway transport officer (RTO), whose job was to check travel warrants, note the time the trains passed and whether they were on schedule or not, and that each train was made up according to the manifest.

More than 1,000 American locomotives plus crews and 7,000 carriages transported troops and supplies to the front, along with thousands of French trains. The standard markings on the French freight rail cars became a byword for the 'Doughboys' (infantry soldiers): *40 Hommes et 8 Chevaux*. Sadly, many Doughboys died on the railways as result of excitement and carelessness. They sat on roofs or hung from the side of trains, little appreciating the narrow tolerance between French tunnels and American rolling stock, and thus came to a sad and grisly end.

*   *   *

Three units that were to play a prominent part in the Argonne Forest campaign started life in America during the summer and autumn of 1917.

The 77th 'Liberty' Division was named after its New York origins and its unit emblem, the Statue of Liberty ('a gift from the people of France on the occasion of the hundredth anniversary of the US Declaration of Independence). It was first raised at Camp Upton on Long Island outside New York on 25 August 1917. The men were mainly city boys from New York's rough and ready neighbourhoods. Most of these men had just a basic education. Irish, Jewish, Chinese, Italians, Armenians and Germans now found themselves rubbing shoulders for the first time and in many cases struggling to speak the same language. The officers tended to come from the better parts of New York, were college or university educated and from the professions.

President Wilson had authorised the formation of several African-American Pioneer Infantry Regiments, known collectively as the '8's after their regiment titles 801st through to 809th. The 805th Pioneer Infantry Regiment initially assembled at Camp Funston on the hot, windy and sand-swept plains of Kansas. Here a stray white tough-looking fighting dog joined them, becoming their mascot. The 'Bearcats' (a person or animal that fights with fearlessness) was the nickname given to them by their commanding officer, Colonel C.B. Humphrey, a regular pre-war officer. The enlisted men came from all over the USA but primarily from the states of Mississippi, Missouri, Louisiana and Kansas. The regiment consisted of three battalions each of 1,000 men, each battalion having four companies, along with support elements making a unit total of about 3,500 men, predominantly African-American with white officers. While still in the USA, the 805th had actively sought to recruit a complete band, but this idea was turned down by the army, as many of the band were over enlistment age. Other aspiring and well known musicians and vaudeville acts did manage to join the 805th, though. Instruments were ordered but failed to arrive before the unit left for France. Only regular pre-war army units were allowed to take bands and instruments to France in 1918.

The 92nd 'Buffalo' Infantry Division was also African-American. It was raised on 27 October 1917 in Camp Funston in Kansas. The division's training was frustrated by an exceptionally cold winter and equipment shortages, and because the unit was scattered across a number of camps in America. This was a deliberate policy, as it was feared that 25,000 African-Americans together in a southern town could lead to friction with locals or other white units. The division contained four infantry regiments, the 365th, 366th, 367th, and 368th, plus the 317th Engineer Regiment and 167th Field Artillery Regiment.

The bringing together of hundreds of thousands of men in close proximity, mainly in tented camps, across America during the summer, autumn and winter of 1917 lead to the outbreak of flu. This was to have far-reaching repercussions, once it crossed the Atlantic with the men to France.

* * *

In October 1917 events took a very serious turn in Russia. Lenin and Trotsky led what became known as the October Revolution. Russian military failures on the Eastern Front fuelled the Bolsheviks, who had become a legal party after the assassination of the Tsar. They now staged a bloodless coup, taking over government buildings, and Russia's continued participation in the war became more precarious.

* * *

Deaths among American soldiers had so far been confined to a few killed under British command. This was about to change. At about 3am on 3 November 1917 German soldiers overcame an isolated party of inexperienced Doughboys under American command. Three members of Company F, 16th Infantry Regiment, 1st Division, were killed while on watch in a front-line listening post, with another eleven men captured. Their first night duty had come to an ignominious end. Privates Thomas Enright and Merle Hay and Corporal James Gresham, entered the history books as the first US casualties of the war, under American command. One was shot between the eyes, one had his skull smashed and one lay face down with his throat cut. They were buried with full military honours in the local cemetery near Bethélémont.

After the war French towns and villages collected money for a memorial to the three men. An unveiling ceremony was held at shortly after the Armistice in 1918. The memorial at Bethélémont was a regular stopping point on French pilgrimages to the front for the next twenty years. On 6 October 1940, in one of the few deliberate acts of vandalism towards First World War memorials, occupying German troops blew it up.

* * *

Pershing's position was clear: there was no time, or spare transport, to take the dead men home. This kept him aligned with the other Allies, who still had to comply with the French law that men couldn't be exhumed or removed from the front. He was also concerned that mothers might glimpse their sons amid the full destructive force of death on the Western Front. His stance didn't help politically back home, where American politicians had started to support a move to bring home the dead.

As 1917 came to end, there was renewed optimism that, with American soldiers now arriving in France, victory was at last in sight. This was tempered, though, by the likelihood that Russia would sue for peace, which would free up large numbers of German soldiers in the east to be moved to the Western Front. It looked as if 1918 would be no less bloody than the previous years of conflict.

Chapter 4

1918

The year began badly with the sinking on 5 February of the SS *Tuscania*, which was torpedoed by a German U-boat while transporting American troops to Europe, with the loss of 210 lives.

In line with Pershing's order that the AEF now hold ninety days' supplies, this task fell to the former LOC, now renamed the Service of Supply (SOS), which began to make the necessary arrangements. While the SOS assembled and equipped the army, Pershing and his staff worked on what the American Army would do and where the various units would be deployed. Pershing was concerned that his Doughboys would become trench-bound, as he perceived the French and British Armies had done. Although initial instruction for most combat units was under either British or French instructors, Pershing wanted to see the American Army fighting out in the open using the rifle and bayonet and American courage. Therefore lessons that had been hard learnt by the British and French were either ignored or discouraged from entering mainstream American Army thinking.

Late in February 1918 the peace talks between Russia and Germany had broken down and German troops advanced on St Petersburg. Russia sued for peace and signed the Treaty of Brest-Litovsk on 3 March 1918. With Russia effectively now out of the war, the very thing the Allies had feared for some time came to fruition. Germany was now able to bring 500,000 troops from the Eastern Front to the Western Front.

Although General Hindenburg was nominally the German chief of staff, it was General Ludendorff who started to plan, in 1917, a decisive Western Front offensive. Using the reinforcements from the east, he hoped to overwhelm the French and British troops before America's new army started to land in large enough numbers to alter the balance of power along the Western Front. But as American troops landed, so too did the flu virus, which took hold in many of the newly built camps on the western French seaboard. Britain and France were well aware that the

German Army of the Eastern Front was on its way to the west, and they anxiously sought to bolster their depleted armies with fresh American troops. This did not sit well with Pershing, who continued to try to prevent the AEF being subsumed into the French and British Armies. By now President Wilson had realised that if this happened, then America would be no more than a side-show in any postwar settlement, despite its significant contribution. Therefore American forces should fight on their own. This message, reinforced by Newton Baker, was that Pershing must find a section of the front where the AEF could stand on its own, commanded by its own officers.

Although the AEF could keep the men in rations and ammunition, it had not yet developed a system for providing men with the other necessities that made life bearable for front-line troops. This task fell to voluntary organisations in the USA, which raised funds and sent out staff to army recruitment camps in the USA and to army camps in France. Chief among these organisations were the Red Cross, the Knights of Columbus (a Catholic organisation), the YMCA, the Salvation Army and the Jewish Welfare Board. In the Argonne area the Knights of Columbus ran a shop in St Ménéhould, and the Salvation Army operated in Clermont. Here men could relax, read and purchase magazines, cigarettes and stationery, and even, after the war, receive a basic education. With over 600 YMCAs now under American control, they were free to add a religious element. They were staffed by American volunteers known as Secretaries, who came from a variety of backgrounds, men and women, black and white. Racial segregation was not encouraged in the YMCA but the hated 'Jim Crow' laws were arbitrarily transferred to France. It usually came down to the personal whims of local commanders. If they asked for separate shops for whites and African-Americans, then that is what happened. Other times it was more random, with signs reading 'No Negroes allowed' found pinned on doors.

In 1917 Marion G. Crandell, who was born in America but educated in France, volunteered to join the YMCA, wanting to help both her American and French friends in the war effort. After training in the USA, she left by ship for France in January 1918. She arrived at the YMCA HQ in Paris on 15 February 1918. Her language skills meant she was attached to the French *Foyer du Soldat* in St Ménéhould on 8 March. Here she helped French front-line soldiers from the Argonne to relax, read and enjoy a meal away from the war. St Ménéhould was now within range of long-distance German artillery and was frequently subject to random shelling. On 26 March 1918 Marion was working in the *Foyer* when it was hit by a shell; she was killed while taking shelter. She was buried a few days later, wrapped in a French Tricolour, in the French military cemetery in St Ménéhould, with full military honours. She was the first woman to be buried in the cemetery, which already contained over 6,000 *Poilus*. After the war she was moved to the American military cemetery at Romagne. Her courage was later remembered in a poem by Harry Webb Farrington, the only American to be commissioned in the French Army during the war:

They Buried Her as a Soldier
They buried her there as a soldier,
This frail, tender woman
Who loved the French.
A hero's coffin will hold her,
So they laid her to rest
Near the front-line trench.
They carried her there as a soldier,
This brave, fearless woman
Who served the French.
She had no rifle to shoulder,
But the cares of the men
From the front-line trench.
They wept for her as a soldier,
This shell-stricken woman
Who cheered the French.
She banished the horrors they told her
By her smile for the men
From the front-line trench
They thought of her as a soldier,
This bright buoyant woman
Who charmed the French.
The colors of France will enfold her,
The flag of her boys
In the front-line trench.
They honored here there as a soldier,
America's woman
Slain with the French.
Her death made every heart beat bolder
To save those back of
To the front-line trench.

Pershing now became sure the war would carry on into 1919 and possibly beyond. He therefore tasked the SOS with drawing up a logistics plan to supply an American army which, by then, would be bigger than the combined armies of France and Britain. It now became crucial to reduce the amount of transatlantic tonnage, and two vital SOS roles revolved around obtaining locally sourced goods and what we would now call recycling. Across France, Spain, Portugal and Italy, SOS men scoured the countryside for food, animals and other raw materials that could reduce transatlantic tonnage. In France, despite strict government controls on all raw materials, extra capacity was found, and wood was cut under French forestry supervision.

Old factories that had been closed down were now reopened to produce, assemble and repair equipment. Farms and land were taken over and planted with food and fruit; such farms were often worked by injured Doughboys. One of the SOS tasks was to redeploy lightly injured men, unlike the British, where a 'Blighty' wound saw a man sent back to Britain for treatment. Doughboys would have to stay in France until the end of the war, other than in exceptional circumstances. The SOS found every man a job best suited to his abilities and physical condition.

Coffee was considered very much part of the Doughboys' staple diet, but supply was a problem because it took up too much shipping tonnage. Into the breach stepped Otto Goldstein, a former German, who had served with the US Cavalry in Cuba and the Philippines. After attaining the rank of sergeant, the furthest he could go in a peacetime army, he left the military and went to Chicago, where he entered the grocery business, going on to open a mail order company. He volunteered for the SOS and initially worked in the problem area of supplying food for the troops; his efforts meant that where only 1,500 men had been fed before, now 150,000 men could be fed. His talents were recognised by a former officer who knew him from his previous army service.

Goldstein was presented with the coffee problem and set out to solve it. Coffee beans were plentiful in France; buyers, trying to stop Germany cornering the market before the war, had warehouses full of bean sacks. What was missing was the ability to roast and grind beans in bulk. Goldstein found an old closed brickyard, which he leased; employing French disabled ex-soldiers, he built a unique coffee roasting and grinding service to supply the whole of the AEF. Having solved this problem, he was then tasked with helping feed the Doughboys' sweet tooth by supplying chocolate. Again this was deemed not important enough to use vital transatlantic tonnage. Closed French chocolate factories were leased and production restarted to bring the men their chocolate. He then applied his skills to biscuits and macaroni, and soon brought them into local production in France.

Another method of saving on shipping tonnage was recycling. America now followed the lead of the British and French reclamation services. This account is taken from an anonymous 1918 report about the French reclamation service:

Every single item of discarded clothing and equipment found at the battlefront, hospitals or in support areas was sent back from the front by train unsorted. Whole trains with 60/70 wagons full of stuff arrived at depots outside Paris. There items were sorted into categories, clothing bundles, broken weapons, shell cases, haversacks, artillery pieces, helmets, blankets, tents, empty wooden boxes, webbing, bayonets and even humble coffee-grinders all found their way into piles. There they were counted and packaged up for onward transport to the appropriate centre for reclamation. Six vast depots were situated across France, each acting as a centre for categories of items, clothing, metal, ammunition, animals, transport, etc. Working on the ammunition reclamation depot was far the most hazardous as live cases inevitably found their way there and many exploded while being handled. Shells were recharged and broken rifles were stripped and made into serviceable weapons, as were all other items, machine guns, trench mortars, field guns and bayonets.

Uniforms that had been gassed were burnt near the front. The remainder of the clothing went to depots to be washed and dried, socks and blankets as well, many of which had lost their colour due to the rain and or sun. Once cleaned and re-dyed it was graded as suitable for further front-line use, and over 300,000 uniforms a month found their way back to the front. 150,000 second-grade uniforms found their way to support staff. Others in poor condition were dyed pea green and marked with P.G., *Prisonier du Guerre* [POW], and handed over to captured Germans to wear. Uniforms, socks and blankets that did not meet the standard were cut up into usable pieces to make repairs. Badges, buckles and buttons were stripped off and sewn onto good uniforms. If possible the remaining fabric was recycled back into fabric to make uniforms and wool turned into underwear. Boots were initially soaked in water and potassium to clean them, then stood on shoe trees to dry in the sun and then re-dyed. They were then treated with fish oil to make them supple again.

Any repairs and re-nailing of the soles was then carried out, 178 hobs per boot. Boots were then polished and sorted into pairs as best they could be. Recycled boots did not go to front-line troops; they were allowed a new pair of matching boots. The recycled boots went to support units and prisoners. Odd and unrepairable boots were sold at auction. Tents were cleaned and repaired and sent back to the front. Those beyond repair were turned into wash bags. Haversacks were cleaned and repaired and sent back for reuse.

At the metal depot, mess tins were either repaired or smelted and turned back into new sets. *Bidons* [water bottles] were likewise repaired and recovered with waste material and sent back. Anything that could not be recycled was sold at auction to the civil population. At the animal depots, discarded skins from food depots were tanned and treated to turn into winter coats, leather belts, pouches, horse bridles and even made into buttons for lower grade uniforms. Animal bones were boiled down for glue.

Nothing was wasted. The SOS soon had a similar operation under way, saving valuable shipping space and money. Meanwhile in America, despite its huge industrial base, uniforms and weapons for the AEF were still in short supply, with many men not seeing a weapon until they arrived in France. As a nation of immigrants, another challenge was language. With many recruits having been in America less than ten years, the widespread speaking and understanding of English proved to be a challenge for many units.

*   *   *

The much-anticipated German offensive finally started on 21 March 1918. Pershing's hand was forced by the rapid British and French retreat, and he was obliged in April to bolster the collapsing front with some of his troops who had just arrived in France. To Pershing's chagrin, they would be commanded by French or British generals – the very thing he had fought against for so long. This also upset the transatlantic shipping programme as the Doughboys were now more urgently needed, which left artillery and engineer support units back in America. This would impact adversely on the troops during the final American autumn campaign.

On 30 May, with the Germans only 50 miles from Paris, two American divisions (including elements of the Marine Corps) were thrown into the path of the advancing German Army in the Chateau Thierry region. Here hard lessons were learnt, with the Americans almost recklessly throwing themselves at the German machine guns. Their casualties were dreadful. The most famous attack was made by the Marines on Belleau Wood on 6 June, where victory came twenty days later – but at a high price, with over 10,000 casualties.

In June 1918 men from the former Czechoslovakian republic fought under the French. Like the Garibaldis in 1914, volunteers had initially joined the French Foreign Legion, but were effectively disbanded after heavy casualties in the fighting around Arras in May 1915. Now in 1918 they were reinforced by American Czech and Slovak volunteers, volunteer prisoners of war (most Czechoslovakians had fought as part of the Austro-Hungarian Empire on the side of the Germans) along with Czechoslovakian men from Russia and Romania. They were now part of an independent Czechoslovakian First Brigade, which fought in the north of the Argonne around Vouziers as part of the French 134th Division. Their hope was that, with the defeat of the Germans and the Austro-Hungarian Empire, Czechoslovakia would once again be a free and independent nation.

As in 1914, the German advance of the spring and early summer of 1918 finally ground to a halt. Just as before, a resolute Allied defence, long lines of communication, insufficient supplies, lack of troop reinforcements and now the difficulty of heaving vehicles and artillery over the already scarred and churned battlefront saw the German advance stall. Unlike the Allies, who could now count on the Americans to make good their 250,000 casualties, the Germans, with similar losses, could not. The offensive had also cannibalised most German divisions of their experienced men, who were selected or volunteered to lead the assault as storm-troops; most were dead now, and their experience was irreplaceable. By early August the offensive had petered out across all sectors of the front. With America landing 300,000 men a month, the balance of power had now firmly passed to the Allies. The flu also abated as summer came.

The French and British high commands, not unsurprisingly, approved of the current mode of operations, with Americans soldiers under French and British command. Pershing, however, still sought an opportunity to find a sector of the front for America. His wish was finally granted at a conference on 24 July. Marshal Ferdinand Foch, now Generalissimo of the Allied armies, announced a plan for a concerted attack across all sectors of the front. Pershing thought this could be achieved if America had its own sector. In exchange for Pershing's support for the plan, Foch allocated Pershing the Lorraine sector and on 10 August the American First Army was born.

Despite American military successes, an infamous incident took place at the village of Fismette, 20 miles east of Rheims in the Champagne sector. Here several futile counter-attacks by the 28th American 'Keystone' Division had taken place, with large casualties and little to show for it. On 26 August the French general Degoutte ordered a small American detachment of 236 men to hold their ground in the village. This was contrary to the wishes of their American commanders, who regarded the position as untenable. After an artillery barrage had reduced the village to rubble and cut off the detachment's escape route over a bridge, German storm-troopers equipped with flame-throwers assaulted at dawn on 27 August. Only thirty men managed to swim back to safety over the Vesle river. Pershing was incandescent with rage; this must never happen again. From now on, Americans would be commanded by Americans, in an American sector.

The first planned American offensive was intended to remove the St Mihiel Salient (a bulge in the Allied line south of Verdun) and then push on towards Metz, the German rail hub for the region. Pershing and his staff went ahead with planning the operation at Chaumont. On 30 August Foch appeared there and cancelled the operation, instead offering the First Army a role in the larger French push further north. Pershing, mindful of the outcome of the Battle of Fismette, was in no mood to support the French. After a heated debate in which tempers flared, Foch left with no American agreement to support his change of plan. A few days later, at another conference, Marshal Pétain, the French army commander, brokered a new deal.

The American First Army would still, first, eliminate the St Mihiel Salient but then, instead of advancing to Metz, would swing north and take over the sector between the rivers Aire and Meuse, including the previously impenetrable Argonne Forest. Pershing agreed, although logistically it wasn't clear how his large army would fight two major battles, 60 miles apart, in a couple of weeks. Pershing was happy, though; at last he had an American sector under American command.

With large numbers of casualties already suffered in halting the German advance and more likely to be incurred in the impending Meuse Argonne offensive, America faced the same problem that the Allies had faced for the last three years: what to do with the dead? Pershing and other American military leaders had agreed from the outset that their dead should remain with their comrades in France. Former President Theodore Roosevelt, whose son was to die in France later in 1918, said he should remain there. The picture was muddied, though, when Secretary of War Newton D.

Baker made an announcement that would have wide-ranging and expensive consequences. To the press he pledged, without any referral to the French in whose remit it lay, that the dead would be repatriated home for final burial. Fuel was added to the fires of debate by embalmers in America offering their services for free; they would go to France and embalm the fallen men and repatriate them. Clearly no real thought had been applied to the practicalities of working in battlefield conditions. Nevertheless, it served as a potent political and public symbol of the desire to bring bodies home, which persisted both during and after the war.

America also now needed to maintain a centralised record of their dead. This task fell to Chaplain Charles C. Pierce, who had been appointed to head up the Army Morgue and Office of Identification in the Philippines, prior to the First World War. He was brought out of retirement in 1917 to take charge of the newly formed American Graves Registration Service (GRS). Based in Tours, France, Pierce and his small staff were quickly overwhelmed by the scale of the task. They worked under difficult and dangerous conditions to deal with the dead on the battlefield. In combat men were buried by their comrades, in individual and communal plots, as all the other armies had done earlier in the war. The GRS followed in their wake, recording the locations of graves as best they could.

* * *

The African-American 92nd 'Buffalo' Division was finally complete in France by July 1918 and moved to divisional training areas in Lorraine. Here, such was the shortage of equipment, the men found themselves with little more than their uniforms. There were no carts, no horses, no grenades, no or machine guns – the list of shortages seemed endless. This already poor situation was exacerbated by the signals unit not functioning, and the fact that the artillery unit was away until the late autumn, training with their new French 75mm guns, which had not been available in the USA. Although the British trained them, they would not let them enter the front on their sector under instruction. It was clearly racist, and it led to a rebuke from Pershing to Haig that regardless of their colour they were all American. Instead they were passed to the French, who took them under instruction on the front in the Alsace. This was a generally quiet sector, with a sort of gentlemen's agreement pertaining since 1914 that neither side, German or French, would attack. Long-range weaponry kept people's heads down while they observed the status quo and took periods of rest away from the main front further north. However, an earlier advance by another American unit had broken the agreement and the 92nd found themselves thrown in the deep end with precious little real training and experience. Now under regular German attack, the American Doughboys had to learn the hard way.

On the morning of 12 September 1918 a section of the 367th Regiment was bombarded with what they thought were gas shells but turned out to be German propaganda leaflets. In good English the leaflets read:

TO THE COLORED SOLDIERS OF
THE AMERICAN ARMY

Hello, boys, what are you doing over here? Fighting the Germans? Why? Have they ever done you any harm? Of course some white folks and the lying English-American papers told you that the Germans ought to be wiped out for the sake of Humanity and Democracy.

What is Democracy? Personal freedom, all citizens enjoying the same rights socially and before the law. Do you enjoy the same rights as the white people do in America, the land of Freedom and Democracy, or are you rather not treated over there as second-class citizens? Can you go into a restaurant where white people dine? Can you get a seat in the theatre where white people sit? Can you get a seat or a berth in the railroad car, or can you even ride, in the South, in the same street car with white people? And how about the law? Is lynching and the most horrible crimes connected therewith a lawful proceeding in a democratic country?

Now, this is all different in Germany, where they do like colored people, where they treat them as gentlemen and as white people, and quite a number of colored people have fine positions in business in Berlin and other German cities.

Why, then, fight the Germans only for the benefit of the Wall Street robbers and to protect the millions they have loaned to the British, French, and Italians? You have been made the tool of the egotistic and rapacious rich in England and in America, and there is nothing in the whole game for you but broken bones, horrible wounds, spoiled health, or death. No satisfaction whatever will you get out of this unjust war.

You have never seen Germany. So you are fools if you allow people to make you hate us. Come over and see for yourself. Let those do the fighting who make the profit out of this war. Don't allow them to use you as cannon fodder. To carry a gun in this war is not an honor, but a shame.

Throw it away and come over into the German lines. You will find friends who will help you along.

Despite some truth in the comments about their conditions and treatment in America, to their credit none took the advice and crossed the line to the Germans.

*   *   *

The St Mihiel offensive started on 12 September, with French support, and brought America its first real victory of the war by 15 September. There was still the small matter of shifting over a million men 60 miles to the north and relieving the 200,000 French troops currently holding that sector. This task fell to Colonel George C. Marshall, an assistant in the operations sector. He had begun his military life inauspiciously as a platoon commander, serving in the Philippine War. It was the mobilisation of the American Army in 1917 that brought him to prominence as a capable staff officer.

Following the change of plan and the altered axis of advance, Marshall's commander, Brigadier General Drum, Pershing's chief of staff, handed him the task of sorting out the logistics. He needed to move most of the First Army from St Mihiel to Meuse Argonne by mid-September, just over three weeks away. The only bright spot was that the French would provide the transport for the move. Marshall pulled his plan together on no more than a couple of sides of A4 and submitted it. He was then summoned to see Pershing, who, to his surprise, approved the plan.

The American First Army began to assemble between the Aire and the Meuse rivers from mid-September and the SOS started to build the ammunition dumps, hospitals, camps and all the other military paraphernalia necessary for what would now become over a million men. Each day thousands of Doughboys arrived behind the front under cover of darkness, most brought by trucks, many driven by French Indo-Chinese soldiers.

The American Army looked north at a sector where the status quo had held since 1915 (apart from the areas near Verdun). Before the First Army lay four German lines of fortification, each five lines in depth. They had spent years building and improving them as part of the overall German Hindenburg Line (named after its architect), that ran south through Belgium and France. These four defensive lines made the best use of the terrain to expose the attackers and hide the defenders. Some 3 miles north of the German front-line trenches ran the first major line of defence running east to west, with Montfaucon-en-Argonne at its centre. From this hilltop (known to the French as Little Gibraltar, due to its impregnability), the Germans had clear observation over all approach lines. Some 4 miles further north was the stronger *Kriemhilde Stellung* line of defence, which ran across the heights of Romagne-sous-Montfaucon and Cunel to Grandpré, north of the Argonne Forest. A further 5 miles north lay the final line of defence, which was not as strongly built as the other two, but still a formidable obstacle to cross. It was being rushed into construction by Russian prisoners to protect the German HQ and important rail junction at Sedan. It was not just the defensive lines that were to challenge the First Army; machine-gun nests carefully sited between the lines and manned by experienced crews caused many casualties, as did the German artillery, firing onto pre-marked positions from their carefully concealed gun pits.

Into the Argonne Forest slipped the 77th Division, bounded on the west by the African-American 92nd 'Buffalo' Division under command of the French Fourth Army and on the east, outside the forest, by the 28th 'Keystone' Division. Rudimentary training had been provided in America and the first men of the 77th were despatched to France in March 1918, where they underwent basic trench warfare training with the British in the Pas de Calais region. In June the men moved south to Baccarat on the French sector where they had their first real experience of trench warfare, albeit in a quieter sector. In mid-August the 77th moved north again, this time to the Champagne sector, and took part in their first real battles along the Vesle river. Here they initially took part in defence but later in counter-attacks against German lines. Here an unassuming officer, Major Charles Whittlesey (known to his men as 'Galloping Charlie', owing to his gait), rose to prominence. A quiet outsider and former lawyer from New England, he had proven to be calm under fire and established a good relationship with his men. Not many of the New York officers had done so. Whittlesey had started to make his mark. After a month of hard fighting, and more than 5,000 casualties, the 77th was now an experienced unit. A new draught of 4,000 men had to be brought in to bring the unit back up to fighting strength, ready for its next challenge.

On 13 September General Peppino Garibaldi and his Alpine unit relieved the 77th in Champagne, and they made their way to the dark, forbidding Argonne Forest. The men of the 77th fanned out from La Harazée to Lachalade and across the forest to the eastern edge. Their allocation to the forest was somewhat ominous, as they had acquired a reputation for getting lost. Most of them were from New York, and so more at home with a street grid system than a map, and most lacked any real sense of direction. An oft-made remark was that you could count on the 77th to get there, you just weren't sure when, from where and from what direction they would appear.

Along most of the Meuse-Argonne sector, most troop movements were carried out at night, so as not to alert the Germans of the impending offensive. Under cover of the forest canopy, at least some work could be done in daylight. Trees were cut, but held in place with ropes until the attack began, to give the 77th's own artillery units a clear field of fire. Guns could not mark any targets or practise. A new phone network was laid, but couldn't be used until battle was engaged, lest the Germans intercepted the messages in English. Meanwhile all the forward posts and trenches continued to be manned by the French, so if there were German trench raids, no Americans would be captured.

Pershing's deception plan was to convince the Germans that the main American thrust would be from St Mihiel towards Metz, where he still held key units. On 22 September Pershing's dream finally came true as he officially took over the whole 17-mile wide sector from the Meuse river in the east to the western Argonne, abutting General Gouraud's French Fourth Army, roughly following the river Aire.

On 21 September the 82nd Division embarked on a four-day odyssey by train, bus and marching to the southern end of the Argonne Forest. On arrival, on 25 September, they set up camp and waited for the main AEF offensive to start on 26 September. They formed part of the reserve for the 77th.

* * *

Until midnight on 25 September the front-line trenches still contained *Poilus*; nothing was left to chance. Behind them, the American First Army was now getting ready for battle under its own terms and with its own leaders. In front of them, though, lay the main lines of the German defence.

Those men of the 77th Division lucky enough to be stationed inside the forest could at least move around under cover of the trees in daylight. Most, such as Whittlesey and his men of the 308th Regiment at Florent-en-Argonne, were packed like sardines inside barns, outbuildings and houses, forbidden to move outside in daylight, and reliant on French villagers to bring them sustenance during daylight.

The 77th Division's advance through the Argonne Forest would consist of the 308th Regiment on the extreme west of the Argonne, with the 92nd American Division, under French command, on their left. Next to them on their right was the 307th Regiment, then the 306th Regiment and finally, on the eastern edge of the forest, the 305th Regiment. Further right, in the main valley, was the 28th 'Keystone' Division. Behind them all were the 200 guns of the 77th Division artillery, camouflaged and hidden amid the forest.

As darkness fell on 25 September the men of the 77th Division began to move into the forest, the American Doughboys heading into the front line as the French made their way out. By midnight the move was complete. At 2.30am on 26 September the camouflage nets were thrown off, the cut trees were pulled down and the artillery assault began. The plan was for the artillery and mortars to cut sixteen lanes through the German wire, four in front of each regiment. Other targets were known trenches and bunkers, German artillery positions and supply dumps. For three deafening hours the barrage fell on the German lines and wire.

At 5.30am the men of the 77th Division fixed their bayonets, climbed up the trench ladders and went 'over the top'. The artillery plan was then to fire 500 yards in advance of the troops. The officers had been instructed the previous day to keep their men as close to the barrage as they could, so as to give the enemy no chance to reorganise. Despite early morning autumnal fog, progress was good; virtually unopposed, the Americans followed their lanes through the wire. All around them lay the remnants of collapsed trenches and smashed bunkers, but the soldiers of the defending German 2nd Landwehr Division were nowhere to be seen, except for the dead and injured. Sporadic firefights broke out here and there, causing deaths and casualties. By nightfall on 26 September the line had been advanced nearly as far as old front line of January 1915, 2km to the north – a distance unheard-of in three years of fighting. The men ate as ammunition resupplies were brought forward and casualties taken back. Watches were mounted for any counter-attacks and the men settled down for a few hours' rest.

At 5.30am on 27 September, after half an hour's artillery preparation, the 77th advanced again. Now, though, the going got tougher. The old French redoubt of Bagatelle, where so much blood had been split in 1915, had come back to life and across the plateau the Germans now responded with devastating artillery and machine-gun fire. The men of the 308th Regiment, on the western edge of the forest, were able to make headway, still virtually unopposed, but the 307th, in front of Bagatelle, and the 306th and 305th found every foot of ground had to be fought for. From carefully concealed positions the Germans raked the advancing regiments with

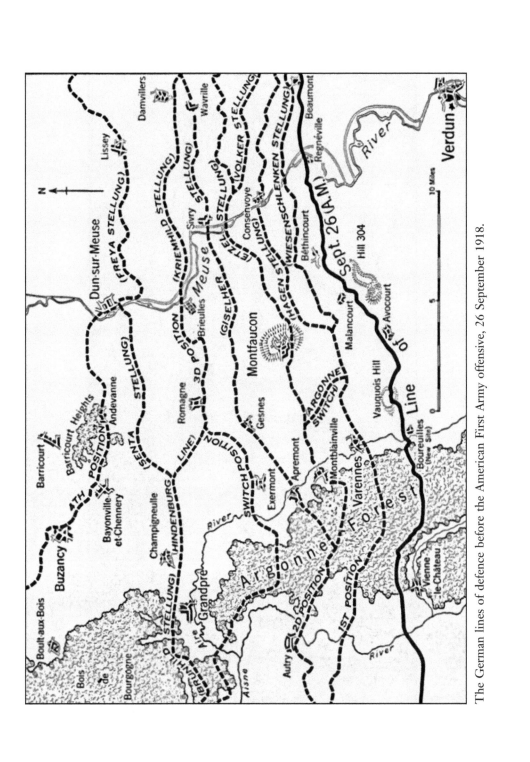

The German lines of defence before the American First Army offensive, 26 September 1918.

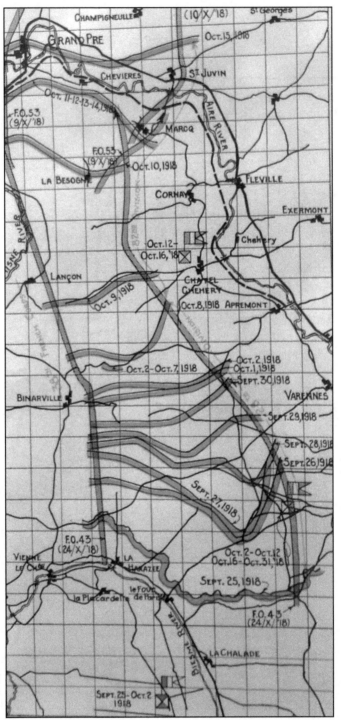

The advance of the American 77th Division through the Argonne.

La Lorraine Illustrée
CLERMONT-en-ARGONNE - L'Éperon Nord, pris de la Route de Vraincourt

ermont en Argonne, *c.*1900. 'Clermont is a beautiful village, situated above a sea of greenery, with church on its head . . .'

ermont en Argonne, *c.*1914: the ruins.

L'ARGONNE - Passavant-en-Argonne
L'Anniversaire du massacre du 25 août 1870, au Monument des Mobiles

Edition E. Moisson, Sainte-Ménehould

Passavant en Argonne, *c*.1900: the memorial to the massacre of the *Mobiles*.

Passavant en Argonne, *c*.1914: the headless memorial. The head was broken off by the retreating German Army in 1914.

L'Argonne Pittoresque
21 - PASSAVANT-EN-ARGONNE

Ici, les Prussiens ont massacré 49 mobiles de la Marne, le 25 août 1870. Lors de leur retraite, au lendemain de la Victoire de la Marne, la horde boche mutila le soldat de pierre.

Visé 8e Région, n° 252

Edit. F. Desingly, Sainte-Menehould

Uncle Bob in his uniform.

Uncle Bob sitting in his car with (*left*) André Citroën.

Lieutenant Erwin Rommel, 1915.

General von Mudra, 1915.

General Henri Gouraud, 1915.

Nicole Manguin, 1915/16.

La Guerre 1914–1915
5 R.P.   Paris   Ils profanent la sépulture Poincaré et y enfouissent leurs morts.

KOLOSSAL KULTUR

German bodies being put in the Poincaré family plot at Nubécourt in 1914.

Bruno Garibaldi dying, 1914.

Garibaldi funeral in the forest, 29 December 1914.

A hand-drawn card depicting a French post in the Argonne forest, Christmas 1914.

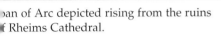
Ce que le Fer et le Feu des Barbares ne pourront jamais atteindre.

Joan of Arc depicted rising from the ruins of Rheims Cathedral.

French *Poilus* fighting in the forest, *c.*1914/15.

German soldiers fighting in the forest, *c.*1914.

Die erbitterten Kämpfe im Argonner Wald.

German soldiers in a trench, spring 1915.

French *brancardiers* in a trench, spring 1915.

Bois de la Gruerie, 1915.

A German cemetery, 1915/16.

A French cemetery of 1916/17, with Cocarde.

La Grande Guerre

FLORENT (Marne) — Le Cimetière où reposent de glorieux héros de l'Argonne

Crown Prince Wilhelm giving out medals, after the summer 1915 offensive.

An AFS 'Flivver'.

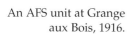

An AFS unit at Grange aux Bois, 1916.

The German *Argonnenbahn*, pictured here in 1915/1916, was a triumph of engineering expertise.

Postcard promoting the *Foyer de Soldat* (YMCA), c.1918.

PAIX SUR LA TERRE
AUX HOMMES
DE BONNE VOLONTÉ

LES FOYERS DU SOLDAT
UNION FRANCO-AMÉRICAINE

Y.M.C.A

General Pershing addressing the crowd at Lafayette's grave, 1917, after the Americans' arrival in Paris.

An African-American
doughboy in the
Argonne, *c.*1918.

Doughboys being fed
by French women.

Doughboys buried in
temporary graves in
the Argonne, autumn
1918.

Survivors of the Lost Battalion, October 1918.

LIEUT. COL. CHARLES W. WHIT-
TLESEY, LEADER OF THE
"LOST BATTALION."

Lieutenant Colonel Charles Whittlesey.

The First Division band playing at the official opening of Romagne cemetery, 30 May 1919.

Louise Baker (*left*), pictured with two local women and their Argonnaise embroidery, Clermont en Argonne, 1919.

Argonne (1919)   La CHALADE   Côte 285

Edit. Mlle L. Nicot

The cleared front line near Côte 285, Lachalade, 1919. Note the absence of topsoil, which hampered regrowth.

The ceremony for Gambetta's heart and the Unknown Soldier, Paris, 11 November 1920.

PARIS - 11 Novembre 1920 — Les Fêtes du Cinquantenaire de la République
Le Soldat Inconnu et le Cœur de Gambetta sur leur Char Place du Panthéon   A. P.

272. ROMAGNE-sous-MONTFAUCON. — Cimetière américain
de l'Argonne, 25.000 tombes. Les tombea fleuries pour la Fête des Morts
Americain Cemetery, 25.000 graves
The graves decorated for Memorial Day 1921 Main Avenue

The graves at Romagne decorated for Memorial Day, 1921.

17. - La Haute Chevauchée - ARGONNE.
M. Poincaré prononçant son discours.

M. Poincaré making a speech at the official opening of the *Haute Chevauchée* memorial, 30 July 1922.

Clermont en Argonne, *c.*1925, with many *Maisons Adrian* visible.

CLERMONT-en-ARGONNE. - Ses Ruines - Vue générale, à droite, l'Église (Mon. hist.), à gauche, le Promontoire Ste-A...
Its ruins - General view, right hand side, the Church (historical monument), left hand side, the head-land of St-Anne.

machine-gun fire. As soon as the advance stalled and the men bunched up, they found artillery rounds landing on them. The forest scrub was all but impenetrable, so the men were forced to use tracks and paths, but each one of these led to a German sniper or machine gun. It was once again the Argonne of 1915, using Mudra's tactics, but instead of months of experience and preparation, the 77th had to learn quickly, and the hard way.

It fell to small groups of Doughboys searching out the concealed gun positions and attacking them with grenades followed by fierce hand-to-hand fighting. No sooner had one position been overcome than another appeared; men quickly lost sight of each other and became disorientated, with north and south looking alike. Germans with years of experience of fighting in the forest knew it like the back of their hand. They appeared in front, to the side and behind the Doughboys. Every yard had to be fought for now. Where the 77th had occupied German trenches, counter-attacks now quickly appeared. As in 1915, once the Germans made it into a trench, the rolling-up process began, with grenades tossed along the trench. Then they advanced sideways along the trench so the men of the 77th found themselves attacked from both front and flank.

The early morning autumnal mists clung to folds in the ground and low-lying valleys. So did the omnipresent German gas; confusion over which was which would cost the Doughboys dear. For a lucky few a nearby oxygen bottle would provide immediate relief, but for others the gas proved fatal. Another tactic that was to bedevil the whole American Meuse-Argonne front now materialised. Germans stood up in front of American troops, apparently surrendering. Thinking they were accepting a German surrender, the 77th called them forward. But as they neared the Americans, the Germans threw grenades at them and then dropped to the ground as supporting machine guns fired into the revealed American positions. Soon no quarter would be given by either side.

Fighting erupted around the former French redoubts of St Hubert's Pavilion, Barricade and Abri du Crochet. By nightfall on 27 September the 77th had managed to advance another 1,500 yards and had captured the depot and German *Argonnenbahn* was rail junction at Barricade. The men began another night of watching and waiting for a counter-attack. It began to rain that night and the men, having discarded their overcoats, blankets and tents during the advance, so as not to impede their progress, now shivered in the cold. Food was becoming scarcer as the resupply lines were extended.

* * *

Meanwhile the men of the 92nd 'Buffalo' Division, having completed their training, such as it was, had moved to the Argonne on 21 September, initially as a reserve division for the AEF's First Army. This plan was changed, however, and they were placed under the command of General Gouraud's French Fourth Army. On 24 September the 368th Regiment was assigned the sector between Vienne-le-Château and La Harazée on the west side of the Argonne, with Binarville as the apex of their advance north. Their sector included the Bois de Gruerie, over which France and Germany had slogged it out over the four previous years. Now the wood was covered in barriers of every description, wire, metal posts, wooden stakes, shattered trees and a German tunnel system. The Americans were still not very well equipped; certainly their wire-cutters were not suitable for cutting thick German wire. Despite this, and with no small machine guns, they set out northwards on the morning of 26 September, the launch day of the massive AEF Meuse-Argonne offensive.

'P.M.F.' of SSU 13 (AFS Ambulancer) wrote the following poem:

American Negro and Senegalese
Their race speaks for them, black replies to black.
They grin with friendship inarticulate,
Old memories strive in vain again to track
Those pathless centuries, before the Great
Tormentor cast the world upon the rack
And tied again the ravellings of their fate.

Using the Binarville Road as their axis, they proceeded north through the first line of German trenches, known as 'Finland', without meeting any Germans. They entered the second line, 'Tirpitz', and moved along it until in the late afternoon they were finally ambushed by Germans with machine guns. Chaos ensued. Men ran or dived into cover; no one returned fire; officers failed to rally the men. With daylight fading fast, the decision was made to turn back to the previous German trench line, Finland, which they were familiar with. Some 200 men were left by the Binarville Road–Tirpitz trench junction for the night. Although under heavy German machine-gun fire, they remained in situ all night, not falling back.

Their orders for 27 September were to push forward to the German third line, 'Dromedary'. Now clear of the old front line, the forest was more thickly wooded and the men soon became separated. Again progress was painfully slow and by nightfall the men were back at Finland trench. On the left flank of the road, though, there had been some progress and

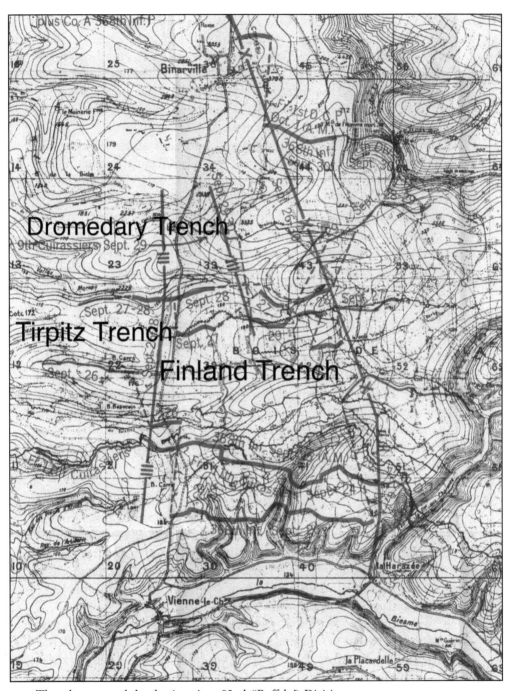

The advance north by the American 92nd ('Buffalo') Division.

men had moved through the Vallée Moreau towards Dromedary. Again the men returned at nightfall to the vicinity of Finland.

On the 28th the men of the 77th moved forward again, after breakfast – their first proper meal in two days. By lunchtime Champ Mahaut had fallen to the 305th, and the redoubts of St Hubert's Pavilion and Bagatelle to the 307th. During the afternoon of 28 September the 307th ran into the second line of defence north of Bagatelle.

Meanwhile the 305th could only stare in wonder at the comfortable support positions they now found themselves in at Champ Mahaut. There were concrete rest bunkers for officers, NCOs and men, beer and flower gardens. There was a concrete swimming pool and heated showers, along with well stocked libraries and an officers' cinema. Signs of a hasty retreat were everywhere, with abandoned pictures of happier times, unfinished drinks on table tops, jackets on the back of chairs, cigarettes and cigars still smoking around ashtrays. All too quickly the men grabbed what booty they could and pushed on north.

On the western edge of the forest, for the 308th under Whittlesey, the going was slow on 28 September, pushing north towards Binarville. Unable to move in a wider formation because of the thick ground foliage and dense forest, the men moved forward in file. By nightfall they were just south of Binarville, on the reverse slope of the ominously named Dead Man's Hill. The men dug in and patrols were sent out to establish links with the adjacent units, the 92nd on their left and the 307th on their right. But the patrols returned having found no one; the 308th were now effectively cut off. Whittlesey decided to batten down for the night and wait for daylight to try to re-establish links with other units.

*   *   *

On 28 September the 2nd and 3rd Battalions of the 368th Regiment of the 92nd, who had been trying to push northwards, finally collapsed, brought down by the complicated Franco-American command structure, lack of experience, poor leadership, and the unforgiving terrain, to name a few reasons. The men just walked back from the front lines in groups, large and small, and refused to move forwards again.

Up stepped the 1st Battalion, commanded by Major Merrill, a somewhat unorthodox soldier, with pre-war experience in the Far East, Persia and with the British Army. He moved up the Binarville road in darkness on 28 September, but his troops soon came under German artillery fire. Merrill immediately took command, quite brutally. As his men began to turn and run, he punched several in the face, thus stemming the rout, and they continued the push north.

That night, back at a regimental command post, Merrill remonstrated with a brigade commander about the lack of equipment and spelt out exactly what he needed to make a successful advance. Overnight some of the equipment arrived and at 10am on 29 September he began his march north, leading from the front. At 3pm his men moved into German trenches 2 miles south of Binarville for the night. He finally brought some organisation to the 368th's front, establishing links with the French to his left and the 77th Division to the right, and spent the night hunkered down in a front-line foxhole.

Next morning, 30 September, Merrill moved across the Vallée Moreau and personally reconnoitred a kilometre in advance. Seeing no Germans, and after watching the French start to move north, he ordered an advance north towards Binarville. He informed his men that if they did not move forward he would open fire on them. They were still reluctant, but after a couple of shots over their heads they started to move forward. Under his continuous prodding, they arrived in Binarville at 4pm, just twenty minutes after the French. But they soon abandoned the position as heavy German artillery fire came down on them. That night Merrill received fresh orders to move back to their start point. His somewhat unorthodox manner had brought a degree of success to the 368th after the failure of the 2nd and 3rd Battalions to advance north. The 92nd lost 279 men killed, injured, gassed or posted missing during their five days' advance. After this, the 92nd moved to the east to join the smaller American Second Army, where they fought on until 11am on 11 November. Their initial reaction to coming under heavy fire matched many units from both the French army and the BEF in the early battles of the war when they experienced similar hesitancy. Their post-war denigration bore little resemblance to their actual participation in further fighting as part of the US Second Army.

* * *

On the morning of 29 September the skies opened up and the rain poured down on the beleaguered men of the 308th. Whittlesey found his chain of runners to the rear had been broken by German infiltration overnight. As dawn broke Whittlesey had a chance encounter with a German officer; Whittlesey was unarmed, as his pistol was being cleaned, but fortunately other men fired quickly and shot the German. Before he died, the officer revealed that his men were behind Whittlesey, with a larger group in front. They were surrounded.

Whittlesey sent back a pigeon with a message outlining their plight and requesting food and ammunition, but saying they would continue hold their ground. A message was sent back to Whittlesey that relief would be mounted from the rear but in the meantime he should consolidate his position. Whittlesey's men dug in, making a rough square, and beat off a few probing attacks during the day. By late afternoon the attacks had become more determined, Whittlesey's casualties were mounting, ammunition was running low and food was non-existent. All they had was rainwater to drink. Two patrols were despatched southwards to make contact with their regimental HQ, but both returned, having been unable to work their way through the German lines. Whittlesey then sent out a larger patrol under Lieutenant Mckeogh, who did eventually manage to wriggle his way through to regimental HQ and report their position; for this action he was awarded a Distinguished Service Cross.

In the meantime Lieutenant Colonel F. Smith, the regimental commander, was making his way forward with a small patrol carrying an ammunition resupply for Whittlesey. Smith was killed in the advance and was awarded a posthumous Medal of Honor in 1922. His citation read:

When communication from the forward regimental post of command to the battalion leading the advance had been interrupted temporarily by the infiltration of small parties of the enemy armed with machine guns, Lieutenant Colonel Smith personally led a party of two other officers and ten soldiers, and went forward to re-establish runner posts and carry ammunition to the front line. The guide became confused and the party strayed to the left flank beyond the outposts of supporting troops, suddenly coming under fire from a group of enemy machine guns only 50 yards away. Shouting to the other members of his party to take cover, this officer, in disregard of his danger, drew his pistol and opened fire on the German gun crew. About this time he fell, severely wounded in the side, but, regaining his footing, he continued to fire on the enemy until most of the men in his party were out of danger.

Refusing first-aid treatment he then made his way in plain view of the enemy to a hand grenade dump and returned under continued heavy machine-gun fire for the purpose of making another attack on the enemy emplacements. As he was attempting to ascertain the exact location of the nearest nest, he again fell, mortally wounded.

Smith is buried in the American military cemetery at Romagne.

*   *   *

After two days of rain, little food and many casualties, relief finally arrived in the late afternoon of 30 September, but the relieving force had orders to press on. Whittlesey made his way to the rear that night, to find that his orders for the next day were 'to push forward without regard for the flanks; once on the day's objective, to dig in and wait to be caught up'. He protested that it was all but impossible to continue forward with the small number of men he now had left and the poor condition they were in. His plea was ignored and the following morning, 1 October, he made his way back to the front and carried on the advance. The outcome was almost inevitable; hence, when people later asked about the 'Pocket', those lucky enough to have survived both encirclements replied, 'Which one?'

* * *

Elsewhere on 29 September the 305th pushed forward another 2 miles past the German base at Abri du Crochet, level with the rear-guard action being fought by the Germans north of Bagatelle with the 307th. The Doughboys were now grasping the intricacies of fighting in the forest, making frequent halts to check direction and to ensure the flanks were moving at the same speed. Short, sharp firefights overcame machine-gun and sniper positions. Supplies were brought forward and casualties evacuated to the rear, to the hospital in the Abbey at Lachalade. The 305th and 306th consolidated their positions, while the 307th was engaged north of Bagatelle and the 308th was fighting for its life near Dead Man's Hill.

The next day proved no less difficult for the men of the 307th who tried to press north from Bagatelle. The forest was now covered in frost, adding to the misery of the men of the 77th. A heavy artillery barrage dislodged the Germans, who merely retreated to another pre-prepared defensive position. With the forest now thickening, and with only narrow tracks and paths to follow, it was proving difficult to bring the artillery forward to support the advance. Another problem was in correcting the rounds as they just disappeared unsighted into the forest. German reinforcements arrived in the shape of the 76th Reserve Division.

Something happened to the men during these cold, wet, dark autumnal days. What the veterans of the 77th would later call the 'Spirit of Argonne' entered them. Despite their lack of warm and dry clothing, the shortage of food, the threat of instant death or injury, and the poisonous gas lying like forest mist in every glade, there was an indomitable will to push forward, to overcome any adversity at whatever the cost against the unseen enemy. They would persevere, and neither the hidden Germans nor the Argonne

Forest would defeat them. An anonymous writer of the history of the 77th Division wrote:

The Spirit of the Argonne

In the mists of the early morning, in the shadows at close of day,
I seemed to see the phantom form, I seemed to hear it say,
'I'm the Spirit of Righteousness, through me battles are won,
So I take this name which shall bring ye fame,
Spirit of Argonne!

'Gird your loins, my fellows – look at your weapons well;
Over the top and do not stop; drive at those beasts of Hell!
Faint not, and fear not of failure; press bravely, firmly on
Till your task, is done and you've crushed the Hun;
Spirit of the Argonne!'

On through machine guns sputtered; on through shrapnel and shell,
On through the red murk of battle, on through the gates of Hell!
Beating back all resistance, smashing the brutal Hun;
'Twas the Spirit's breath in defiance to death – the
Spirit of the Argonne!

And each of them gave the best in him, and some gave precious life,
To a noble and holy cause, for the end of sinful strife;
Think not 'twill be forgotten, the work by these heroes done,
Inspired by Right and conceived in the might – of the
Spirit of the Argonne!

'Twas the spirit of personal sacrifice, the gift of brave men's all;
The liberty should not perish, that righteousness should not fail;
And our country (God bless her!) is better for the deeds her sons have
    done.
May this spirit march through the ages to come – the
Spirit of Argonne!

*   *   *

Into the forbidding forest fire-storm came, unexpectedly, the Y Secretaries. Mr E.T. Banks, from Dayton, Ohio, was one; he was also a sometime preacher. He accompanied American soldiers for two days carrying food, cigarettes and helping the injured. On the last night, while giving first aid to a wounded African-American soldier in no man's land, he was fired on by a German machine-gunner. Despite being under fire, he successfully brought the injured soldier back into the safety of the American lines and was cited for his meritorious service. An officer wrote personally to Banks thanking him: 'When the full story of the Argonne is told, the Red Triangle represented by Mr Banks will add beauty to the rainbow reflected from the silent tombs of those who sleep the sleep of death that Democracy may not perish from the earth.'

Another Y Secretary in the field, William B. West, later described the scene:

> We were on a forest trail. The mud from recent rains covered our leggings and heavy hobnail boots. We came to a crossroads in the heart of the forest. Our wounded on stretchers were everywhere. I can see now the bandaged eyes of the gassed patients, the armless sleeve or the bared breast with bloody dressings. I can see the silent forms of those who will never fight again ... The Y man with his pack always received a sincere welcome.
>
> There was a smile of gratitude as a piece of chocolate was placed in the mouth of one of those whose hands were useless, or a cigarette and light given to another whose whole frame is a-quiver from the shock of battle. There are eager requests of the Red Cross men for extra supplies for the boys whom they would see when Mr Y Man was not with them.
>
> ... The deepest cave was connected by a tunnel with a railway system that had branches everywhere through the forest. When we found the head surgeon we told him we had chocolate for his patients. He took us to one of the wards where thirty men were crowded into four small rooms. The odor of death was in the air. The laboured breathing of unconscious men cast a gloom that was hard to shake off. ... We went from cot to cot with a piece of chocolate for each, gripping the hands of some and looking in the eyes of others too far gone even to speak.

On 2 October, after seven days of fighting, the men of the 77th were ordered to advance on the *Etzel-Giselher Stellung*, the first main line of German defence. Whittlesey with the 308th received his orders for the day: 'Advance due north and then west, occupy the slope above Charleveaux valley, take the mill, reorganise and await further orders to advance.' This was reinforced by a no-turning-back order. Whittlesey again demurred; he had only just escaped from being surrounded by Germans a few days previously at Dead Man's Hill. He had lost many men; those he had left were poorly equipped, insufficient in number and mostly untrained for the task. He was ordered to press on regardless and also, crucially, to ignore his flanks, which would be protected by other units. On their left flank French forces would be advancing towards the old Charleveaux Mill. On their right flank men from the American 307th Regiment would advance to link up with them.

It was this order that was to write Whittlesey and his men into the annals of American military history. He advanced with a mixed group of men from the 308th and 306th Regiments. During the advance on 2 October Whittlesey found a gap between the German defensive line, the *Giselher Stellung*. He worked his way up through the gap, with the German strongpoint at La Palette Pavilion on the hill to their left, up on to Côte 198 (hill), and then they dropped down across what looked like a German parade ground at the bottom of the Charleveaux valley. On the slope slightly north of the stream they stopped on their objective, just below the Binarville–La Viergette road. Whittlesey reorganised and awaited further orders.

Here he was joined by Captain McMurtry and men from the 2nd Battalion of the 308th Regiment. They set up a defensive perimeter, in what later became known as 'the Pocket'. Assuming that reinforcements and fresh orders would arrive soon, patrols were sent out to find the units on their flanks and a message was sent back through the chain of runners left along the route. The men sat down to eat the few rations they carried and dug in. As dawn broke on 3 October, Whittlesey and his second-in-command McMurtry realised their position was parlous. They had only iron rations, no blankets, and precious few overcoats against the cold, and they were reliant on a local stream for water. Patrols had shown there appeared to be no flank support.

Although the commanders at Divisional Head Quarters were pleased to learn Whittlesey had reached his objective, the realisation now dawned that he was isolated, and reinforcements from the 307th were despatched that night to join him. They made their way in darkness through the same gap in the German line and on to Côte 198 – and then things went wrong.

The Germans had not been idle. Discovering the breach in their line, they had begun to encircle Whittlesey and his men in the Pocket. Before the breach was closed, Captain Nelson Holderman of the 307th arrived in the Pocket with his K Company, and assured Whittlesey that at least two more companies from the 307th would be arriving imminently. But these companies became separated in the dark and never made it to the Pocket. The combined force in the Pocket now numbered approximately 700 men.

A newspaper reporter, Fred S. Ferguson, attached to the AEF, made an initial report on Whittlesey's unit, moving in front of the general AEF advance. His editor in the USA wired back, 'Send more on the Lost Battalion'. So was born the legend of the 'Lost Battalion'. The story ran across American newspapers for five days, enthralling millions of readers, as Whittlesey, his officers and men held their ground. The Lost Battalion was not in fact lost at all. Whittlesey knew where he was, as did 77th Division HQ, to within a couple of hundred metres (the dense Argonne Forest tree cover prevented the AEF aero units from locating the exact position of Whittlesey's unit) – but so did the Germans.

In the east of the forest the 305th and 306th Regiments had little luck in moving north on 3 October; apart from Whittlesey, it looked like the advance of the 77th had ground to a halt. The 306th incurred such heavy losses that they had to be pulled back into a support role. The 305th was pinned down by machine-gun fire. The remaining companies of the 3rd Battalion, 308th Regiment, made an attempt to break through but heavy fire from La Palette and Côte 198 opposite and thick barbed-wire entanglements forced them back.

A plan was hatched later that day at Corps HQ for the units on either side of the 77th Division – the French on the west and American divisions in the east of the forest – to stage a major attack on the following day, 4 October. All the 77th had to do was maintain pressure in the forest front and let the units outside the forest outflank the Germans.

On 3 October, as the morning progressed, the Germans ratcheted up the pressure on the Pocket with trench mortars and machine-gun fire. The only thing in the Pocket's favour was that the Germans had overestimated the strength of the force holding it. As Whittlesey assessed the situation, the words of Major General Alexander, commanding officer of the 77th Division, rang in his ears: 'We are not going back, but forward.' This was backed up by threats to shoot any man who ordered a retreat. To a New York lawyer like Whittlesey, the situation was clear: he would remain on the objective as per his orders and await further orders to advance. It was a position that none of his officers sought to disagree with. It was confirmed in a written order sent to all his officers in the Pocket: 'Our mission is to hold this position at all costs. No falling back. Have this understood by every man in your command.' The die was cast.

Later that afternoon the Germans made their first assault on the Pocket, but they were beaten off after an hour of intense fighting. That evening Whittlesey sent a message by pigeon. He gave their grid reference, using the established French mapping protocol, and listed his casualties –

9 dead, 140 injured – and noted that he had 245 men still capable of fighting. He also emphasised their dire need for more ammunition. That evening men tried to fill their canteens with water from the stream. The Germans, aware that this was the only water collection point, ambushed it and killed them.

At 5.30am on 4 October a major American offensive started, with the 77th looking to break through on the left flank, next to the French, using the same route Whittlesey had come through. In the Pocket men silently cheered as they heard the mass of artillery and machine guns open up on the German lines; help was at last on its way. A half-hearted attack on Le Palette and Côte 198 on 4 October by the remaining men of the 308th petered out with nothing to show for their sacrifice. The French advances on the west were treated with a degree of scepticism by the Americans. By lunchtime it was clear that the 77th advance had stalled again despite many casualties, and the Pocket remained surrounded. But it wasn't all bad news: out to the east of the forest a concerted thrust by the First Army was showing some reward and sucking Germans away from the Argonne.

Whittlesey now sent one of his last four pigeons, saying he was short of food, some American artillery fire had fallen on the Pocket and he had casualties that needed evacuation. He was growing concerned lest more officers were killed or injured. Without strong leadership, he feared his men would abandon the Pocket. The men, predominantly New Yorkers,

The Lost Battalion and the pocket.

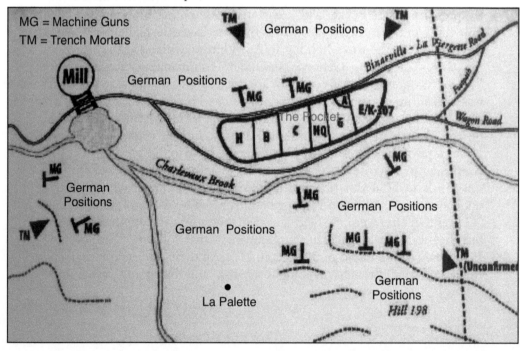

took a dim view of their officers, whom they regarded as coming from the 'wrong' side of New York. The outsider Whittlesey, though, had moved up in their esteem after his earlier conduct at the Vesle river. Always calm, with time for everyone, he constantly walked around, seemingly oblivious to incoming fire.

Now he kept the men busy digging latrines and burying the dead, whenever there was a lull in the fighting. Only recycled first aid dressings were available. At 10.35am he sent another message by pigeon, outlining the dire straits they were now in, down to 235 fighting men, and asking, 'Can support be sent at once?' By midday the American relief attack had failed across the whole sector behind them. In the Pocket all the men could now do was wait for the next German onslaught. Among the injured, gangrene started to spread.

Back at 77th Division HQ, after the guns had cooled down, they would start suppressing fire around the Pocket, to try to protect it. Later, in what men said was the cruellest twist they suffered in the Pocket, friendly artillery fire from the Americans rained down on them. A misunderstanding about the precise location of the Pocket had brought the shells down on Whittlesey and his men. The Germans opened fire with machine guns as they saw the men try to move to safer positions, seeking better cover from the murderous shells.

Whittlesey called for the last two pigeons, but one escaped from the cage after the handler fumbled with it. There was only one pigeon left, named Cher Ami. Whittlesey penned the message: 'We are along the road parallel 276.4. Our own artillery is dropping a barrage directly on us. For heavens sake stop it.' The pigeon handler, Richards, threw Cher Ami into the air, but it merely went to roost in a nearby tree. He threw stones and sticks at it, but the pigeon simply moved to another tree. In desperation, Richards climbed the tree to shoo Cher Ami on its journey. At last it took off, but the Germans had seen it and opened fire on the bird. At 4pm Cher Ami arrived in its coop, minus a leg and an eye, and with an injured chest. The message was hastily removed and first aid given to the bird. The American fire on the Pocket was finally halted at 4.15pm. With a lot of their cover blown away, the Germans now had clearer sight of the Pocket and poured in machine-gun fire. More than a hundred men had been killed or injured in the American artillery firestorm, including two officers, adding to Whittlesey's main worry – a lack of leadership.

That evening four captured Americans were led in to the German HQ. On their way in, they had agreed their story: there were about 1,500 men in good shape in the Pocket, with plenty of food and ammunition. Under interrogation they stuck to this story, which merely confirmed the earlier German suspicions and they now summoned reinforcements to take on such a large number of Americans.

*   *   *

On 5 October the Americans and French planned another relief attack. McMurtry, now himself injured, was organising the covering of the dead. The men no longer had the strength to dig graves for them. Whittlesey made his rounds, doing what he could to keep up moral and try to help the injured. They lay in pitiful rows, many wanting water, which was all but unobtainable. Whittlesey was now forced to place armed guards to stop men trying to get water from the stream and getting themselves killed. As the early morning mist cleared, the Germans began their machine-gun fire into the Pocket and the trench mortars rained down on the trapped men.

In the Pocket, men broke into a cold sweat as they heard the same sound as yesterday: an American artillery barrage creeping closer and closer. At the point when the men's nerves were most stretched, the barrage began to drop into the German lines in front and behind them; a cheer rose from the beleaguered men. Meanwhile above them planes from the 50th American Aero Squadron flew overhead trying to locate the Pocket and dropping much-needed resupplies; sadly these fell straight into German hands. Locally, the Germans now had the upper hand, having stopped both the French and American attacks on the flanks of the Pocket. Across the broader Meuse-Argonne front, though, the German Army was now in retreat to new positions further north. With a lull in the incoming fire, men came out of their foxholes to enjoy some warmth from the autumnal sun. The American fire earlier had quietened the Germans down. They could only look up in despair as they saw glimpses of the 50th Aero Squadron's planes fly overhead, fruitlessly looking for them. In the late afternoon the Pocket came under a renewed German attack for an hour or so, but nothing was achieved except more casualties on both sides. German HQ now requested that stormtroops be sent up to finally break the Pocket. Whittlesey, still miraculously uninjured, spoke to McMurtry. They needed to make another attempt with a runner to try to get through the German lines. There seemed to be no other way to let 77th Division HQ know their dire situation. Private Botelle set off to attempt the journey.

On 6 October a fresh American division arrived, the 82nd, with orders to push west into the forest above the Pocket, outflanking the Germans and thus relieving the trapped men. In the Pocket Whittlesey did his morning rounds; today he noticed a change in the men, they were now resolute, they could endure. They had found the 'Spirit of the Argonne'. His earlier worries of mass desertion disappeared, and the men knew their leader was a match for their situation. McMurtry oversaw the covering of the dead and Whittlesey chased men to use the latrines they had dug. Botelle returned badly injured; his attempt to break through the German lines had been unsuccessful. The men watched forlornly as the 50th Aero Squadron again tried to locate the Pocket, and once more dropped their precious resupplies into German hands.

In one of the de Havilland DH-4 planes, pilot Lieutenant Harold Goettler and Observer Erwin Bleckley thought they caught a glimpse of the 'Lost Battalion' through the early morning mist. But their plane was so badly damaged by German fire that it was grounded on its return to base. Determined to try to find the Lost Battalion and drop supplies, they took off in another aircraft. This time, flying even lower, their luck finally ran out; the plane was shot down and both men were killed. However, the plane came down behind the French lines, and their map coordinates provided more valuable information about the Pocket's exact location. Both Goettler and Bleckley were awarded a posthumous Medal of Honor for their courage.

Meanwhile German HQ had given the local commander thirty-six hours to drive out the Americans in the Pocket and then retreat. The overall German position along the front was becoming untenable. At 3pm men in the Pocket braced themselves for the inevitable German assault that usually came around that time. This time the attackers included flame-throwers, the most feared method of attack, yet somehow the Pocket still held firm. Whittlesey went round cajoling the men and moving them to reinforce any breaches.

That night, though, Whittlesey's mood darkened. The perimeter had shrunk, valuable weapons had been lost and there were only three functioning senior officers: Whittlesey himself, and McMurtry and Holderman, both injured but still mobile. Today had also been the most effective German attack carried out since the Pocket was formed. His only consolation was that the aircraft overhead indicated that help was at hand, although they had yet to receive a successful drop. Once again they came back to the need to get a messenger through. McMurtry went out and found eight volunteers to try to creep through the lines, in the hope that at least one would get through. Four of the men became lost in the dark and returned to the Pocket. There were still four men out there, though. However, none got through: they were either killed or captured.

On 7 October, as Whittlesey made his rounds, his optimism of forty-eight hours earlier was now crushed as he received the first report of a group of men abandoning the Pocket. Whittlesey spoke to Holderman and asked him if he had a man who would take his chance in daylight to try to get through to HQ. He offered Private Krotoshinsky, who appeared in front of Whittlesey for a briefing, and was joined by two other men, also willing to give it a go. As they disappeared into the bush a machine gun opened up. Not long after, one of the men returned badly injured and said the other was dead, but of Krotoshinsky there was no news. Whittlesey asked for two more volunteers to try to make their way through. Two men, Privates Brown and Kozikowski, stepped forward. Again Whittlesey outlined the precariousness of their position and the urgency of their mission. Off they set on the route given them. Around that time a bogus American panel placed by the Germans was incorrectly identified by the 50th Aero as the Pocket.

Outside the Pocket, the 1st, 28th, 77th and 82nd Divisions, all desperate to relieve the men trapped in the Pocket, finally started to gain some traction and break the stiff German defences of the *Gishelher Stellung*. The German force surrounding the Pocket would have to retreat soon if they were to save themselves and their equipment.

The previous night heavy artillery fire had been directed against La Palette to try to cut through the wire surrounding the hilltop in preparation for another French attack. Once more this failed, as did the French attack, which was unable to make any progress through the wire or against the well dug-in Germans. But events outside the forest to the east were finally bearing fruit. The attacks towards Chatel-Chéhéry were a success and the German positions in the forest were becoming more precarious as they risked becoming enveloped from the rear by the 82nd Division. By noon, the 305th, at the extreme eastern end of the forest, found they could at last move forward, as could the 306th next to them. German resistance in the forest was at last starting to crumble.

The Germans around the Pocket had earlier captured an injured but still mobile American, Private L.R. Hollingshead, possibly one of a group of eight men who disappeared while searching for dropped supplies. Lieutenant Heinrich Prinz interrogated him in perfect English, having lived in Seattle for six years before the war. Prinz asked Hollingshead to go back into the Pocket with a message. Given a stick to support his injured leg and a white flag, he was blindfolded and taken to within a few hundred yards of the American position. There the blindfold was removed and he was pointed towards the Pocket. Challenged by the guard, he said he had a message for Whittlesey from the Germans, and asked to be taken to him. Whittlesey was talking to McMurtry about how they could hold out against the afternoon attack, due any time soon. The note, asking Whittlesey to surrender, was handed to him. Whittlesey passed it to McMurtry, who passed it to Holderman. McMurtry cried, 'We've got 'em licked, or they wouldn't have sent this.' Whittlesey told Hollingshead to go back to his position and the next time to make sure he had orders to leave the Pocket. Reluctantly, in case the Germans or his own men thought them a signal of surrender, Whittlesey had taken down the white marker panels that were intended to alert the 50th Aero Squadron to the exact location of the Pocket. Inevitably, though, this action removed any chance that their position would be located from above. Later, Whittlesey's post-operation report merely remarked, 'No reply to the demand to surrender seemed necessary.'

Within minutes, though, word had gone round the Pocket that the Germans had asked them to surrender and Whittlesey had told them 'to go to hell'. The men's backs were up; the 'Spirit of the Argonne' was back. Surrender? Never! Even the sick made their way to hold the line for the anticipated attack. The assault came and was bloodily repulsed. Holderman was the hero of the hour; injured yet again, he still rallied the men and held off the enemy.

The 307th Regiment held the key to relieving Whittlesey, but their attack was short of manpower and relied on an element of surprise. They would attack, but they needed to cut through the thickets of German wire first. Their commander was Colonel Houghton, who had arrived earlier in the war with the Canadians and had participated in most of the Western Front campaigns. He had seen what looked like some gaps in the wire; he just needed time to cut through them. During the day Lieutenant Tillman cut the wire and men from the 307th's 1st Battalion were able to move through in small groups, unnoticed by the Germans. By nightfall they were behind the Germans in a battalion-sized group. Astonishingly, Private Abe Krotoshinsky, the runner sent by Whittlesey from the Pocket, now ran into a forward patrol of the 307th. After a coffee and a tin of beef to eat, he led them in the dark back down towards the Pocket. An hour later, they fell into a guard's foxhole at the perimeter of the Pocket and asked for Whittlesey. A soldier appeared in the dark in front of Whittlesey and said an American officer was on the road to meet him. Whittlesey came forward to the previously dangerous road and greeted Lieutenant Tillman of the 307th at about 7pm. He was given a sandwich.

McMurtry, who had remained hidden in the Pocket, had become suspicious when he heard Whittlesey was moving up to the road, which until then was held by the Germans. He moved up to the road, but all he could say when he saw Whittlesey eating was 'For God's sake Charles, give me a bite of that.' At 7pm the Pocket was officially relieved.

As the relief force made their way into the Pocket, the sight was one of utter desolation and destruction. The dead lay everywhere, and the sick crying out for help. All the living men wanted was food and water. Later that night Privates Brown and Kozikowski also made it through to the 307th. All three runners were awarded the Distinguished Service Cross for their efforts to reach the American lines. With the Pocket now relieved, the 77th Division front across the forest was again unified and linear from east to west.

On 8 October, after five days of unrelenting siege, men could finally sit out safely, and eat and drink in safety; the sick were treated and evacuated by a steady stream of ambulances arriving by road. General Alexander, the commanding officer of the 77th, found Whittlesey and immediately announced his promotion to lieutenant colonel. At that point there began one of the great deceits of the Lost Battalion as Alexander insisted that it was French artillery that had fired on them. This would later be changed to German artillery fire. Many of the 194 men from the Pocket who were still uninjured, having eaten and drunk, then moved forward with the rest of the division in pursuit of the Germans.

Of the approximately 700 men believed to have been in the Pocket at the start of the siege, only 194 walked out. Another 197 were killed in action, with the remainder either injured, captured or posted missing. In the 77th Division's Official History there is an account of the end of the siege: 'The crash of the Minenwerfers and the whine of bullets is stilled. But if the trees on this torn slope of France could break the silence they would say "By these splintered wounds you see upon us, we live to mark the valor of the Americans".'

One of the greatest feats of arms in American military history had been successfully concluded. The story of the Lost Battalion in the American newspapers had been slavishly followed all over America for days. Whittlesey, the unassuming Boston lawyer, had now unwittingly become one of America's most famous military heroes, stepping onto the pantheon alongside men such as Colonel Custer, Davy Crockett and Jim Bowie.

Meanwhile, the Germans had now gone into a broader retreat, fearing envelopment from their flanks. By midday on 8 October units of the 77th Division on both the eastern and western edges of the forest had been able to move into open country on the move north. This also allowed their artillery to be pulled forward for the first time in days and thus to fire more accurately on the German lines. Inside the forest, progress was slower for the 307th and elements of the 308th. The wire and thick forest still held German machine guns and snipers who mounted a stiff rear-guard action, slowing down the American advance.

*   *   *

The 82nd Division, advancing on Chatel-Chéhéry to relieve the Pocket, was to throw up another unlikely hero. Alvin C. York, a deeply religious backwoodsman from Tennessee, who had initially refused to bear arms, was to write himself into American army folklore.

At 8pm on 6 October the 82nd finally received orders to move forward into combat. A difficult night march through the chaos of war brought the unit to its forming-up position, just east of Chatel-Chéhéry, with orders to seize the eastern slopes of the Argonne, as part of the attempt to relieve pressure on the Lost Battalion. The 1st Battalion of the 328th was to clear Côte 233 or Castle Hill, just north of the village. Further north, the 327th was to clear Côte 180. York had a ringside seat as the men of the 328th began their assault under cover of advancing artillery fire on the morning of 7 October, and by lunchtime the hilltop was under American control. The Germans soon launched a counter-attack; through the night and into the early morning of 8 October the battle ebbed and flowed on the hilltop, with each side clinging tenaciously to the top. York's unit was prevented from moving by German artillery and machine-gun fire that cut a swathe through the unit. Even so, it was ordered during the night of 7 October to move west to cut the vital forest road and railway supply route which ran north–south through a valley to the west of Côte 223.

Meanwhile fresh German units were arriving to push the Americans back off Côte 223 and 180. Lieutenant Paul Vollmer, commanding the Germans, had been in the Argonne since 1914 and knew the ground well. He prepared the men to defend their ground against the impending attack of York's unit. The German plan was simple: to hold Côte 223 for as long as possible, and then retreat, luring the Americans into the open valley to the west. Here, with the Germans occupying the high ground all around, they would kill the attacking Americans before counter-attacking to retake

Côte 223 and 180, thus controlling the Aire valley and beyond onto the Meuse plain.

In the early morning of 8 October York's battalion moved into the village of Chatel-Chéhéry and on towards the top of Côte 223 in the dark. Soon the Germans spotted them and artillery fire and gas rained down on them, slowing their advance as they donned gas-masks and stumbled on in the pitch dark. On the top of Côte 223 the survivors of the 1st Battalion on the western edge thankfully greeted them. With York was a man called Cuttings, who had suspicions as to whether York was capable of killing Germans, given his deeply religious background. At 6.10am, despite the absence of support artillery, York and his men pressed forward. Soon they found Germans, in front, behind and to the side of them, hidden in the dense forest cover.

As per the German plan, once they ran short of ammunition they pulled back westwards across the valley to set the trap. York's men looked aghast as they cleared the forest and looked across the open valley at the forest on the far side, from where the Germans now began to machine gun them. To add to their difficulties, their flanks were exposed as well, due to fresh orders given to their support troops to alter their own lines of attack.

York's 328th Regiment was now literally advancing on its own. The men were moving in a north-westerly direction towards the German defensive hill position called *Humserberg*, when their leader Lieutenant Stewart was cut down and command fell to Sergeant Parsons. The men, now pinned down, began to dig in, out in the open, as best they could to try to find cover. Parsons saw that the main machine-gun fire being directed at them was coming from *Humserberg*. He ordered Cuttings, York, Early and Savage to take their squads and silence the machine guns. Early, as acting sergeant, was in overall command of the four sections.

Now under German artillery fire, Early identified what he thought was a gap in the ridge due south of them which would provide cover to flank the German machine guns. Just as they began to move, into the face of almost certain death from German artillery fire, the American barrage belatedly began to drop on the Germans, giving Early and his men time to disappear south into the forest.

The seventeen men could hardly believe their luck; at last they were safely out of carnage of the valley bottom and were now safely hidden in the dense forest. They pressed westwards and found an ancient trench which marked a border. Taking cover in the trench, they continued to move westwards, arriving on the supply road that they briefly followed before arriving at a stream. There were two Germans filling water bottles, who fled before Early and his men could stop them.

Meanwhile, further north, German reinforcements had arrived to help the counter-attack on the Americans that was expected to take place about 10am. Vollmer made his way back to see the new men and could hardly believe his eyes when he saw them eating breakfast, with no weapons to hand. To add to the confusion, the two men who had gone for water now arrived shouting that the Americans had arrived. Out of the corner of his eye he could make out a group of Americans charging towards them. Vollmer drew his pistol and urged the men to pick up their weapons, but it was too late; assuming that Early and his men were part of a much larger force, they surrendered. The key *Humserberg* defence commander Vollmer could do nothing. Early and his men had captured seventy Germans by sheer surprise. Just above the captured Germans, Lieutenant Lipp realised what had happened; wanting to save his comrade Lieutenant Vollmer and his men, he shouted in German to the men below to take cover. The prisoners dived for cover and in the chaos that followed as Lipp and his machine gunners opened fire, six of the Americans were killed and three more injured, as were several Germans.

Savage was dead, and Early was badly injured, as was Cuttings, leaving York as the only able-bodied NCO, with seven men. The men were scattered in the meadow grass, calling to one another to find out who was dead and who was alive. The Germans lying alongside them were just as likely to be shot as the Americans, such was the confusion. York now seized the initiative. With Beardsley firing the machine gun and the six others giving what covering fire they could, he moved towards the German machine gun above. Working himself into a position to overlook the machine gun, and using his backwoods marksman skills, he killed nineteen Germans.

On his way back York was spotted by another German officer, Vollmer's friend Lieutenant Endriss. He hastily organised a bayonet charge against York, who now dropped to the ground beside Beardsley. Using his Colt pistol, York fired into the charging Germans, supported by Beardsley; he killed at least six Germans. The last to fall was Lieutenant Endriss, shot in the abdomen. York had now killed twenty-five Germans in total.

Vollmer, seeing his friend dying, asked York to desist, promising that he would get the Germans on the hill above, under Lieutenant Lipp, to surrender. Lipp and his remaining men duly came down to surrender to York and his seven able-bodied men. York now had over a hundred prisoners, plus the wounded Americans and Germans, to take to the rear. He set off with Vollmer and Lipp at the front, with his pistol aimed at Vollmer's

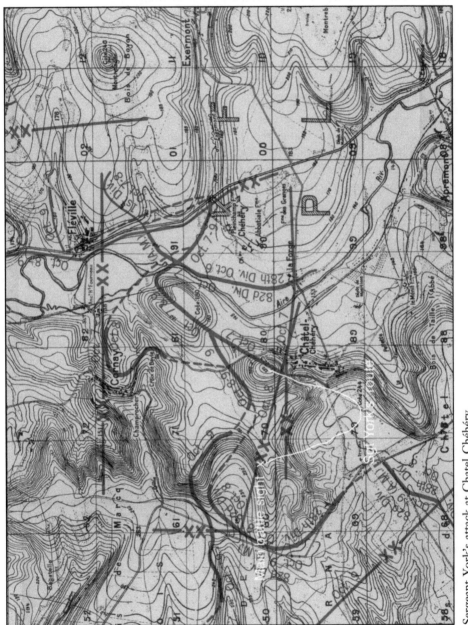

Sergeant York's attack at Chatel Chéféry.

back. On the way back York asked Vollmer to persuade another platoon of Germans under Lieutenant Thoma to surrender and join their column. On Hill 223 Lieutenant Woods of the 82nd assumed that such a large group of Germans heading in their direction must be a counter-attack. Gathering a group of men together to meet the attack, he then noticed that they were unarmed and were in fact prisoners. York then stepped forward and said 'Company G reports with prisoners, Sir.'

Woods ordered York to proceed further back to Chatel-Chéhréy. He counted 132 German prisoners. The wounded were left at the Chatel-Chéhréy aid post while York marched the remainder back to Varennes. There they were photographed by an official US Army photographer, with Lieutenants Vollmer, Lipp and Thoma clearly identifiable at the front of the column.

York returned to his unit on 9 October and continued the advance northwards. The Germans finally left the Argonne on 10 October 1918, four years after they had first occupied the area. Since then, over 150,000 men on each side had been lost and countless more injured in the mud, trenches, mines and thick undergrowth. York pressed on for another three weeks and engaged in more intense fighting. On 1 November the men of the 82nd Division were finally relieved, exhausted, sick and with over a third of the original men killed, injured or missing. Miraculously, York and his seven companions, who had marched out with Vollmer and his men from the *Humserberg*, were all still alive.

* * *

On the eastern edge of the forest the 305th and 306th Regiments of the 77th Division pressed north, capturing the villages of Marcq and Chevières on 10 October. This was an advance of some 10 miles in two days, a rapid advance by any measure. All the time the 77th came under shellfire from the German guns on the hills behind Grandpré and St-Juvin, where the *Brunhilde Stellung* joined the *Kriemhilde Stellung*, northern sections of the Hindenburg Line.

Attempts to cross the river Aire to capture Grandpré on 12 October were frustrated by heavy and accurate machine-gun fire coming across the river from the town. The only consolation for the 77th was that their artillery fire was increasingly accurate and kept the Germans' heads down. Having cleared the apparently impregnable forest fortress of the Argonne, the 77th assumed they were due a rest after sixteen days of non-stop combat and heavy casualties. This was not the case; yet more was demanded of them.

Across the river Aire stood the second major line of German defence, the *Kriembilde Stellung*, dominated by the two towns of Grandpré and St-Juvin. The latter had already defied three assaults by the 82nd Division. Now the 306th Regiment of the 77th was ordered forward to mount an assault on St-Juvin. On the morning of 14 October they managed to cross the river Aire, although with heavy casualties, and assaulted St Juvin, or what was left of it after days of artillery assault. After a tough day's fighting, they secured part of the town and Hill 182 to the north of the town, from where much of the machine-gun and artillery fire had come. The honours were shared with the 82nd Division, which had also captured part of the town, despite the confused divisional boundaries. Both divisions were given St-Juvin within their boundaries, which was an oversight somewhere in the staff planning section, and a wrangle would run for some time between the two divisional commanders as to who captured the town.

On 15 October the 307th and 308th mounted an assault on Grandpré crossing the river Aire after managing to build a footbridge unseen. Daybreak on 16 October saw the main assault begin on Grandpré, with the 307th encircling the town and fighting their way into the centre, led by Lieutenant Tillman, who had led the relief of the Lost Battalion. Meanwhile, the remainder of the division marched to the rear for a well-earned rest. The 77th Division's 15-mile advance through the sometimes impregnable forest had exacted a high price: it had lost around 600 men killed and over 3,000 injured or missing. The 78th Division now took its place.

* * *

By the second week of October more than 340,000 American Doughboys were either hospitalised, lying in trenches or support areas unable to fight. With the onset of cold weather, the flu had returned with a vengeance, finding a ready breeding ground among so many men in poor physical condition and living in very close proximity. Great lengths were gone to in order to hide the scale of the outbreak from both the Germans and the other Allies. The seriousness of the outbreak only came to light after it crossed the Spanish border, where there was no news censorship. This is why it became known as the Spanish flu. It went on to claim over 500 million victims globally, killing an estimated 20–50 million of them, between 1918 and 1920.

* * *

The three battalions of the 805th Pioneer Infantry Regiment left the USA at the end of August 1918. The 1st Battalion sailed from Canada to

Britain and then to France, while the 2nd and 3rd sailed a few days later on different ships, one of which narrowly missed a German mine in mid-Atlantic. They took the same route, via Britain and then France, arriving in late September 1918. Not long after their arrival in France, while they were in a tented camp undergoing gas training, Spanish flu began to appear among the men. Despite this, they were soon despatched by train to Clermont en Argonne. Here they were to join the First Army Division Engineers as part of the AEF advance. The first men started arriving early in the morning on 2 October.

With the late arrival of the 1st Battalion, their ship having turned back to Canada after a couple of days, the regiment was finally complete by 10 October 1918. The men took up residence in the tented Camp Bondet on the top of the hill behind St Anne's Church, Clermont, overlooking the main AEF line of advance. The unit was now assigned to the Department of Light Railways and Roads. With their unit motto 'Why Not Excellent?', they set about supporting the war effort. After cleaning up Clermont, the companies were posted to the surrounding villages and engaged in a variety of tasks, building ammunition dumps, rebuilding rail-heads and driving railway tracks forward, towards the advancing front line. They were joined by the 317th Engineer Regiment of the 92nd 'Buffalo' Division and were then given the vital task of maintaining the roads running north on either side of the Argonne Forest (the Les Islettes–La Harazée road on the west and the Clermont–Varennes road on the east), supporting the AEF advance. Maintaining these roads in appalling weather and clearing the battlefield obstructions were huge tasks, not made any easier by the general lack of equipment. Their masterstroke, though, was linking the French 600mm narrow gauge railway that terminated near Maison Forestière in the Argonne Forest with the German 600mm narrow gauge railway that had terminated near their old front line. This was in spite of reservations by the First Army's railway staff at HQ that the link couldn't be made. In a few days the connection was made, despite the engineering difficulties involved in crossing the battle-strewn no man's land. This enabled hundreds of tons of ammunition to be moved forward by train away from the overloaded road system.

'Bearcat' men out in the field in the AEF advance positions soon experienced their first gas and artillery attacks. Men left in Clermont were not safe either; as an important road and rail-head, it was bombed at night by German planes. On their right, the 802nd Pioneer Regiment extended the standard gauge railway line north from after Aubréville to Varennes, to keep supplies rolling forward to the front line. By moving supplies, particularly heavy shells, by rail, the single carriage road north from Clermont to Varennes could be used by men, ammunition convoys and returning casualties. The 'Bearcats' were tasked with maintaining this road, which with the autumn weather and excessive use was in a constant state of disrepair.

*   *   *

Early on 11 November it was clear to most commanders that the ceasefire would take effect later that morning. In a war that consumed an average of over 2,200 men a day, this day would be even bloodier, despite the impending ceasefire. Officially, more than 10,000 men were killed, wounded or posted missing that morning.

The guns finally fell silent at 11am on Monday, 11 November 1918, after four years, three months and two weeks of continuous, savage warfare. For the first time in over four years a silence swept across the front that was as deafening as the roar of artillery had been only a few short minutes earlier. There were very few men remaining alive on the front who could look back to the summer of 1914, when expectations on both sides had run so high. The landscape over which their opening salvoes were fired, golden cornfields scattered with blood-red Poppies and blue cornflowers, were now replaced by a turgid seascape of unrelenting death and destruction. The rich farmland soil that provided the shell-scrapes from which the Belgian, French and British soldiers had engaged the unending 'grey mist' of advancing Germans was now soaked deep in the blood of friend and foe alike. For the last men officially killed in combat on the Western Front in the war, there would be no quiet moment of reflection in the silence at 11am.

Among the French, who continued actions on various sectors of the front, over 1,100 men fell that morning. The tragic honour of the last French death of the war came at 10.45am to *Poilu* Augustin Trébuchon who was taking a message to troops by the river Meuse that soup would be served after the Armistice was declared.

More than 3,000 Americans would be killed, wounded or posted missing that day. The 313th Infantry Regiment, 'Baltimore's Own', continued the advance further south-east in the Ville-devant-Chaumont area. At 9.30am the unit advanced towards the enemy through the autumnal mist, unsure where the enemy was or where they were, either. Soon German artillery fire rained down on them, causing some casualties. Nevertheless, the advance continued, with no let-up, until just before 11am. Private Henry

Gunther had been a sergeant before setting sail for France, but for writing what was perceived as a defeatist letter, he was demoted to private. It was said he was looking to redeem himself in action against the Germans and win promotion again. With rounds whistling over American heads, the Germans assumed they would remain stationary as the final minutes ticked away. But Gunther continued his advance, possibly seeking some last-minute glory.

The Germans fired a short burst; one bullet hit Gunther in the head, killing him. The time on his colleague, Sergeant Powell's watch was 10.59am. Private Henry Gunther of Baltimore, originally of German extraction, was recorded by General Pershing as the final American killed in the war. Gunther and Trébuchon, along with a Canadian and a British soldier (who had arrived with the BEF in August 1914) killed further north, entered the history books as the last official Allied deaths in combat of the First World War.

* * *

Outside the forest, the main AEF Meuse-Argonne offensive took place across the land between the Argonne Forest and the River Meuse. The 47-day offensive fought here from 26 September to 11 November was, and still is, the greatest campaign fought by America, in terms of the numbers of soldiers involved and the numbers of casualties.

The 77th 'Liberty' Division was only a small part of the 1.25 million soldiers from twenty-two divisions and support elements that fought in the campaign. More than 26,000 American soldiers, airmen, marines, nurses and other support workers died in the Meuse-Argonne offensive and a further 100,000 were injured: casualties on a scale America had never seen the like of, either before or since, in a single campaign.

The epic AEF campaign under General Pershing during the autumn of 1918, with its army built from scratch, its vast scale and its vital contribution to the overall Allied victory, remains little known outside interested military aficionados. The American Civil War battles (with the possible exception of Gettysburg, where records were not kept with the same diligence), D-Day on 6 June 1944, the Battle of the Bulge from December 1944 to January 1945, and the Pacific battles in 1945 at Iwo Jima and Okinawa were all fought on a lesser scale and with fewer deaths. But these battles, along with Korea and Vietnam, resonate more today with the broader American public than the Doughboys' victory in the cold autumnal mists and mud of the Meuse-Argonne offensive of 1918.

Pershing believed the Armistice of 11 November would not hold, so training for all units continued just as intensively and new men replaced the dead and injured. He had wanted to carry the offensive into Germany and on to Berlin and decisively crush the German Army. If they didn't do so, he counselled his Allies, they would be back within a generation to finish the task.

John B. Whitton of TMU 133, American Field Ambulance Service, wrote a poem to celebrate the Armistice:

Armistice Day
As Paris, joy-mad, waved her flags above
The boulevards, nor spared her finest wine,
And London's cheers and dance and song,
New Yorkers' whoops and whistles' whine,
A crazy world, with pent-up spirits rang!
Out there –
A soldier dropped his weary gun and slept,
And cooling cannon by their gunners lay
Untended, when 'cross that martyred field of pain
The long-awaited word arrived to say
Hell's own war was done and men could live again.
Were there hurrahs acclaiming France was saved?
Did deaf'ning cheers and whistles split the air?
Or cannon roar to humor wine and song?
Not so, the *Poilus* – perhaps they knelt in prayer, –
With silence welcomed peace the fighting throng.

*   *   *

On Saturday, 14 December 1918 a general election took place in Britain. There had not been one for eight years. Lloyd George had led the coalition government since the end of 1916 but now he needed to legitimise another coalition, to oversee the peace. All men aged over 21, men over 19 who had served in the war and women over 30 who occupied property or who held a degree from a British university could vote for the first time. Women could also stand as Members of Parliament for the first time. The mass registration of British overseas servicemen meant that the vote could not be counted until after Christmas, to allow their postal ballots to reach Britain.

Chapter 5

Après La Guerre

After the war Piatt Andrew, founder of the American Ambulance Field Service, commented, 'If the fallen French soldiers lined up in ranks of four and marched by at 10,500 per hour, it would take six days and five nights for them all to pass by.'

The former front was approximately 400 miles long as the crow flies. In reality though, it was a vast network of 25,000 miles of trenches, predominantly in France. Scattered in and around the desolate landscape were the dead, nearly 4 million of them. There were around 800,000 British and Empire dead, around 1.3 million French and Colonial dead, around 50,000 American dead, and around 1.5 million German dead, not to mention thousands of others who had rallied to France's cause. France was now their custodian. In order that the country did not become some vast dystopia of the dead being shunted around, along with real public health concerns, their 1914 order of no removal of the dead from the *Zone des Armées* held firm.

The *Corps du Génie Rural* (Agricultural Engineering Corps) was established in 1918 to oversee rural reconstruction, road and bridge repair, and electrification. They produced a colour-coded system for maps of the war-damaged lands. Zone Green comprised areas that had been used in the war, mainly for activities such as storing men and equipment en route to the front, with a modest amount of damage. Zone Yellow comprised areas where there had been occasional fighting, but were mainly behind the lines; these areas had some trenches, shell holes and unexploded ordnance, but had a workable road network. Zone Red comprised areas that by and large were the main areas of combat, with large amounts of unexploded ordnance, polluted water supplies, dead animals and people to be buried. The local infrastructure was destroyed; there were few houses other than army shelters, no electricity, and agricultural and forestry land would require extensive work to bring it back into production. Most of the Argonne Forest was designated Zone Red, particularly along the former front line at *Haute Chevauchée* and Bois de la Gruerie.

In the Argonne Forest there was another crucial task to be undertaken before the removal of the dead could even be considered. The 805th Pioneer Infantry Regiment, AEF, known as the 'Bearcats', continued with road repairs and other tasks until 18 November. Then they were ordered to Varennes for a new tasking, leaving the Department of Light Railway and Road, First Army for the SOS. The 'Bearcats' were now tasked with clearing and salvaging abandoned equipment and with demolishing live and dud ammunition. Even with more than 3,000 men, it was a huge logistical task. Their sector covered over 500 square miles of the Meuse-Argonne battlefield, including the entire Argonne Forest. As the autumn turned to winter, the men were posted to company locations around the forest, including the villages (or remains of them) of Florent, Varennes, Lachalade and Clermont, with their new headquarters at the Château de Chéhéry just outside Chatel-Chéhéry, as of 25 November. The forest was divided into sectors and the men began to salvage and sort French, German and American equipment. Railway rolling stock, weapons, artillery pieces, iron shelters, clothing, bedding, radio equipment, stakes and barbed wire were just a few of the salvageable items. Almost everything in the forest had to be manhandled through the winter mud and rain to a navigable road.

Large teams of men pulled and shoved massive artillery pieces to positions where a vehicle could finally take over. With little transport and poor roads, progress was slow until additional vehicles could be found. Their arrival speeded up the movement of the items to the rail-head stores at Varennes, Les Islettes, Clermont and Aubréville. There they waited for onward movement by train to central collection and salvage areas. Some 'Bearcat' companies were lucky and found a solid roof over their heads in villages or in French or German bunkers. Others lived in forest trenches and many had nothing more than their pup tents to shelter them from the harsh Argonne winter. Although most of the sixty-one unit deaths through the winter were from Spanish flu, several men were killed in the process of shifting and blowing ammunition, and by German booby traps. Where dead bodies were found, these had to be buried and details of their graves recorded. As some of the last to arrive in France during the war, this meant they would be some of the last to leave.

Spirits were kept up during the long hard winter by the 805th's band and various vaudeville acts. At Varennes a large tent was erected; called the Bearcat Oprey House, it contained a large stage and orchestra pit and seating for 800 men. Electricity was installed and each night some form of entertainment was held. Army touring shows visiting the 805th could hardly believe such a venue existed at the old war-torn front.

*   *   *

Following the relief of the Lost Battalion, Whittlesey had immediately been promoted to lieutenant colonel and sent back to America. He and McMurtry, along with Holderman, were each awarded a Medal of Honor on 6 December 1918.

Lieutenant Colonel Charles Whittlesey's citation read:

> The President of the United States of America, in the name of Congress, takes pleasure in presenting the Medal of Honor to Major (Infantry) Charles White Whittlesey, United States Army, for extraordinary heroism on October 2–7, 1918, while serving with 1st Battalion, 308th Infantry, 77th Division, in action at Charleveaux, Binarville, Argonne Forest, France. Although cut off for five days from the remainder of his division, Major Whittlesey maintained his position, which he had reached under orders received for an advance, and held his command, consisting originally of forty-six officers and men of the 308th Infantry and of Company K of the 307th Infantry, together in the face of superior numbers of the enemy during the five days. Major Whittlesey and his command were thus cut off, and no rations or other supplies reached him, in spite of determined efforts that were made by his division. On the 4th day Major Whittlesey received from the enemy a written proposition to surrender, which he treated with contempt, although he was at the time out of rations and had suffered a loss of about 50 per cent in killed and wounded of his command and was surrounded by the enemy.

Captain George McMurtry's citation read:

> The President of the United States of America, in the name of Congress, takes pleasure in presenting the Medal of Honor to Captain (Infantry) George G. McMurtry, United States Army, for extraordinary heroism on October 2–8, 1918, while serving with 308th Infantry, 77th Division, in action at Charleveaux, Argonne Forest. Captain McMurtry commanded a battalion which was cut off and surrounded by the enemy and although wounded in the knee by shrapnel on 4 October and suffering great pain, he continued throughout the entire period to encourage his officers and men with a resistless optimism that contributed largely toward preventing panic and disorder

among the troops, who were without food, cut off from communication with our lines.

On 4 October, during a heavy barrage, he personally directed and
supervised the moving of the wounded to shelter before himself
seeking shelter. On 6 October, he was again wounded in the shoulder
by a German grenade, but continued personally to organize and direct
the defense against the German attack on the position until the attack
was defeated. He continued to direct and command his troops, refusing relief, and personally led his men out of the position after assistance arrived before permitting himself to be taken to the hospital on
8 October. During this period the successful defense of the position
was due largely to his efforts.

Captain Nelson Holderman's citation read:

While in command of Company K, 307th Infantry, which company
held the right flank of the force consisting of six companies of the
308th Infantry, two platoons of the 306th Machine Gun Battalion
and Company K, 307th Infantry, and which force was cut off and
surrounded by the enemy for five days and nights in the Forest
d'Argonne, France, from October 2nd to October 7th, 1918. Captain
Nelson M. Holderman, though wounded early in the siege and suffering great pain, continued throughout the entire period leading
and encouraging the officers and men under his command. He was
wounded on the 4th of October but remained in action during all
attacks made by the enemy upon the position, personally leading his
men, himself remaining exposed to fire of every character. He was
again wounded on the 5th of October, but continued personally
organizing and directing the defense of the right flank against enemy
attacks.

During the entire period he personally supervised the care of the
wounded, exposing himself to shell and machine-gun fire that he
might help and encourage his men to hold the position. On October
6th, though in a wounded condition, he rushed through shell and
machine-gun fire and carried two wounded men to a place of safety.
This officer, though wounded, continued to direct the defense of the
right flank and on the 7th of October was again wounded but continued in action. On the afternoon of October 7th this officer and one
man, with pistols and hand grenades, alone and single handed, met
and dispersed a body of the enemy. Killing and wounding most of the
party, when they attempted to close in on the right flank while their

forces were at the same time making a frontal attack, thus saving two machine guns from capture as well as preventing the envelopment of the right flank. Again on the evening of the 7th of October and during the last attack made by the enemy upon the position, a liquid fire attack was directed on the right flank; though in a wounded and serious condition Captain Holderman remained on his feet, keeping the firing line organized and preventing the envelopment of the right flank.

He refused to let his wounds interfere with his duty until after relief was effected. The successful defense of the position was largely due to his courage. He personally led his men out of the position after assistance arrived and before permitting himself to be attended. The courageous optimism and inspiring bravery of this officer encouraged his men to a successful resistance in spite of five days' fighting, hunger and exposure.

Lieutenant Ernest Goettler's citation read:

1st Lt Goettler, with his observer, 2nd Lt Erwin R. Bleckley, 130th Field Artillery, left the airdrome late in the afternoon on their second trip to drop supplies to a battalion of the 77th Division which had been cut off by the enemy in the Argonne Forest. Having been subjected on the first trip to violent fire from the enemy, they attempted on the second trip to come still lower in order to get the packages even more precisely on the designated spot. In the course of this mission the plane was brought down by enemy rifle and machine-gun fire from the ground, resulting in the instant death of 1st Lt Goettler. In attempting and performing this mission 1st Lt Goettler showed the highest possible contempt of personal danger, devotion to duty, courage and valor.

Lieutenant Erwin Bleckley's citation read:

Second Lt Bleckley, with his pilot, 1st Lt Harold E. Goettler, Air Service, left the airdrome late in the afternoon on their second trip to drop supplies to a battalion of the 77th Division, which had been cut off by the enemy in the Argonne Forest. Having been subjected on the first trip to violent fire from the enemy, they attempted on the second trip to come still lower in order to get the packages even more precisely on the designated spot. In the course of this mission the plane was brought down by enemy rifle and machine-gun fire from the ground, resulting in fatal wounds to 2nd Lt Bleckley, who died before he could be taken to a hospital. In attempting and performing this mission 2nd Lt Bleckley showed the highest possible contempt of personal danger, devotion to duty, courage, and valor.

Two further Medals of Honor were won by troops trying to relieve the Pocket. The first was awarded to Sergeant Benjamin Kaufman of Company K, 308th Infantry Regiment, 77th Division, whose citation read:

> He took out a patrol for the purpose of attacking an enemy machine gun which had checked the advance of his company. Before reaching the gun he became separated from his patrol and a machine-gun bullet shattered his right arm. Without hesitation he advanced on the gun alone, throwing grenades with his left hand and charging with an empty pistol, taking one prisoner and scattering the crew, bringing the gun and prisoner back to the first-aid station.

The second Medal of Honor was awarded to Private Archie Peck of Company A, 307th Infantry, 77th Division, whose citation read:

> For conspicuous gallantry and intrepidity above and beyond the call of duty in action with the enemy in the Argonne Forest, France, on October 6, 1918. While engaged with two other soldiers on patrol duty, Private Peck and his comrades were subjected to the direct fire of an enemy machine gun, at which time both his companions were wounded. Returning to his company, he obtained another soldier to accompany him to assist in bringing in the wounded men. His assistant was killed in the exploit, but he continued on, twice returning safely, bringing in both men, being under terrific machine-gun fire during the entire journey.

Altogether seven Medals of Honor were awarded for the battle to save the Lost Battalion: the most to be awarded for a single action in the First World War.

*   *   *

The 'Bearcats' continued to be without musical instruments until 1 January 1919, apart from improvised handmade pieces. On 28 December 1918 the 805th Adjutant, Captain Paul Bliss, was sent by the commanding officer to Paris to seek instruments for the New Year's party and to keep the men entertained at night after a hard day's work. Bliss visited the YMCA, the Knights of Columbus and the Red Cross, looking for instruments. He returned by train late on 1 January 1919 with seven cornets, six clarinets, five saxophones, four slide trombones, four alto horns, two base tubas, two baritones, a piccolo, a snare, a bass drum and some 'jazz band' effects. These came from mainly from the Red Cross. The same afternoon they formed an orchestra – The Bearcat Entertainers – which played at a party that night. Soon more musical instruments found their way to Chatel-Chéhéry. The first concert away from the Chateau was given in the military hospital at Froidos.

The band, though, had to be led by a white officer. Lieutenant Leonce R. Legendre was in charge of the show and the band, with George L. Polk as assistant band leader and conductor. The 805th's orchestra was formally organised by regimental order on 24 February, allowing men in other companies to transfer to the HQ Company at Chatel to participate. Soon a jazz band offshoot sprang up to entertain troops and villagers in the region. The mainstay of the vaudeville show was William 'Billy' Higgins from Kansas City. Before the war he had been a well-known singer, songwriter, entertainer and comedian. While at Camp Funston in the USA, Colonel Humphrey had spotted his talent to entertain the men and had secured his services for the 805th. All the way from the USA to France, and then during the long cold winter, Higgins had kept the men entertained. Now he had a real venue and set about building a show with other peacetime and aspiring entertainers. Before long he had a show that filled the Bearcat Oprey House. Higgins went on after the war to become one of the most popular stage comedians in America.

* * *

French legislation published on 12 January 1919 prohibited the exhumation and transportation of bodies of Allies and Germans alike for three years outside the Zone Red. The only exception granted was for the collection of bodies from the thousands of sites inside the Zone Red into more centralised, easier to manage and larger formal military cemeteries. Sites with good vehicular access were being identified all along the front to gather the dead in their final resting places. Although Russia, Germany and France had greater numbers of war dead to be reburied, none had the depth, scale of vision or funding of the British Imperial War Graves Commission (IWGC). Rudyard Kipling later compared the scale of it to the building of the pyramids in ancient Egypt.

The French legislation suited Fabian Ware and the IWGC well. It was now agreed government policy between Britain and its Empire that their dead should remain in France and other overseas battle sites. Crucially it also avoided the topic of the cost and logistics of potentially moving nearly a million dead back to Britain and the Empire. Sir Frederic Kenyon, Director of the British Museum, was asked to examine the varying schemes proposed by architects for the IWGC. He visited France during the winter of 1917 and early 1918 and observed it was not all 'larks and poppies'. He held extensive consultations with soldiers, the families of the deceased and Empire representatives. Britain would bear the lion's share of the building programme (80 per cent), but each Empire country would help share the cost on a proportional basis (according to the number of their dead). Even before the war's end, they had been busy planning for this moment, and the architects and gardeners already had their designs worked out.

No sooner had the guns fallen silent on 11 November 1918 than the IWGC started on a small number of experimental cemeteries in the vicinity of Etaples. They wanted to work through the real practicalities of the work, which was so far no more than drawings on a board in London. They were keen to see how the theory of their work would relate to actual circumstances on the ground, such as the effect of the weather on stone and planting, and how long cemeteries would take to scale up, from burying ten to a hundred or a thousand men or more.

The Germans had no choice, as France firmly controlled access to their dead and the burial of them. Their wartime overseas graves organisations were disbanded. All burial work outside Germany was now under the guardianship of whichever country they lay in. France forbade any repatriation of German war dead from French soil.

*   *   *

The 'Bearcat' forest salvage operation was complete by the end of January 1919, but there was still no let-up for the men. They were moved to the local rail-heads to help count and store the salvaged goods and then load them into train cars. As spring appeared, the men were tasked with trench filling, mainly across Argonne farmland, adjacent to the forest, so crops could be planted again. The huge task was finally completed by the end of the first week of March 1919. By then, 3,000 full rail cars had been sent to centralised salvage depots across France.

With spring approaching, a baseball diamond was built in front of the Château de Chéhéry. The YMCA and the Knights of Columbus supplied the necessary equipment. The 'Bearcat' baseball team was the pride of the regiment. Captain George M. Bragan, a white officer, managed the team to an undefeated 10–0 record. The success of the team was no fluke. The team roster included several players who would go on to play professionally in the African-American Leagues after the war. Some inter-unit matches attracted crowds of several thousand to the château diamond.

The bands and the baseball teams continued to maintain troop morale while the 805th began its long journey home, starting in May 1919. They played their last baseball game against the 807th in Brest, where Colonel Humphrey was heard to boast that the 805th had the best baseball team, the best Vaudeville and the best jazz band in the AEF. By 27 June all the men were back in the USA.

*   *   *

In March 1919 the first meeting of the American Legion took place in Paris over two days. The idea was part of an early 1919 initiative to help improve morale among troops waiting to sail home. Initially held in an officers' club on 15 March, it had moved on to the Cirque de Paris by 17 March, with over 1,000 men and officers dropping in at some point during the proceedings. By the end of the caucus they had adopted the name American Legion, and drawn up a constitution.

In May 1919 the most famous war-time American jazz band leader died. Lieutenant James Reese Europe had served in the 369th 'Harlem Hell Fighters' Regiment both with his band and on active duty. It was claimed he brought jazz to France with his band, and his jazz version of *La Marseillaise* brought the French president Poincaré to his feet, clapping. After the war, with his new-found fame he toured America until he was tragically murdered by a fellow bandsman.

*   *   *

Despite the work in Zone Red to bury the dead in a fitting and appropriate manner, the public and politicians in the USA and France clamoured for repatriation. It was an unstoppable force, which gathered momentum as time passed.

An American government delegation arrived in France in early 1919 but, confronted by the scale of the task and likely repatriation costs, soon agreed a slightly different strategy, to promote the men remaining in France and assure the public that the new cemeteries would be places of great beauty.

The situation remained unclear for all parties; the military wanted the men to remain, as did many politicians. They wished to support the military and avoid the likely cost of such a massive repatriation project. Some members of the military, including Chaplain Pierce, did express concern about the dead remaining in France. Looking at the historical precedents, they could see that invading armies might cross the region once again and disturb the dead Americans. This would necessitate a response from a future American government.

With no specific mandate from the French government yet to permit repatriation, the American government sent out a ballot in March 1919 to over 70,000 known next of kin. What would they prefer: to have their loved one returned to America, or left in France? American mothers were the people nominated to make the choice.

As they could only be moved within Zone Red, eight American sites were selected for gathering their dead: six in France, near the main American battle sites, one in Belgium and one in Britain, at Brookwood. For the Meuse-Argonne offensive, Romagne was picked as the assembly site. The French government's land purchase scheme did not always meet with approval from local French residents, who did not see the need for individual graves. They thought ossuaries a more suitable place for soldiers' remains; these would also take up less of their land.

Romagne was in the centre of the 500 square mile American battlefield. It benefited from good road links, to bring the dead in by truck from the surrounding areas. The new American cemetery was established on 14 October 1918, on land taken by the 32nd Infantry Division in September. This land was subsequently ceded, tax-free, to the USA in perpetuity by the French government to establish a permanent burial site for dead Americans of the Meuse-Argonne offensive. Romagne already had another military cemetery, a German one, in the town itself, which had originally contained a few bodies of men killed in the 1914–15 fighting. As the town was out of French artillery range, it soon became a base for German hospitals. During the German Verdun offensive of 1916, thousands of casualties were brought here, primarily from the fighting at Morte-Homme and Côte 304. Over 6,000 of them died in the Romagne hospitals and were buried in the town's military cemetery. The Romagne cemetery also contained many graves of victims of the Spanish flu pandemic, which killed almost as many serving Americans as were killed in action or died of wounds. Around 51,000 servicemen and women died in both the USA and Europe from the influenza, which swept across the world during and after the war. This amounted to 44 per cent of America's total wartime deaths.

The flu struck down men of all colours, all religions, and did not distinguish between the men burying the dead or those who were waiting to go home. Private Josh Lee wrote a poem, *The Flu*, in 1919:

The Flu
It stalked into camp when the day was damp
And chilly and cold.
It crept by the guards
And murdered my pards
With a hand that was clammy and bony and bold;
And its breath was icy and mouldy and dank,
And it killed so speedy
And gloatingly greedy
That it took away men from each company rank.

The grim and awful task of exhuming the dead from the Meuse-Argonne battlefield now fell to the 813th (which also had burial companies further north at Château Thierry), 815th and 816th Pioneer Infantry Regiments, and the 332nd and 349th Labor Battalions, all African-American units. None of these units appears to have maintained a record of their thankless but important work as they scoured the battlefield looking for the dead from American GRS reports and local information.

During the winter of 1918 and 1919 the dead were dug up, identity checked and reburied. It was evident to the GRS, after exhuming the dead, that the men were unfit now for embalming. Too much time had passed and decomposition had set in, even for the most recent casualties. The French would have expressed surprise at the article in the American *Stars and Stripes* on 4 April 1919, given that they had only recently been forbidden from removing the bodies of the dead out of the Zone Red:

America's dead will be carried back to America or left to sleep close to the French fields where they gave their lives for her, according to the expressed wish of the next of kin. This is the substance of a War Department ruling just made public. Meanwhile the bodies are being lifted from the widely scattered, hastily made graves, dug in the heat and rush of the battle, and are being assembled in great cemeteries.

The largest of these is on the edge of Romagne sous Montfaucon. There because the spot is the focal centre of the area which saw the most violent American effort and heaviest American losses. Approximately 25,000 American graves will be enclosed within this one cemetery when it is completed. The work is being rushed, and a visitor to Romagne these days would think a big American contractor had embarked on some mammoth construction project there. Acres of mud, unrelieved by so much as a single spear of grass, plank roads laid to give the trucks some sort of pathway, in and out, and then a gently sloping hillside, alive with the toiling figures of 5,000 negro soldiers.

Each truck sets forth in the morning with its grave crew, headed by a sergeant with a map and handful of papers, each slip giving co-ordinates that will lead to where some Yankee soldier lies buried. In the big cemetery the officers will be grouped in the centre. Another part is set aside for the chaplains, nurses and men of the auxiliary services who were killed in action. The unidentified dead will lie in their separate portion of the cemetery, but it will not be a big portion; each day's work in the field reduces, with unexpected success, the number of nameless graves that the cemetery must hold.

In the centre of the camp a long barracks shelters the papers and records of the Graves Registration Service. One look at the chart shows why the outskirts of Romagne was chosen to place the largest of all our American cemeteries. Within a space of 10 square kilo-metres, 17,000 American dead lie scattered over the most difficult battlefield American troops encountered.

It is a dreary panorama now, the view from the edge of the cemetery, but in the course of time the ground will be smoothed and there will be turf and hedges and flowers. Probably a great shaft will rise to honour the dead and beckon pilgrims who will come by thousands from across the sea. For it may be guessed that the greater number of these dead will lie there always. No one knows, for no one can say what will be in the mind of the families at home. Each request is acknowledged and filed away, and no body will be shipped back till all that are ever going can be sent home as part of one enterprise.

Not only the scattered graves are being shifted to the main cemeteries, but also the impractically placed groups of graves, many of them inaugurated by men who did not know what conditions would make possible a decent maintenance, and above all, by the men who had not consulted the very rigorous laws of France governing such matters.

Visitors to the battlefields are likely to run across certain graves to which special attention has been paid: graves marked off with stones, piled high with wreaths and perhaps fenced in. In all such cases it means that earlier French authorities have sought to express goodwill or that some friend or kin of the dead has found his way to the grave and done the work himself.

In no case will the Graves Registration Bureau confer any distinction on one man's grave above another's. The Army authorities will not accept wreaths or flowers, being unwilling to do to one grave what cannot be done to another. While the cemetery on the outskirts of Romagne is by far the biggest of all, there are many others where work continues.

The main source of information about the reburial process comes from magazines published at the time and from a book written in 1920 by Addie Waites Hunton and Kathryn M. Johnson, *Two Coloured Women with The American Expeditionary Forces*. Hunton and Johnson travelled from the USA to France in 1918 as YMCA Secretaries, describing themselves as 'in quest of democracy'. Their job was to help run the Ys. These were located in a variety of places, including huts, tents and other temporary buildings. Here they provided men with medical help, religious services, a home from home environment, help and support, particularly for those unable to read or write. There was a regular programme of entertainment, usually films and shows put on by the men. The prerequisite for all programmes was that they 'be wholesome'. Hunton and Johnson told the story of their fifteen months in France working for the YMCA with the AEF. The book lifted the lid for American readers on the discrimination experienced by African-American soldiers in France, both during and after the war. Having served in Ys in a number of camps in France, mainly at the ports, Hunton and Johnson desired nothing more than to serve in a Y at the front, but this was denied them.

In May 1919 Addie Waites Hunton found herself among the men burying the dead and provided probably the only contemporaneous account of life at Camp Romagne in the spring and summer of 1919. Having reached Verdun, Hunton tried for a number of days in early May 1919 to reach Camp Romagne, only for the commanding officer there to say he did not wish women to be at the camp with 9,000 African-American men. This was of no concern to her, having already worked with far larger numbers of men at a variety of camps. Permission was eventually given and Hunton arrived after a long, dusty drive on Sunday, 9 May 1919 – Mothering Sunday. She set to work in the Y and soon, over a glass of lemonade or hot chocolate, she was able to gain the confidence of the men. She usually began with 'Where are you from?', and soon a common friend or experience would break down the barriers, in a way men from the Y could not.

Conversations would discuss life on return to the States, family, returning to a farm, going to college and their other hopes.

Here is Addie Hunton's account of life at Camp Romagne:

Here was a tremendous task for the surviving American soldiers, but far more sacred than tremendous. Whose would be the hands to gather as best they could and place beneath the white crosses of honor the remains of those who had sanctified their spirits through the gift of their lifeblood? It would be a gruesome, repulsive and unhealthy task, requiring weeks of incessant toil during the long heavy days of summer.

It also meant isolation, for these cemeteries for the American dead would be erected on or near the battlefields where the men had fallen. But it would be a wonderful privilege, the beauty and glory of which would reveal itself more and more as the facts of the war should become crystallized into history.

Strange that the value of such a task did not gather full significance in the minds of all American soldiers. Strange that when other hands refused it, swarthy hands received it! Yet, perhaps, not so strange, for Providence hath its own way, and in those American cemeteries in France we have strong and indisputable evidence of the wonderful devotion and loyalty and the matchless patience and endurance of the colored soldier.

We recall an incident at Romagne. Even though it was May the nights were winter cold, so that when one was snuggled between army blankets in the tent, it required a bit of heroism to crawl out. This particular night we had just retired when shots were heard, fired in rapid succession. Without thought of the cold we began dressing and were sitting wrapped in cloaks thinking rapidly about what was happening when someone called, 'It's only a fire!' What a relief it was! What did it matter if the whole camp burned in comparison with our boys being goaded by prejudice beyond reason!

Another anonymous account describes the fire:

It was the burning down of the Knights of Columbus tent and placed thereon was a sign to keep colored soldiers away. The colored soldiers, heartsore because they, of all the soldiers, German prisoners, etc., that there were in France, should alone be forced to do this terrible task of moving the dead from where they had been temporarily buried to a permanent resting place, immediately resented the outrage and razed the tent to the ground. The officers became frightened lest there should be mutiny, mounted a machine gun to keep order, and commanded the four colored women who were doing service there to proceed at once to Paris.

Addie Hunton's account continues:

Rations were often scarce and poor at Romagne because we were so far from supplies, hence we prepared and served food for the soldiers all day long. But this was but a small task compared with that of keeping the men in good spirits and reminding them again and again of the glory of the work they had in hand.

Always, whether in the little corner set aside in the Y barracks as our reception room, or among the books they liked so well to read, whether by the side of the piano or over the canteen, we were trying to love them as a mother or a dear one would into a fuller knowledge and appreciation of themselves, their task and the value of forbearance. We had gone from Romagne, women of fine spirit had taken our place and were lovingly ministering to the needs of these soldiers, when things happened too grievous to be calmly borne. At one stroke down came tents of discrimination and injustice, but the work there went on and the soldiers completed the difficult task assigned them. For weeks at Romagne we watched these men fare forth with the dawn to find the dead on the 480 square miles of battlefield of the Meuse-Argonne. At eventide we would see them return and reverently remove the boxes from the long lines of trucks and place them on the hillside beside the waiting trenches that other soldiers had been digging all the long busy day.

Far into the night we would sit in our darkened tent looking out on the electric-lighted cemetery, watching the men as they lowered the boxes into the trenches. Sometimes we could hear only a low murmur of voices, and sometimes again there would come to us a plaintive melody in keeping with the night hour and its peculiar task.

Mr William G. Shepherd wrote the following account in the *New York Evening Post*:

As we moved about the battlefield later, we saw in fields, in groves, on hillsides, and even in the yards of what had been the houses of French villages, groups of Negro soldiers at their worthy but infinitely slow task of calling the roll of our American dead and gathering them together at the hillside rendezvous of Romagne.

One of the burning pictures of all this war to me was a view of these Negro sexton-soldiers working on a hilltop one rainy evening at dusk. They were outlined against the gloomy sky. Their huge motor-truck stood near by, ready to carry their burden to Romagne. I thought of the home back in the United States where this one doughboy's empty chair held its sacred place; of how the 'home fires', of which our doughboys had so often sung, had been kept burning for him. I thought of how the heart-love in that home would flash across the Atlantic to this bleak French hilltop faster than any wireless message if the homefolk only knew. It was good to know that he was being taken from his solitary bed, in the mid of the battlefield's desolation, back to the crowd of his buddies at Romagne. This, that I saw on the sky-line, was his second mobilization.

Not this time will he sing and romp and play and joke and fight; after his second mobilization at Romagne he will just lie still and rest with all the other thousands of his fellow soldiers, his job well done, until it is time for us he saved to take him back home.

Addie Hunton's account of life at Camp Romagne goes on:

We have yet another picture. It was the day before the 30th of May, 1919. Every soldier was helping to put the Romagne cemetery in readiness for its dedication by General Pershing on the next day. Looking out from our little kitchen window of the Y barrack, we saw what seemed to us a wonderful sight.

Two long lines of soldiers were before us, one moving slowly over the hill and the other coming up the main road, each man bearing on his shoulder a single white cross that would rest above the grave of a fellow-hero.

Quickly quickly our minds traveled back over the centuries to Him who had borne the cross toward Golgotha, and we saw in these dark-skinned sons of America bearing those white crosses, something of the same humility and something of the same sorrow that character-ized the Master, but we also beheld in them the Christ spirit grown large, beautiful and eternal with the ages.

Behind the vivid picture drawn by Mr Shepherd, and behind this other picture, one sees not only the twenty-two thousand homes represented by these crosses at Romagne, but the ten thousand real Americans, colored men of the pioneer infantries and labor battal-ions, who, through the sweat of toil, linked that place of sainted pilgrimage on the Western Front with those American homes.

Our outstanding impression of those faithful ones who wore the insignia of Alsace-Lorraine is their strict allegiance to the trust imposed upon them, with heart and purpose fixed to pay the price entailed in the completion of their severe task. Whether they sought their comrades by the winding Meuse or on the battle-seamed heights of no man's land; whether they found their bodies in the shadows of the ruined cathedrals of Rheims, Soissons or Ypres, always they were making an unconscious challenge to the very heart of the United States for the rights of the twelve millions of its citizens whose loyalty had thus endured the test.

May we not hope that as the heart of this homeland finds its way to those American shrines in France, a real peace, born of knowledge and gratitude, shall descend upon us, blotting out hate and its train of social and civil injustices? Then shall we realize the value and meaning of the pain and sacrifice of these dark-browned heroes of ours.

The American *Stars and Stripes* described the events at Camp Romagne in more prosaic terms on 16 May 1919:

One tenth of the graves in America's greatest cemetery in France, near Romagne, in the heart of the Meuse-Argonne battlefield is now filled. The cemetery when completed will hold 30,000 American dead. Officials of the Graves Registration Service at Romagne are making every effort to transfer first all the bodies whose location and identification present the most difficult problem. The transfer of bodies from smaller cemeteries already developed will be left until the scattered graves have been cared for. Parties from Romagne are now exploring the countryside daily in successful searches for isolated graves or groups of graves.

An idea of the task sometimes presented to these searchers may be gained from the fact that at Fléville, south-east of Grandpré, 91 graves were found recently, wholly submerged by the flooded river Aire, which had torn up the crosses and left them floating around in hopeless confusion. The water was drained off, the bodies exhumed and every one identified. The 91 now lie in Romagne. To prevent any possibility of wrong identification, five separate checks are made on the location of every grave in the big cemetery. The American Memorial League, whereby it is planned to have French women care for some particular American soldier's grave, has been formed at Cosne.

The league was formed at the suggestion of two American chaplains, and two French girls have been made president and secretary.

The objects of the league are: To care for graves in France of American soldiers who have died in France, whether in action or in hospital. To select 30 May as an annual Memorial Day on which graves shall be decorated with appropriate services; and to get in touch with the parents of soldiers and inform them of the care being taken of the grave and furnish photographs on request. Each local league will be composed of French women, the number to be determined by the number of graves in each community, and each mademoiselle or madam selects one or more graves for which she volunteers to be responsible.

On 30 May, Memorial Day, General Pershing attended the camp to dedicate the largest AEF cemetery in France. The bands of the 815th and 816th Regiments played, weeping as they performed their homage to the dead.

* * *

In early 1917 Nicole Mangin had been promoted to captain and posted to the newly opened Edith Cavell Hospital in Paris. Although she had finally secured a paid medical post, she was not allowed back to the front. She spent the remainder of the war at the Edith Cavell, seeing her promotion as a twisted way of removing her from the front and preventing women from working in front-line hospitals in any capacity other than nursing. She taught theory and practice to nursing sisters. She asked her friend Marie Curie to teach radiology and she continued her study into cancer, with her beloved Dun still at her side. In late 1918 she found herself at the forefront of the fight against the Spanish flu outbreak. By the end of the war she was mentally and physically exhausted. In the summer of 1919 she was due to embark on a worldwide tour, lecturing on her experiences during the war, but on 6 June 1919, aged just 40, she was found dead in bed at her home in Paris. Next to her lay a number of medications; she had taken an overdose. The cause of her death was put down in part to overwork caused by the war and delayed shell shock due to her time at Verdun in 1916. She died having received no campaign medals for her army service, nor any form of recognition for her bravery at Verdun.

* * *

With America and the Allies still maintaining huge armies in France, it was thought necessary to keep the men occupied while they waited for demobilisation. Quite whose idea the Inter-Allied Games was is unclear. The 1916 Olympics had been cancelled due to the war, and although there were plans for Olympic Games in 1920, something was needed to keep the troops' minds off their current situation. So, a two-week games spectacular, with thirteen main events, was planned for all the Allied armies. With the American YMCA funding the stadium and American Army engineers stepping in at the last minute to see the stadium completed on time, it was not unsurprisingly named Stade Pershing. It was built near the 1900 Paris Olympics site at Joinville-le-Pont. After the closing ceremony, Pershing presented the stadium as a gift to the French nation.

Over two weeks from 22 June to 6 July 1919 more than 500,000 Allied servicemen and women witnessed an Olympic-style opening and closing ceremonies and a veritable feast of sport. All the Allies competed, including Arabia. African-Americans were allowed to take part, but not women. Many stars of the past and future were on display, including Gene Tunney (future world heavyweight boxing champion) and French tennis star André Gobert, winner of two Olympic gold medals for tennis in Stockholm in 1912. Another star was swimmer Norman Ross; Olympic champion in 1920, he won three gold medals and set thirteen world records in the pool.

*   *   *

In America the summer of 1919 became known as 'the Red Summer' after hundreds of African-Americans died. A perfect storm of events turned towns and cities across the whole country red with the blood of dead African-Americans, especially returning African-American servicemen who were expecting to enjoy the privileges they perceived they had fought for. Others who died included southern men and women moving north to escape the hated Jim Crow laws. African-American and white veterans clashed while looking for what precious little work there was available.

Nowhere was immune from the riots, from the big cities of New York, Washington and Chicago to the small southern towns; everywhere lives and property were lost. The very thing America had worried about in 1917 when African-Americans volunteered or were conscripted into the army had come to pass. Returning servicemen armed and organised themselves into self-defence groups to protect their families and properties. By the end of the summer more 250 African-American men, women and children had been murdered by white mobs. Their deaths were as grisly as those in the trenches had been; they were lynched, burnt or beaten to death. Set against this, a very small number of white people also died.

*   *   *

Statesmen at Versailles signed the peace treaty with Germany on 28 June 1919. The Allied armies wanted their day in the sun, so 14 July, Bastille Day, was selected. On that day countless thousands of Allied troops, led by disabled and blinded French veterans, saluted the Catafalque, next to the Arc de Triomphe on the Champs Elysée. The Catafalque – a decorated wooden framework supporting the coffin of a distinguished person during their funeral or while lying in state – was of great historic significance. One had been used for Victor Hugo's body to lie in state in 1855.

Troops from Britain and her Empire, France and her Empire, men from America, Japan, Portugal, Romania and Italy, to name but a few, passed by. Men and women of every colour and religion proudly marched by the assembled dignitaries and received the crowd's applause. The victorious wartime generals and regimental bands passed by to great cheers. But not a single African-American was present that day to receive the adoration of the Parisian crowd, despite their contribution both during and after the war. Nor was there a single Russian.

Almost as soon as the day was over, the Catafalque was removed, despite the best intentions of French architect and veteran André Mare to commemorate victory and the dead with it. French premier Georges Clemenceau demanded it be dismantled, as he deemed it too Germanic. However, prior to the parade it had already caught the eye of British premier David Lloyd George, who commissioned Edwin Lutyens to build a similar temporary remembrance structure for the British Peace Day Parade due to be held on 19 July in London.

On 19 July the victorious British and Empire servicemen and women passed by the newly unveiled temporary wood and plaster cenotaph (lit. 'empty grave'). Its non-religious impact was immediate, as it became the focus for grieving widows and relatives with no body to mourn and no grave at home to tend. Floral tributes stacked up around the cenotaph, and more than a million bereaved people passed by before it was dismantled. A permanent replacement was subsequently commissioned; it was to be made of Portland stone and permanently sited in Whitehall, and was to be ready in time for the armistice ceremony in 1920. One inscription on it, that was not used in France, read 'The Glorious Dead'.

* * *

If the American 805th, 813th, 815th and 816th Regiments and the Labor Battalions had faced a huge task, clearing the battlefields and reburying their dead, the French task was colossal. The Argonne Forest front alone, although representing only 5 per cent of the total front line, had more than 10 per cent (150,000) of France's battlefield deaths, all needing to be located and reburied. A similar number of German dead also needed to be located and reburied. In addition, the trenches and bunkers created over four years of conflict had to be dismantled and the land made re-usable. The most dangerous task was locating and digging up unexploded artillery shells which had sunk below the muddy surface, a large number of which contained gas.

The French army began another sweep of the battlefield, clearing ammunition, shells, barbed wire, tin shelters and other battlefield detritus. There were no metal detectors then, so the task had to be painstakingly undertaken by hand with shovels and long metal poles pushed down into the ground. The French Army and German prisoners of war then began the grisly task of locating their dead. The French and German dead lay under four years of battlefield carnage and for the most part were no more than bones.

If a map indicated a possible grave location, these would be marked. For the men, most of whom had served on the front, body location required a degree of detective work. Signs were looked for – protruding body parts and equipment, rat holes with discarded waste, rich coloured grass, dirty water – each became a clue for the exhumation parties. Possible body sites were marked and then began the gruesome task of digging up the dead.

Any possible clue to the identity of the remains was carefully put to one side, ranging from the straightforward ID disk to items of kit bearing a regimental number, a letter or even a jaw for identification through dental records. For every positive identification made, there was one less family grieving for a missing soldier. The men with no discernible identity joined the ranks of the unknown soldiers. Known men were placed into creosote-soaked canvas bags and prepared for moving to the nearest cemetery.

The French dead were moved to cemetery concentration sites around the edge of the forest, some of which had already been used as wartime cemeteries, such as Les Islettes, Florent, La Harazée and Vienne-le-Château. Men from French Indo-china, Annamites, who had served in the war carried out much of this work and now, like the African-Americans, found themselves handed the most thankless of tasks. The men who could be identified were given a marked grave; the others, often no more than bones, were placed in ossuaries in the same cemeteries.

*   *   *

For French villagers already resident or returning to their destroyed or partially destroyed villages, the French government published a pamphlet in 1919 to help them through the bureaucratic minefield of claiming compensation. Claims needed various supporting documents, which in most cases were lost in the fighting and or destruction of their property. Property and land owners needed to prove the loss of fruit trees, forestry, vines, cattle, other livestock, outbuildings and machinery, much of which would have been paid for with cash over many years. Town halls, if they still survived, had lost cadastre maps of towns and surrounding areas. Some villages in Verdun and the Champagne area had ceased to exist in any meaningful way. Trigonometric points on high ground, which could have enabled new mapping, had also disappeared.

Boundaries to houses, property and land were difficult or impossible to re-establish. Small plots of land, houses and other property commonly had multiple owners, who in many cases could not agree what they wanted to do. In other cases owners had simply disappeared. To add to the bureaucratic confusion, if the cost of reconstruction was greater than the land value, then the state would purchase the land.

Boureuilles on the east of the Argonne was so entirely destroyed by the war that it was rebuilt a few hundred yards away. In the fields surrounding Neuvilly, following clearance, a new programme of tree sapling planting started. For the Argonne and surrounding forests to regain their pre-war use, they would have to be replanted from scratch. An experiment with self-seeding had shown only a 25 per cent success rate. So thousands of oak, silver birch, ash, beech and pine saplings were planted out, for future sowing in the surrounding forest remnants.

Most of the houses in the villages on the eastern side of the forest were destroyed. Here, returning locals took matters into their own hands, using whatever materials they could find – old bricks, wood, beams and stones – for the walls. There was a sort of justice for many in reclaiming their building materials from German trenches and rest camps. Some used army-issue tin, boards and tarpaulins for roofing, with old roof tiles holding them down. Others took refuge from the elements in cellars and wartime bunkers. During the American advance, they had dynamited most of the German strongpoints, fearing that a counter-attacking German army would re-occupy their old positions. Many of the rest camps, though, remained untouched and would provide rich pickings for locals for years to come. Items as diverse as pianos, bed and table linen, and table glasses were said to have been recovered by grateful locals in the years following the war.

The French government was not oblivious to their plight. A French Army engineer officer, Louis August Adrian, had left Metz as a child in a cart after the annexation of Alsace by Germany following the 1870–1 Franco-Prussian War. He joined the French Army as an engineer, working his way up through its ranks to become deputy director in 1907. On his way he had rooted out corruption and fraud, making many enemies among both the army and the civilian military equipment suppliers along the way. He had retired, exhausted by these battles, in 1913. At the outbreak of war he was brought back and immediately managed to save 4,000 tons of cloth during the capture of Lille by the Germans. He was soon at work. The greatest danger to the *Poilus* was shrapnel; 70 per cent of all wounded were shrapnel head injuries, and 80 per cent of these proved fatal. Initially Adrian designed a metal skullcap to place inside the kepi, but this had limited success. Next he designed a metal helmet, the M15 *Casque Adrian*, which was soon in general production and became standard issue to the French Army in 1915. By 1916 head injuries from shrapnel had been reduced to 22 per cent of battlefield casualties, with fatalities accounting for fewer than 50 per cent of these. The *Casque Adrian* saved hundreds of thousands of *Poilus* during the course of the war. Adrian was already working on his next tasks: trench boots and sheepskin jackets for use in the long, cold winters in the trenches. Goggles to shield the eyes from shrapnel splinters and armoured turrets for aircraft also appeared under his stewardship. France was faced with a massive shortage of accommodation for troops not serving at the front line. In the centre and south of the country it was Adrian who brought in a prefabricated, quick-to-assemble wooden hut modelled on France's African Army barracks.

Around the Argonne, for the returning villagers, it was a small house designed by Adrian that saved the day. Prefabricated in wooden sections for easy movement by train to local stations, these houses were no more than a couple of basic rooms with a central chimney poking out of a tar paper roof. Insulation was non-existent, but the *Maison Adrian* did provide accommodation for the *sinistres* (as the claimants from the state were known) while they pursued their claims. A few examples remain to this day in the quiet backstreets of some Argonne villages.

Help with civilian house-building came from an unlikely source: the American Friends Service Committee (AFSC), a Quaker organisation set up in the USA in 1917. Their aim was to provide an alternative national service for Quakers who objected to serving in the army, but wished to contribute to the war effort. Mennonite objectors also joined their ranks. Many of them, having first served prison terms in the USA for refusing the draft, started to arrive in the Argonne region in early 1919. Their first task was to rebuild Sister Gabrielle's Hospital in Clermont. They then moved on to building temporary housing (*Maison Adrian*) and setting up food co-operatives and shops in each village. The poor state of the roads and lack of communications with the outside world meant food for civilians was hard to find.

One AFSC worker described the roads as so bad that for every hour a vehicle spent on the road, an equivalent amount of time had to be spent in the garage for repairs. Funds and supplies were collected through the Quaker and Mennonite networks in the USA and shipped to France. They brought in farming machinery, fruit trees and animals to help locals feed themselves and start farming again. In their two years in the region they built 773 houses in twenty-four different villages, including 100 in Varennes, 79 in Montfaucon, 76 in Aubréville, 72 in Neuvilly, 71 in Boureuilles and 76 in Montblainville.

*   *   *

Mary Louise Baker was born into a Quaker family in Alliance, Ohio, on 4 August 1872. She finished her education in Pennsylvania and later taught in some small local schools. At the turn of the century she achieved her ambition to study art at Pennsylvania Museum School of Industrial Art. Afterwards, she undertook many different aspects of art, including teaching, illustrating, and making architectural technical drawings. In 1908 she began her lifelong love of Mayan pottery, producing a series of archaeological illustrations in colour. Despite suffering poor health since childhood, she volunteered after the First World War to join the Quaker AFSC in France to assist in postwar reconstruction. Although painting and illustrations were her forte, she also had a lifelong interest in embroidery. She was assigned to the Embroidery Depot at Verdun in 1919. From there she was sent to Clermont, where she helped returning local women re-master the lost art of Argonnaise embroidery. She helped to sell their work across France, lifting the women from postwar poverty. In August 1920 she returned to America and continued her work on Mayan art.

*   *   *

For the French *sinistres*, struggling through the bureaucracy, progress on their claims was slow. The shortages of building materials and skilled men and the high cost of materials added to the length of time everything took. They were also resistant to the proposed 'improvements' in their homes and villages, which the government sought to introduce, partly in response to their grief for loved ones lost and homes destroyed, and partly because they wanted the pre-war situation reinstated. They wanted their homes and villages back; their houses, streets, shops, churches and town halls all exactly as they had been before the war, not interfered with by some distant government busybody. This added to the delays as each plot of land was examined, and properties and houses aligned to their pre-war positions. Everything had to be the same.

People supported each other, though, and like the food co-operatives, building co-operatives soon appeared and neighbour helped neighbour to rebuild, with the assistance in many cases of German POWs. The materials used were often partially reclaimed from their old houses and properties. There were, though, two public hygiene improvements to housing in the rebuilding programme that the government could take credit for. One was the separation of animals and people; traditionally they had been housed together, albeit in separate rooms, but now separate barns were built for livestock. The other was the removal of dung piles from in front of their houses. Local tradition had it that animal dung was piled in front of the houses for later removal and use as fertiliser. American soldiers had been shocked by this on their arrival in the Argonne and had spent hours clearing piles away, only for them to reappear later.

With much of the Argonne Forest in Zone Red, and unlikely to be of any economic value in the foreseeable future, the government set about purchasing it from its private owners. The only permitted activities in the forest were army camps, reclamation, commemoration visits and forestry work.

The government was now beset by another problem: the lobbying of the veteran groups. With many veterans now government deputies, they also had a view on what should be done with the land along the front. Many subscribed to the idea of a *'Via Sacra'* along the front line, as proposed by the British and French earlier in the war, to be kept in perpetuity for remembrance of the sacrifice. This brought many challenges, not least, as to the exact location of the front in a war that had ebbed and flowed. Some landowners may have been happy to accept compensation for having such a path across their land; others, though, especially where it passed close to their house, or cut off their land from their house, were not so willing.

The *Via Sacra* eventually materialised in the form of ninety-six roadside markers made from pink granite, marking the furthest points reached by the Germans on 18 July 1918. On the top of each metre-high marker was a *Poilu*'s helmet. They were erected between 1921 and 1927 by the Touring Club of France and their Belgian counterparts. Marshal Pétain oversaw the placement of the markers, which were made by the Parisian sculptor

Paul Moreau-Vauthier. One of the few still remaining is on the Four de Paris– Varennes road.

*   *   *

In northern France, where so much government revenue had been lost as a result of the war, there was pressure from landowners and businesses to clear Zone Red as quickly as possible. The imperative here was to get the arable land back into production to feed the nation, and for businesses and mines to be reopened both to provide employment for returning veterans and to produce revenue for the government. However, the veterans could take some consolation from the fact that the areas of Verdun, Fille Morte, Côte 304 and the Argonne Forest had no such potential and thus would remain as sites of pilgrimage. Army camps and training areas also sprang up in the areas either side of the forest.

The first Michelin Guide for tourists and pilgrims visiting the former front lines was published even before the end of the war, and early in 1919 the French government officially sanctioned battlefield tourism, although poor local infrastructure meant it didn't really take off until a few years later. Once the roads and railways were functioning, and accommodation and catering services had been built for people wishing to visit, a growing number of visitors did start to arrive. Outside France, wealthier war widows, children, parents, veterans and the plain curious from America, Britain and the Empire began to make their way to the battlefields and cemeteries.

For French veterans, grieving widows, parents, orphans and other family members a visit to the Argonne Forest immediately after the war started with arrival at Les Islettes railway station. Then, depending on their means, they either walked or took a donkey-cart or ox-cart along the rough bumpy tracks up into the forest. Locals and former soldiers became adept guides, taking people around the sights and cemeteries. As nature rapidly reclaimed much of the old forest and brambles spread over the cleared areas, battle sites became difficult to access. There were graves for a lucky few, but for relatives whose loved ones had simply disappeared into the mud, there was nothing at all.

*   *   *

German prisoners of war, as the French did, cleared the battlefields and dug up their dead. They then searched for each soldier's identity and moved their dead into larger concentrations at cemeteries all along the front. For the Germans it was the same process: identified men had a grave, although not always a single one, while unidentifiable bones were placed in ossuaries. Although they secured a few larger sites, they were small compared to many of the Allied cemeteries. This led to the construction of ossuaries to house the remains of the unidentified and *Kameraden Graben* (comrades' graves) for those who were known, usually four men to a plot with one cross. German Argonne cemeteries were built across the region including at Apremont, Servon and Romagne.

Dr Siegfried Emmo Eulen, an ex-German army officer who had been responsible for the burial of war dead in Poland and Turkey, decided to look after the war dead buried outside Germany. On 16 December 1919 he founded the *Volksbund Deutsch Kriegsgräberfürsorge e.V.* (People's Community for the Care of German War Graves). Its principles were simple: to be voluntarily funded, non-political and open to all.

* * *

As 1919 came to an end, some sort of order now prevailed at the front and villagers had begun to rebuild their lives. It was not, though, the end of the problems and 1920 was to prove no less challenging for the politicians. In early 1920 the French government's hope was that once their new cemeteries started appearing, with their symmetrical lines of white crosses, families would have a focus for their grief. But this proved not to be the case, and the unauthorised macabre trade of moving the dead continued much as it had done for the previous four years. The poor were left with no focus for their grief, while the rich could take some comfort from their illegally acquired loved one – or someone else's. The debate was further stirred up by America having gone to a ballot the previous year regarding the returning of their dead.

Over 60,000 ballot papers been returned to the American authorities by January 1920. Despite family controversy, and many next of kin being unable to respond as they had moved or died, or incorrect details had been sent out, the overwhelming response was clear: they wanted their sons and husbands brought home. As a result of this, Congress approved funds to begin the work, despite there being no approval from France. Even if the French did concede on the matter, they could hardly do so before they had made repatriation arrangements for French widows and parents.

* * *

By 1920 Great-Uncle Bob was back in his marital home in Paris. Following General Gouraud's departure to the Dardanelles in April 1915, Bob had been discharged from the French Foreign Legion. He entered the

British Army Service Corps as a second lieutenant and made his way back to the front in the autumn of 1915 as a driver's mate. As he was not a French citizen, he was unable to undertake translation duties. In the spring of 1916 he had been sent to Cambridge military hospital with flu and neurasthenia (shell-shock). Although passed fit for service later in 1916, he was still clearly unwell, as he didn't return to the front until the autumn of 1918. In May 1919, nearly five years after he first enlisted in the French Foreign Legion, Bob was finally discharged from the British Army. His request for a 1914 Mons Star and clasp was turned down as he was 'not serving in a recognised unit in the BEF'. The French, though, did acknowledge his service and on 7 October 1919, he was gazetted in the *London Gazette*, awarded the *Croix de Guerre Avec Etoile de Bronze* by the French government. The citation is sadly lost. He returned to his Paris home in the Rue Eugene Manuel near the Eiffel Tower.

On 12 April 1920 Uncle Bob left his Parisian home, telling his wife he was off on family business to London. On the night of 12 April 1920 he departed Le Havre on the SS *Hantonia*, bound for Southampton. When it docked in Southampton the next morning, Bob was missing. His cabin was searched and his case recovered. In it was found a note: 'I have had a bad life and as no one would wish to attend my funeral, I shall have it by myself.' His death was recorded in the ship's log as suicide, 5 miles off the coast of Le Havre, where a fellow passenger had reported seeing someone acting suspiciously on the boat deck the previous evening. His body was never recovered.

* * *

On 16 May 1920 Joan of Arc was officially canonised in Rome as St Joan of Arc. One of the officiates was Cardinal Merry del Val, a distant cousin. In London more than 100,000 people crowded around Westminster Cathedral to listen to the service, broadcast from Rome, and see a solemn street pageant to celebrate her life, including a figure of her in armour mounted on a horse. Her prominent role in the French war effort meant the intended date of her sainthood (in 1931, to coincide with the 500th anniversary of her death) was brought forward. Her influence as a rallying point during the war had spread from France to Britain, where she was depicted in armour on posters appealing to women to purchase war savings certificates. In America, similar imagery was used to appeal to American women to buy war savings stamps. Cecil B. DeMille made a film about her life in 1916, *Joan the Woman*, which began and ended in a trench. Former French president Raymond Poincaré wrote of her sainthood, 'Joan, the

English and us, we fought on the same side in the world war, like her for the reign of right and justice. In her spirit let us remain united for the good of mankind.'

* * *

On 30 May 1920, Memorial Day, the American Memorial League staged their first service at the American military cemetery at Romagne. The Mayor of Romagne and the village priest led several thousand people up to the cemetery. Many had set off at dawn from villages further away to make the pilgrimage. Carried in the mid of the procession was a large wreath of wild flowers, so big that it took twenty-three men to support it.

In front of each of the 22,000 crosses flew the flags of America and France. A chain of daisies, made by local schoolchildren, linked all the crosses. Around the large central American flag was a star made from yellow pansies. The American general Henry T. Allen, who had commanded the 90th Division in the war, presided over the occasion. Now commanding American forces in Germany, he brought with him a company of American soldiers and a band. General Duport represented the French Army.

Meanwhile, the lack of an Argonne memorial was about to change. On 21 July 1920 a service was held at the Cimetière National de la Forestière, in the centre of the forest. Attending the service was the Countess de Martimprey, whose husband Captain Jean de Martimprey had disappeared on 13 July 1915 at Côte 285 near *Haute Chevauchée*. She decided to launch an appeal to build both a memorial and an ossuary, under the guidance of a new Commemorative Committee of the Argonne. With the help of the priest of Lachalade, Abbot Bouilly, she was able to ask General Henri Gouraud to chair the committee, which was formally created on 12 June 1921. The former French president Raymond Poincaré, who was from nearby Nubécourt, became the honorary president.

Public pressure for the return of bodies mounted in France among groups such as the Union of Fathers and Mothers whose sons had died for their country. Externally, political pressure for body return from America was increasing.

On 31 July 1920 a law was passed in France to provide for free coffins and transport of the remains of military personnel killed in the war back to their homes. Forms were sent in August 1920 to town halls all over France to be completed by grieving families and returned to the *Service Général des Pensions* by 2 January 1921. Unlike America, in France it was widows who had the say-so unless the men had died unmarried, in which case it was the mothers. This process had to be extended to 15 February owing to insufficient forms being available. Exceptions to the deadline were made for families whose loved ones had not yet been identified by that date. They would have three months to register following notification of identification of a body. Problems soon arose as some widows wanted the bodies returned while parents did not, and vice versa. These disputes had to be settled in the civil courts.

This move towards repatriation had a knock-on effect in Britain. A last-minute debate in Parliament in May 1920 set out to scupper the work of the IWGC and enable repatriation, but the motion was defeated. Work on the IWGC cemeteries could now get under way in earnest. The Portland stone headstones lay in neat symmetrical secular rows. Each headstone carried the following: a national emblem or regimental badge, name, rank, unit, date of death and small family inscription. For the unknown, there would be no ossuary but an individual grave with a headstone inscribed with Kipling's touching words: 'A Soldier of the Great War. Known unto God.' Despite the apparent military order, each cemetery was also indicative of the chaos of war as neither the names, the units nor the year of death followed any sort of order.

In Britain after the war memorials inscribed with the names of the dead appeared in almost every town and village, and each served as a focus for grief and commemoration. For those few people with sufficient funds, it was possible to go to France and visit the battlefields and see the grave of a loved one. A cottage industry sprang up in Belgium and France to place wreaths for those who could not afford the trip. Many were unemployed British war veterans; some did their job diligently, and placed a wreath or flowers, while others just exploited the grieving, took their money and did nothing.

In 1920 there developed another public movement. Amid the continued absence of focus for the public's overwhelming sense of grief, there appeared a body for veneration: the Unknown Soldier. The original provenance of the idea is disputed between France and Britain. For Britain, the credit lay with the Reverend David Railton MC, a chaplain with the British Army in France. In 1916 he had noticed a sad and forlorn white cross, bearing the words 'An Unknown Soldier (of The Black Watch)'. This notion of an 'unknown soldier' remained with him for the duration of the war. In 1920 the idea was put forward but initially turned down by the King. Nevertheless, it found support from Prime Minister Lloyd George, who had read the public's mood better than most and had already witnessed the success of the Cenotaph. The newspapers also supported the idea of an Unknown Warrior (as the British body was now known) being brought back from France and buried in Westminster Abbey as a focus for the national grief.

The French felt that they had had the original idea of honouring an Unknown Soldier and it was taken from them. In 1916 Francois Simon, president of the *Souvenir Français*, an association founded in 1887 to keep alive the memory of the dead of the Franco-Prussian War of 1870–1, proposed that an Unknown Soldier be buried at the Pantheon in Paris, home of France's national heroes. After the first anniversary of the Armistice in 1919 it was proposed that an Unknown Soldier be buried in the Pantheon. However, veterans believed the burial place should be the Arc de Triomphe, the great memorial to the dead of the Revolutionary and Napoleonic Wars.

A site near the Arc had been used as a temporary Catafalque during the Victory Parade of 14 July 1919. The argument swayed back and forth, and the waters were muddied further by another event, the impending fiftieth anniversary of the Third Republic. Added to this was the desire to inter the heart of another national hero, Leon Gambetta, a leading politician during the Franco-Prussian War of 1870–1, who had campaigned for the return of Alsace-Lorraine. Now the two provinces had been returned to France, it was felt that this was suitable time to commemorate him. After nearly a year of prevarication, and despite the British getting ready with their own ceremony, nothing had been agreed in France except to take Gambetta's heart to the Pantheon.

At the end of October a former French soldier wrote to a national paper saying he and his comrades would exhume for themselves a soldier from the battlefield and bar the way to the ceremony for Gambetta's heart at the Pantheon. Quickly the three events were now merged and preparations began.

In remarkably little time an operation was organised to exhume a body from France and return it to Britain in time for the Armistice anniversary service on 11 November 1920. The IWGC, which originally forbade such an exhumation, fell into line. The French government had to hastily change its legislation to permit the removal of bodies from the front, whether to Paris or London.

Four unidentified soldiers were exhumed, one from each of the main British battlefields at the Aisne, the Somme, Arras and Ypres. The men had to still have some remnant of their British Army uniform, to avoid any doubt about their nationality, and to be skeletal in order that there were no health concerns. The four sets of remains were placed in a room under guard, with no indication of which battlefield they had come from. At

midnight on 7 November General Wyatt, the General Officer Commanding British troops in France, placed his hand on one of the four coffins.
This was duly selected to start its journey back to Britain.

The coffin was carried across France in an ambulance, together with
earth taken from each of the battlefields. On 10 November the coffin was
put aboard HMS *Verdun* for passage to Britain. Solemn crowds at every
station marked its journey from Dover to London by train. On 11 November 1920 the coffin was mounted on a gun carriage and conveyed across
central London to the newly built stone Cenotaph, where the King laid a
wreath before he led the cortège to Westminster Abbey. The pall-bearers
were made up of commanders from all the wartime services, and there was
a guard of honour comprising 100 Victoria Cross holders. The guests of
honour included a group of about 100 women, chosen because they had
each lost their husband and all their sons in the war. A short service was
held, and then a two minutes' silence at 11am. Then the coffin containing
the Unknown Warrior was lowered into his grave in the west nave. The
King scattered a handful of French earth over the coffin. More than
200,000 people filed past the Cenotaph and the warrior's tomb during that
day, and another million more, before he was finally buried under more
soil brought from France a week later.

The French exhumed eight unidentified bodies, one from each of
France's main battlefields: Artois, Flanders, Somme, Ile de France, Chemin
des Dames, Champagne, Verdun and Lorraine. The same care was taken
over their selection; they had to be in a French uniform and in a suitable
state of decomposition. The bodies were gathered in the Citadel of
Verdun in oak caskets. The person selected to choose the coffin was a hero
of the Chemin des Dames and Verdun, but he fell ill with typhoid fever
and had to stand aside. Instead, 21-year-old August Thin, a private from
the 132nd Infantry Regiment, was selected. Thin had lost his father earlier
in the war fighting at Verdun and had himself participated in the war; he
was gassed and one of only a handful of survivors from one battle in
Champagne. On 10 November the eight coffins were put on display, each
covered with a French flag. Thin, resplendent in a new uniform, walked
around once briskly and then again more slowly. He made his choice,
placing a bouquet of red and white violets on the sixth coffin. Later he
said the reason for his choice was that he was a member of the Army's
6th Corps and it was the total of his regiment's number (1 + 3 + 2 = 6). The
coffin, under military escort with Thin, was then carried through the
snow-covered streets of Verdun to the railway station, for onward transportation to Paris.

On the morning of the 11th two carriages left the overnight resting place in Paris, a chapel; one was the gun carriage carrying the Unknown Soldier, resplendent in full military honours, while the second was a grand hearse containing the urn with Gambetta's heart. They were conveyed to the Pantheon, where a service was held. Both were then taken to the Arc de Triomphe, escorted by French marshals. Thousands of mourners lined the streets of Paris and clung to every vantage point. At the Arc a small religious service was held. The two coffins lay side by side under the Arc de Triomphe as thousands of Parisians filed by. At sunset the Unknown Soldier's coffin was placed in a chapel on the first floor of the Arc, where it remained under constant guard until it was time for burial. The urn containing Gambetta's heart was conveyed back to the Pantheon for interment. The Unknown Soldier was finally buried beneath the Arc de Triomphe at 8.30am on 28 January 1921, after extensive support work had been undertaken to enable the grave to be dug. The Unknown Soldier was awarded the French *Legion d'Honneur* prior to burial on behalf of a grateful nation.

The seven other bodies from the Verdun citadel were reburied in a cemetery in Verdun, with Thin in attendance.

One of the escorts on 11 November was the famous Albert Séverin Roche the 'First Soldier of France'. Albert's story is one of the most remarkable of the entire war. In 1914 he volunteered for service at the front, but was rejected, much to his father's relief, as he was too puny. But Albert changed regions and was accepted into the 30th Battalion of Chasseurs, known to the Germans as the Blue Devils after the colour of their berets. He arrived at the front with the 27th Battalion in July 1915 and was soon in the thick of the action. Over the next three-and-a-half years he fought on all fronts, captured 1,181 German prisoners, was wounded nine times and was awarded numerous decorations for bravery. His closest escape from death came after he had spent ten hours rescuing an injured captain from no man's land. He was later found collapsed with exhaustion; court-martialled for sleeping at his post, he was sentenced to death. Just before his execution, however, the captain woke from his coma and vouched for him. Albert was selected to be present in the citadel at Verdun for the choosing of the French Unknown Soldier and later carried his coffin to the interment under the Arc de Triomphe.

For the Americans, the suddenness of the burials of the Unknown Warrior in Britain and Unknown Soldier in France meant they were unable to make a similar arrangement in 1920. Chaplain Pierce also wanted to be quite certain that the American Soldier chosen was really 'Unknown'.

Now that France had changed its position on the repatriation of the dead, America began to plan the return journey home for their dead, albeit at the American taxpayers' expense. Trains and canal boats were requisitioned, lined coffins made, labour sought. The aim was to be ready to start the process in 1921.

In the meantime, to add to the confusion, many families had changed their minds, now wanting their loved ones to remain in France. Added to this, in an immigrant nation 'home' could be anywhere; in the end, some 700 dead went to Europe, including Germany. Negotiations had to be entered into with a multitude of governments, to bring the dead back to their final resting place.

Given the scale of the task, with more than 250,000 requests for repatriation of French remains, the government had to make one department solely responsible for the work. The battlefields would be assigned into nine separate zones, each of which would be further subdivided. The work of returning the bodies would be paid for by the state but fulfilled by private contractors, who would arrange trains and the storage and delivery of bodies all over France. For corpses that were mummified or already skeletal, they were to use basic metal-lined oak coffins free of adornment, which were supplied in two standard lengths, 1.7 and 1.9 metres. For corpses that were still decomposing they would use zinc-lined coffins that were welded shut. If a family wanted to use their own coffin, this would have to comply with the government regulations and be with the contractor at the point of disinterment.

Families were invited to be present at the disinterment, which could prove very distressing, given the advanced stage of decomposition all the bodies were in. The coffins were then moved to the local railway station ready for transport across France. All this had to be organised by battle zone and by final destination, not to mention the need to maximise rail network efficiency and minimise the time the bodies spent disinterred, for the sake of public health. Wagons and later vehicles had to be sealed and the coffins accounted for at all stages of the journey. Once they arrived at their final destination they had to be placed in safe storage and under guard until their reburial. The trains' arrival was usually greeted with a sombre local ceremony attended by most of the town's residents. In the warmer parts of France such activity had to be scheduled for night-time so as not to subject the coffins to too much heat.

Exactly what the French government had wanted to avoid when they forbade the repatriation of the dead in 1919 began to happen in 1921. The country became a ghoulish web of the dead being transported across the country. Bodies were heading to the USA, bodies of Frenchmen were being taken home and now bodies of French dead from overseas started arriving home. After a delay due to Italian legislation forbidding the repatriation of the war dead, they too began to go home from their consolidated cemeteries. The 500-plus Garibaldi men who had died in the Argonne Forest in 1914 and 1915 had lain in and around the forest ever since, mainly opposite the Abbey at Lachalade. Now they began their journey back to Italy (226 of them), or were reburied in local French military cemeteries around the forest. Others were sent back to French villages at the request of the parents or widows, or to the main Italian war cemetery at Bligny. Here they were finally laid to rest in an Italian-modelled garden.

In an operation of such scale and complexity, problems inevitably occurred: French families arrived at disinterments only to find it was the wrong person in the grave, or families were not notified in time to attend; contractors cut corners on costs and coffins broke; coffins arrived at local stations but families were unaware their loved ones had returned; the wrong body was delivered to the wrong station or to the wrong family. However, given the huge numbers brought home between 1921 and 1926 from both France and overseas, 250,000 to 300,000 in total, the problems were relatively insignificant.

In 1921 the French government brought in a new law that established the right to a free annual pilgrimage for families wishing to go to the grave of their buried relative. This was part of the broader incentive programme to avoid body repatriation.

Elsewhere the line between battlefield tourism, and its intention to help bring much-needed rejuvenation to the damaged villages, and pilgrimages of veterans and widows to graves was a fine one and subject to much debate and anger. Villagers in the devastated regions had no wish for outsiders to see their grief and destroyed homes, and former soldiers had no wish for tourists to seek souvenirs on land they had shed blood for.

*   *   *

By mid-1921 bodies of the American dead started to move back across the Atlantic. General Pershing was present at Hoboken in New Jersey on 21 July 1921 to welcome the first ships bringing the dead home. Among them were the caskets of Privates Thomas Enright and Merle Hay and

Corporal James Gresham, the first men to die under American command. Pershing placed flowers on their coffins. They were then sent out across America for reburial either in family plots or in national army cemeteries. Eventually even Private Henry Gunther (America's last man killed on 11 November 1918) found his way home to be buried in Baltimore. African-Americans had fought alongside their white comrades, buried them and then dug them up for sending home. Now they found there was still no equality as they were consigned to coloured sections of the national cemeteries, including Arlington.

Of the approximately 115,000 American war dead, many of whom had died in America, approximately 45,000 made their way home. Charles Pierce, whose valiant efforts in France with the GRS and earlier in the Philippines, died of pneumonia in France in 1921. He was repatriated and buried in Arlington. By the mid-1920s the remaining 35,000 in Europe were consolidated in eight cemeteries, the largest of which is the Meuse-Argonne American cemetery at Romagne. Here lie more than 14,000 men and women in the largest American military cemetery in Europe. The spirit of the Argonne glass-makers even prevailed in the chapel, where special glass was commissioned.

* * *

On 24 July 1921 General Duport, commander of the 6th Corps, placed the first memorial stone at *Haute Chevauchée* in the Argonne Forest, launching the public subscription. The Countess de Martimprey organised dozens of meetings in Paris, and wrote to veterans' groups in France, Italy and America, and to thousands of families of the missing to raise funds for her project. She remarked, 'the more humble the person donating, the more important the donation'. As funds flowed in, the Countess was able to commission two war veterans, Paris architect Alexandre Bollore to design the monument, and sculptor Edmond Becker to start work on the stone statue. The 9 metre high sculpture, entitled 'Aux Morts de l'Argonne', is topped with the figure of a *Poilu*, whose face is that of Becker's son, killed in 1915. On each side of the memorial are inscribed the names of the 275 French regiments, 18 Italian regiments, 32 American divisions and the Czechoslovakian volunteers who saw service in the Argonne sector. On the rear an inscription commemorates the 150,000 Allied dead who were killed in the Argonne sector between 1914 and 1918. The monument was inaugurated on 30 July 1922, a little over a year after the fund-raising campaign was officially launched. Not only had the Countess raised the funds and overseen the building of the monument in such a short period, she had also negotiated with a multitude of different vested interests, any one of whom could have brought the project to a halt: the French Army, responsible for administering the land; the Ministry of Liberated Regions and their agencies working in the forest; a multitude of veterans' groups; and the local communes on whose land the statue would now stand, along with its access, which required a stone path to be built. Raymond Poincaré, once again Prime Minister and Senator for Meuse, gave the opening speech, in which he spoke vociferously of the need for more war reparations from Germany.

The following year, on 17 June 1923, General Henri Gouraud officially inaugurated the crypt in the ossuary beneath the statue, where the bones of more than 10,000 unidentified men from all armies were placed side by side. In the small crypt were three raised coffins, each draped with the French Tricolour and decorated with flowers. Under each coffin was a brief description of the battlefield from where the unidentified bones had come from. On the left are remains recovered from the Bois de Bolante, in the centre are remains from Fille Morte and Côtes 285 and 263, and on the right are remains from Ravin des Meurissons and La Gruerie. Unidentified bones continued to be placed in the ossuary for another fifty years.

*   *   *

Back in the USA Congress had originally wanted the American Unknown Soldier to be buried in Arlington in time for Memorial Day 1921 (the last Monday of May). Pierce of the GRS, however, argued that more time was needed as they had to be sure that the body was really unidentifiable. A compromise was reached, and four unidentified bodies were exhumed on Memorial Day 1921 in France. Sergeant Edward F. Younger, a wounded and decorated serving soldier, was taken to the city hall in Châlons-sur-Marne, France, on 24 October 1921, where there lay four identical caskets. He placed a bouquet of white roses on the third casket from the left. This one was transported back to America for the ceremony at Arlington on 11 November 1921. The three other caskets were taken to the Meuse-Argonne military cemetery in Romagne. On that same day all across America veterans of the American Civil War, the Spanish and Philippine Wars and now the First World War gathered to commemorate the dead around the newly built town memorials.

Given Britain's position on repatriation of the dead, it is said that America had to remove war dead for repatriation from Brookwood military cemetery under cover of darkness. The vehicles that took them to

Southampton were similarly inconspicuous and they were put aboard the ship at night.

*   *   *

The weight of the dead and injured men of the Lost Battalion bore down on Whittlesey relentlessly. Added to this, segments of the press now began to voice similar concerns: was the Lost Battalion as glorious as was first made out? To add to Whittlesey's woes, he had acquired a hacking cough, probably a result of the German gas encountered in France, which kept him awake at night.

On the third anniversary of the armistice, 11 November 1921, Whittlesey was in attendance, along with President Wilson, General Pershing, and numerous other dignitaries. He and other Medal of Honor holders, including Holderman, McMurtry, York and Woodfill, were there for the interment of the American Unknown Soldier in the sarcophagus at Arlington national cemetery. Many of the veterans were now haunted by their own personal demons. Whittlesey said, 'I keep wondering if the Unknown Soldier is one of my men killed in the Pocket? I should not have come. It's been too unnerving.'

On Friday, 18 November 1921 he booked a passage to Havana in Cuba for 25 November. He changed his name to avoid recognition and took a starboard cabin, which meant he could move to the promenade deck unseen. Over the weekend his father visited him in New York and found him 'in good spirits'. On Sunday, 20 November he was present at what was to be his last official function, sitting on the stage with disabled American veterans at a dinner to honour Marshal Foch, the former Generalissimo, in New York City. He spent the following week tidying up his affairs, rewriting his will and leaving client instructions. On Friday, 25 November he paid in advance for his lodgings, later meeting a female friend at a show, after which he boarded the SS *Toloa* at midnight. On Saturday evening, 26 November, he mingled with fellow passengers but such was his fame it was not long before he was recognised and the captain asked him to dine with him.

That evening, by way of a change, Whittlesey's mood appeared to have lightened. Both at the table and in the lounge after, with fellow passengers, he found himself, for the first time in three years, able to talk about the war. But at about 11pm Whittlesey was seen for the last time. The following day the ship hit bad weather, with most passengers spending the day in their cabin.

It was not until Monday, 28 November that Whittlesey was missed. A cabin search revealed that his room and bed had been unused. On the bed were a request to telegraph his parents and instructions for his law firm, as to where to find his client instructions. He left four letters to personal friends, none of whom was prepared to divulge the contents. They agreed with the press's story that he was 'a battle casualty'.

At his memorial service, Colonel N.K. Averill of the 308th Regiment spoke of Whittlesey's life:

> Let us briefly review his war service. Answering at once his country's call and coming from his quiet, scholastic life of a city lawyer, he was thrown almost immediately into the fiercest fighting the World has ever known.
>
> How heroically he rose to the emergency suddenly thrust upon him, history will always tell, but what a mental strain it must have been on that shy, retiring, kindly and lovable man, when he could do nothing to relieve the suffering or the agony of those gallant men dying beside him – and this after he had reached the last stages of physical exhaustion due to a hundred hours' constant fighting and hunger; with this were the unspeakable conditions and the horrors of the battlefield where it had been impossible to bury the dead, and the sole responsibility rested on him. Whittlesey had that rare and moral courage which makes men great, and in that emergency he held on, to the everlasting credit of the American Army.

Years later one of his letters emerged in a college archive. It was written to his lifelong friend John Bayard Pruyn, with whom he spent Thanksgiving in 1921, just before he sailed to Cuba. It said:

> Dear Bayard: Just a note to say good by[e]. I'm a misfit by nature and by training, and there's an end of it.

* * *

Much of the remaining wood in the Argonne Forest was unsuitable for anything other than firewood. The wood was sick from the chemicals used, blasted by shells and damaged by machine-gun bullets that had ripped into the trees. Once the trees were damaged, rot set in, further impacting their condition. The bullets regularly blunted the axes and saws of forest workers felling the trees. Between 1919 and 1926 hundreds of thousands of cubic metres of wood was cut down and sold to the locals for firewood. As it was deemed to be polluted, it was not supposed to be used for cooking, but it may well have ended up in local bread ovens and home stoves. Even to this day, over a hundred years later, as the last of the mighty First World War trees are felled, it is still possible to see machine-gun bullet marks burnt in their centres.

By 1922 the work of the French Army was concluded in the Argonne Forest, with most of the dangerous military hardware removed and bodies reburied in nearby cemeteries. Work was now handed to private contractors to salvage whatever was left. This included lead and copper and, more controversially, the disposal of the thousands of chemical shells still known to be in the forest. The contractors and villagers were also paid by the US Army GRS 20 francs for bodies identified as American. Some 500 hundred bodies a year, mainly French (only about half of whom could be identified), were dug up for a decade after the war ended.

In March 1923 the American government created the American Battle-field Monuments Commission (ABMC) with General Pershing as president. Initially tasked to oversee the construction of battle monuments, it later took over responsibility for managing the cemeteries. Postwar arguments in America, which was overwhelmingly Christian, over how to officially mark graves caused endless delays. As a result, the 'temporary' white wooden crosses remained in the French cemeteries. Eventually it was agreed that a headstone similar to Britain's, which was a copy of the old American Civil War headstones, would be used, including a Jewish engraving where appropriate.

There the matter lay until 1923, when out of the blue it was changed. Pershing was still the army chief of staff, which kept him away from the ABMC much of the time. Nevertheless, on his regular trips to Europe to monitor the work on the American cemeteries, he had been impressed by the work being carried out by the Allies on monuments in Europe. In his absence, Senator David Reed, an Argonne veteran, instituted white marble crosses, rather than the previously agreed secular headstones, for the cemeteries in Europe. The crosses would be inscribed with the name, rank, unit, state of origin, date of death and any decorations. Representations were made from the Jewish lobby for the Star of David to be used atop the marble to mark the graves of Jewish dead. As with Britain, the unidentified would each have a plot with a cross, engraved with the words: 'Here Rests in Honored Glory an American Soldier Known but to God.'

In America the main pressure was from veterans wanting their old unit wartime memorials and monuments in France preserved. These informal monuments, ranging from old artillery pieces to decorated mounds, were disappearing as the French reclaimed the land. Pershing was no fan of these and wanted nothing less than divisional-level formal memorials. He demanded that the French government remove many of the 'private memorials', but to little avail. He was also conscious that other state-sponsored memorials were appearing before the American government had erected anything, although the state of Missouri had erected a memorial to its men in the 35th and 89th Divisions at Cheppy near the Argonne in 1922.

*   *   *

In 1924 the Countess de Martimprey oversaw the redesign of the French military cemetery in the centre of the Argonne Forest. The original cemetery had been started in 1914 for those who had died fighting nearby or in the adjacent aid post at Maison Forestière. Many of the Garibaldis were originally buried there, before being returned home to Italy after the war or removed to Bligny. Here, unlike in any other French military cemetery, flowers were planted at the entrance and on each grave. Red, white and blue perennial hydrangeas, the colours of the French Tricolour, made it a garden rather than a cemetery, similar in design to the IWGC cemeteries in the north. The only other French exception was the Douaumont Ossuary at Verdun, where at its inauguration in 1932 the 16,000 graves in front of it were each planted by an orphan with a single rose.

*   *   *

In 1924 the Argonne Forest was entrusted to the recently formed Water and Forests Administration. By now 66 per cent of the forest was in government hands, with just 33 per cent still in private hands. The forest was not yet suitable for replanting as there was still much clearing to be done. Some people also voiced the opinion that the land should be left to heal itself. In 1926 the earlier epicentre of the trench warfare, Bois de la Gruerie, finally cleared of the detritus of war, was handed back to its original owners. They just left the forest to reseed itself. This section was cut regularly between the wars.

*   *   *

In 1925 the ABMC decided to back three monument projects, one for each sector of the front: one at Montsec near St Mihiel, to commemorate the offensive there; the second at Montfaucon, to commemorate 'the greatest battle in American history'; and the third at Château Thierry to commemorate American operations in the Marne region. Arguments would continue with the French for years regarding the purchase and building of these three memorials.

Despite this, both the ABMC and Congress were under considerable pressure from individual units wanting to have their own memorials built. As these were less than divisional size, Pershing brushed them aside. The 93rd Division, an African-American unit that had fought with the French, applied for a memorial but the request was denied on the basis that it had not been a 'proper' division since its artillery was left in America during the war and the troops had fought under the French. However, memorials were permitted for white units that had served further north with the British.

* * *

By 1927 the military reclamation work was completed, with 60 million cubic metres of wartime rubbish removed from the Argonne battlefields. Another 22 million tons of ammunition and shells had been blown up. The clearing of the French, American and German gas shells continued to cause controversy. Record-keeping was poor and allegations were rife that in order to save money the private contractors had burnt the gas shells in the forest or dumped them in nearby rivers and lakes or as far away as the sea.

In the spring of 1927 the main forest replanting could began in earnest; up until then it had been left to nature. The contractors had used over a million cubic metres of soil to fill in trenches and bunkers. This turned soil made for an ideal base for the saplings. Initially softwoods were planted, particularly in the worst affected areas, as it was felt they would draw out the poisons from the soil and make the land ready for replanting with hardwoods later. The softwoods could also manage with little top soil in areas where most had been blown away in the war.

In 1930 Jean Baptiste Allure, a wounded veteran now working for the *Office National des Forets* (ONF) made the case for planting pines along the former front lines of the Argonne around Fille Morte, Côte 304 and the heights above Verdun: 'Trees will remove the undergrowth, stop flooding and the washing away of the trenches and craters. Furthermore they will provide a quiet place of meditation and reflection, while listening to the sound of the wind.' He won the argument and the planting of pines along the former front lines began soon after. As the pines grew, another unexpected benefit appeared, as dappled light filtered down through the branches creating a Cathedral-like atmosphere over the former front lines.

For five years 5–6 million saplings were planted each year, 250 per man or woman per day. The programme ended in 1933, with most of the forest now replanted. The return of birds during this period was welcomed as a further sign of nature healing itself. The same joy was not felt at the return of wild animals, rodents and snail collectors. Protection had to be added to prevent the young saplings being trampled or eaten.

All along the Western Front the war had changed the biodiversity of the whole front. Previously, flower seeds could travel no further than wind or birds could carry them. But with horse feed coming in from all over Europe, and later America, alien seeds entered the area. Added to this, men often arrived at the front with seeds caught on their uniforms. In parts of the Argonne Forest, kept away from the public eye, the ONF maintains small sites where persist some of the rare and beautiful specimens that arrived accidentally from America.

*   *   *

The majority of the French dead remained at the front with their comrades, and their remains continued to be centralised in cemeteries and ossuaries near where they died. With government coffers now empty and the burden of repatriation, the circular of 24 February 1927 from the Ministry of Pensions regarding the construction of cemeteries made no reference to any architectural message, unlike their British and American counterparts. The austere plans were drawn up by technocrats, and envisaged a standard layout to be used after 1928 at all cemeteries. The French flag would be the central point, with graves stretching out in rows, similar to army lines. Crosses would be made of white wood, with only four types of emblem on display: a Latin cross (where the vertical below the horizontal is the longest part, like the cross of Jesus's crucifixion) for Christians; Muslim headstones; Jewish headstones; and a special stone for free-thinkers and agnostics – the only country to do so. The Muslim graves tended to be grouped together where practicable.

Affixed to each headstone was a metal plaque bearing the inscription 'Mort pour la France', along with the man's name, unit and date of death. No other adornments were permitted to avoid any distinction between the graves. There would be no individual plants on grave plots, although in the *Cimetière National de la Forestière* in the Argonne, almost uniquely, each plot does have a plant, red, white and blue hydrangeas matching the French Tricolour. Such planting as there was elsewhere would consist of red roses planted around the periphery of the cemetery. In the interceding years the white wooden crosses have rotted away and have now been replaced by white concrete crosses and other religious denomination headstones.

For those with no bodies or graves to grieve over, the government permitted the building of war memorials in each village. These would have inscribed on them the names of local men who were killed or died during the war. In the Argonne region these memorials also included the names of civilians killed. The commemoration of the dead offered a chance for the Catholic Church to put itself back into heart of local politics and the community, a role that the 1905 Separation Act had sought to remove. The church now became pivotal in organising and fund-raising for local war memorials dedicated to the dead.

Despite the involvement of local and central government, with design guidelines and permissions required, fierce debate soon broke out regarding the artistic merit and appropriateness of many of the memorials. This inevitably led to commercial firms entering the fray, with promises of anodyne statues that would pass scrutiny and get permission and state funding to be erected. Funding was expected to be mixed, with a third raised from local donations, a third from local council funds and a third from the state. Evidence of funding and details of the proposed memorial would have to be approved by the state before permission to site a memorial was granted. Many small communes had insufficient money to pay for a memorial, or their population had not yet recovered from the war, so could not afford a memorial, but more than 36,000 memorials appeared under the auspices of local communes. The largest Argonne memorial is in St Ménéhould, where the figure of a *Poilu* stands with his dog, looking towards *Haute Chevauchée*, the former Argonne Forest front line. In the region of the Argonne people looked back to the region's glass-making past. Church windows were specially commissioned to commemorate events as well as the dead. The churches of Le Neufour and La Harazée, and the Chapel of the St Marie Hospital of *Soeur* Gabrielle in Clermont, are among thirty-two Argonne locations displaying forty-six commemorative stained-glass windows.

Once the memorial was complete, a service would be held dedicating it to the local community. There then followed a procession of local dignitaries, fund-raisers, widows, children and parents of the dead, and veterans. Speeches were made and the names on the memorial were read out. After each name the assembled crowd spoke as one, 'Mort pour la France'. As some memorials had hundreds of names, this process could take time. Although the Church may have been instrumental in organising the memorials and fund-raising for them, there was not permitted to be any religious aspect to these dedications. Religious services had to be held in the local church, away from the memorial.

*   *   *

The *bluet de France*, or cornflower, became the symbol of those who died for France – more than 1.4 million men and women. The cornflower was omnipresent across the devastated battle areas of France in the summer months, and also symbolised the change in uniform from the red trousers and blue overcoat of 1914 to the new 'Blue Horizon' uniforms of the conscript army in 1915. Suzanne Leenhardt, former head nurse at Les Invalides, whose husband had been killed in 1915, and Charlotte Malleterre (daughter of the Commandant of Les Invalides), whose husband had lost a leg in the fighting in 1914, saw the need to help men recover from their wounds. The first paper cornflowers were made by their injured veterans in 1916 and sold to the public as a means of earning a small income.

France's final tribute to the dead was the *Livre d'Or des Morts pour la France* (the Golden Book of the Fallen). In these volumes each commune listed its dead alphabetically by surname, also giving their forename, date and place of birth, rank, regiment and date of death, but only included those born in or residing in the commune at the time of mobilisation. This, along with the fact that war memorials were being erected in the period 1920–5, before the work on the books was complete (1929), is why there is often a difference between the names on the memorials and listed in the books. One set of the books was placed in the Pantheon.

*   *   *

The German cemeteries in France were classed as temporary burial sites until 1926, when the French allowed them to become permanent. The VDK secured the services of Robert Tischler, a former German soldier turned architect. He designed cemeteries to blend into the local environment, in keeping with the German concept of mythological communion between man and nature. Oaks, the national tree of Germany, were planted at many sites to grow alongside other local species. These provided a natural cemetery perimeter to 'Watch over the eternal rest of soldiers'.

Planting was avoided, and the wooden crosses were painted with tar to preserve them, all to avoid costs and excessive maintenance. The Argonne German cemeteries resemble wooded glades cut into the forest. Headstones and other memorials did not start appearing until the late 1920s.

These cemeteries were in complete contrast to the Imperial memorials and graves of the victorious Franco-Prussian war of 1870–1. The work came to a halt again in the 1930s as the Nazis took control and the VDK was forced to align with their policies.

The German flower of commemoration is the forget-me-not; this originated in a German myth which tells how God named all the plants except one, which cried out 'Forget-me-not, O Lord!', to which God replied, 'That shall be your name.' The flower is worn to symbolise the dead, gone but not forgotten.

It was not until 1966 that the German war cemeteries were given permanent status, and much of the work viewable today was concluded subsequently. Unlike the Allies, who commemorate the dead on 11 November every year, Germans commemorate Volkstrauertag (People's Day of Mourning) two Sundays before Advent.

*   *   *

The poppy initially became the American symbol of remembrance, although many poppies had been sold for fund-raising in Britain from 1916. Like the *Bluet*, it somehow survived the destruction of the war to grow prodigiously along the front. In the spring of 1915, shortly after losing a friend in Ypres, a Canadian doctor, Lieutenant Colonel John McCrae, was inspired by the sight of poppies growing in battle-scarred fields to write his now famous poem, 'In Flanders Fields':

In Flanders fields the poppies blow
Between the crosses, row on row,
That mark our place; and in the sky
The larks, still bravely singing, fly
Scarce heard amid the guns below.

We are the Dead. Short days ago
We lived, felt dawn, saw sunset glow,
Loved and were loved, and now we lie
In Flanders fields.

Take up our quarrel with the foe:
To you from failing hands we throw
The torch; be yours to hold it high.
If ye break faith with us who die
We shall not sleep, though poppies grow
In Flanders fields.

McCrae is alleged to have thrown the poem away, dissatisfied with his work, then entitled 'We Shall Not Sleep'. Another officer, Cyril Allinson, retrieved the poem and handed it to his commanding officer, who posted it to London for general publication. The *Spectator* rejected the poem, but *Punch* published it on 8 December 1915, anonymously. McCrae subsequently died of pneumonia in 1918, while still serving at the front.

The poppy was first introduced as a symbol of memorial in America in 1920, and its provenance sits between two women activists. Moina Michael, an American author working in the YMCA, was moved by McCrae's poem, which she read on 9 November 1918. She started to wear a poppy herself, and in her spare time made and sold others to friends. The proceeds of the sales she donated to ex-servicemen. Her poppy was entwined with a victory torch. In 1920 she persuaded the Georgia Legion to adopt it as their symbol, and in September 1920 the National American Legion Convention adopted the poppy as the country-wide symbol of remembrance to be worn on Memorial Day in May. Frenchwoman Anna E. Guérin had likewise became fixated on the poppy symbol, both during and after the war. In her self-styled Horizon Blue uniform, based on that of the Alpine Chasseurs (the 'Blue Devils'), complete with matching hat and decorations, she was actually present at the American Legion Convention in 1920. It is more likely that it was Madame Guérin who took the poppy symbol to America, as she toured the country speaking publicly both throughout the war and afterwards. As America was neutral until 1917, speaking in public places in support of the war was forbidden. Instead, Madame Guérin spoke about French history and often dressed as historic French women, such as Joan of Arc. After speaking, she would raise funds for French orphans and invalid veterans. For the entire war she would crisscross America, speaking and fund-raising in the winters, while in the summers she generally returned to France by ship. Once America entered the war, her historic tableaux were replaced by descriptions of real life in wartime France and the subsequent hardships suffered by children and the disabled. She now wore her theatrical self-styled French uniform, complete with decorations. She sold poppies made in France by widows and orphans to raise funds for them; these were billed as Poppy Days.

In October 1919 she addressed the Baltimore Gold Star Mothers, who agreed to adopt the poppy for fund-raising. Later in the month she oversaw the manufacture of 10,000 poppies for sale in Baltimore. From April 1920 Poppy Days or Poppy Drives became a regular feature of her visits to American cities. On 19 September she gained permission from the Grand Army of the Republic (a Civil War veterans' group) to use their

Decoration Day for her annual Flanders Poppy Day. On 27 September, resplendent in her uniform, she persuaded the second National Convention of the American Legion to adopt her proposal for an inter-Allied Poppy Day.

On 11 November, the second anniversary of the Armistice, Poppy Days were held to raise funds for her American-Franco Children's League. By 1921 she was widely recognised in the American press as the French Poppy Lady, and 28 May 1921, just prior to Memorial Day, was nominated Poppy Day, with fund-raising carried out by the American-Franco Children's League. At the end of May she arrived in Canada to promote the inter Allied Poppy Day, and in July she despatched an emissary to South Africa, Australia and New Zealand for the same purpose.

Madame Guérin arrived in London at the end of August 1921 to garner support for her Poppy Days. It is not clear whether she met the Prince of Wales or Earl Haig, now president of the newly formed British Legion. But she must have met someone of influence as the British Legion sent an emissary to France to check that she could manufacture poppies and kept appropriate financial records. The British Legion then ordered thousands of poppies for 11 November. Since the Legion was short of funds, and owing to the short notice, Guérin gave them credit for the poppy purchase. On 16 September the British Legion adopted the inter-Allied Poppy Day scheme. New Zealand then followed suit, as did America, Canada and Britain on 26 September. In promoting the day, Earl Haig described 11 November as Remembrance Day or Poppy Day. Guérin then returned to America, where in October 1921 the third National Convention of the American League dropped the poppy in favour of a daisy, because the poppy was not considered an indigenous American floral species, unlike the daisy.

Following the success of the 11 November Poppy Appeal, the British Legion adopted the poppy for itself and took over the manufacture of the poppies in Britain by disabled ex-servicemen. In 1922 the American Legion re-adopted the poppy and Guérin imported millions of French poppies for Memorial Day.

As the 1920s progressed, more and more of the countries who had adopted the poppy switched manufacture from France to their home countries to give work to disabled ex-servicemen. Records show Madame Guérin still regularly crossing the Atlantic later in the 1920s and 1930s but there is no further mention of her fund-raising or poppy activities, which dominated the press during and after the war. Despite her heroic efforts to promote the poppy and raise funds, history appears to have airbrushed out her contribution. Nor did she receive any broader formal government recognition of her contribution to what is now the most ubiquitous Remembrance Day symbol worldwide.

*   *   *

As well as the American Legion founded in Paris in 1919, another organisation came to the fore in America in the 1920s: Gold Star Mothers Inc., for women who had lost one or more sons or daughters in France. Service banners, officially defined as a white field with a red border, and bearing a blue star, hung from American homes, proudly indicating a son or daughter in wartime service. As early as 1918 women who had lost sons in France started to wear a gold star, which was initially worn on a black armband. As the Gold Star movement grew, banners began to display not only a blue stars for each member of the family in service, but also a gold star to show the loss of a loved one.

This nationwide movement was founded by Mrs Grace Darling Seibold in Washington DC, who lost a son in France on 4 November 1918. He became one of the missing, with no known grave. She began a group to help support other bereaved mothers and to help injured soldiers in American hospitals miles from home. Although locally grouped, they initially had no formal national structure. On 4 June 1928 twenty-five of these mothers met in Washington DC and formally became Gold Star Mothers Inc., to help and support mothers nationally who had lost a son or daughter in the First World War. In their earlier, less formal associations, working alongside the American Legion, the Gold Star Mothers had lobbied for state-funded pilgrimages to visit their sons' graves in France. With potentially 14,000 or more mothers qualifying, the bill was voted out in 1924.

The complexity of the American domestic political landscape became apparent in the 1920s. The Nineteenth Amendment to the Constitution, which passed in 1919, allowed women to vote. In the presidential election held on 2 November 1920 women and men aged over 21 were permitted to vote. This did not universally apply: exceptions included African-American men and women, American Asians and Hispanics, and native Indian women.

The American Legion was open to African-Americans and women who had served. In the southern states black membership was not welcomed as it gave them voting rights in Legion matters, rights that did not exist in general elections. The Legion therefore deferred to individual states and their segregation laws. In the northern states African-Americans had equal membership. In the south black members made their own groups. Like their British and French contemporaries, the American Legion became very politically adept and introduced numerous bills into Congress to support ex-servicemen and women. Annual conventions in cities around the USA became a hallmark of the Legion. While bringing tourists and their cash to these cities, they also brought with them heavy drinking and rowdyism. In 1927, at the invitation of the French government, the Ninth Annual American Legion Convention was hosted in France from 19 to 22 September. This gave veterans their first official chance to visit their former battlefields and see the new cemeteries and memorials. A small fleet of ships, described by some as a second AEF, set off with over 18,000 veterans and their families. Only two African-Americans made the trip and attended the parade on 19 September,. They had to pay for themselves, and segregation policy on the ships meant they could not travel with their white comrades. Their names were William J. Powell, a veteran who had been gassed on the very last day of the war, and his friend Burrel Neely, and they would write themselves into African-American history.

After the opening ceremony on 19 September the American Legion paraded with their former French comrades through central Paris, where over a million Parisians assembled to watch the veterans march past. Their route took them past the Tomb of the Unknown Soldier, onto which flowers were flung.

Trips to Le Bourget had been arranged for American veterans staying in Paris. Four months earlier Charles Lindbergh had arrived at night at Le Bourget after his epic 33-hour flight across the Atlantic. *The Spirit of St Louis* landed on 21 May 1927, after the first solo non-stop transatlantic flight. At Le Bourget, Powell and Neely took their first flight over Paris, including a spin round the Eiffel Tower. Both were soon hooked on flying. When they returned to America, the segregation laws meant Powell was unable to get pilot training in Illinois, so he moved to Los Angeles. After qualifying as a pilot, Powell, with Neely as his business manager, set up the Bessie Coleman Aero Club, the first pilot training school open to men and women of all races. It was named after the first African-American woman to hold a pilot's licence.

The very first African-American pilot was Eugene Bullard, who made his living in Paris before the war as an impresario and boxer. He joined the French Foreign Legion on 19 October 1914 and served in combat with the FFL on most of the French sectors of the front and was injured several times. He gained his pilot's licence with the French Army in 1917.

For the American Legion veterans and their families, despite postwar austerity as France grappled with its debts, life in Paris appeared relatively normal. Frenchwomen, though, were taken aback by the American women in the Legion and the power they wielded. Like Britain in 1918, women in the USA had taken huge steps forward, with full enfranchisement in 1920. Frenchwomen had to wait for another war to end before they enjoyed similar rights.

After the close of the convention, the veterans made their way from Paris to their old battlegrounds. Much had been repaired, the battlefields cleansed and most of the bodies gone. Some battlefields had disappeared, back under the plough or for other commercial uses, while nature had started to reclaim others. Sections of the Argonne Forest were overgrown with thickets of all but impenetrable brambles.

In rural France the sombre ritual of mourning, which had long since lost favour in America, was still omnipresent in the villages counting the cost of the war. French cemeteries were austere, but those who ventured near the British cemeteries could only stand and gaze in awe at the work of the IWGC. Although work on the cemeteries was coming on, the ABMC had yet to complete any of its three chosen memorials, much to Pershing's frustration. The memorials that did exist were either state-sponsored or constructed by the men themselves.

*   *   *

The Gold Star Mothers and the American Legion continued to lobby without success for trips for mothers to see their sons' graves. In 1928 the newly formed GSM Inc. joined representatives from other women's organisations and the American Legion to again lobby for the pilgrimage. This time they succeeded, and one of President Calvin Coolidge's final undertakings was to sign the act to make the pilgrimages possible. There was still no funding, though, and inevitably wrangling broke out about who was eligible; should they include not just the mothers but also widows, widows who had remarried, fathers and children? They all considered themselves eligible. Another group consisted of relatives of the American volunteers who had gone to France and died before America formally joined the war. They were not permitted to travel.

Funding was finally approved in 1930, with the first GSM group leaving in May, amid much media attention. Between 1930 and the autumn of 1933 more than 6,000 women, out of 11,000 who were eligible, travelled on the summer pilgrimages funded by the American taxpayer.

For African-Americans, the politics of race came into play as surely as it did for the American Legion veterans trip to the Paris convention in 1927. The government announced that the GSM trips would be segregated. Uproar ensued in black America, already bruised by the treatment of returning veterans. This was further evidence, if any were needed, of government-sponsored discrimination. But for most African-American mothers and widows the chance of a free trip to France to see the grave of a loved one was too much to turn down, despite the segregation. Seven African-American women declined the trip because of segregation. The African-American women travelled together on pilgrimages arranged exclusively for them. Apart from their ships being of lower quality, all the other arrangements were exactly the same as for the white mothers and widows. Noble Sissle, a former vocalist with James Reece Europe's famous AEF band, was on hand to greet the women as they arrived in Paris.

*   *   *

The 1920s saw America join Britain in the revival in spiritualism; the deaths of so many men in France, Italy, Russia and from Spanish flu saw people flocking to clairvoyants. Conan Doyle became a regular visitor to America, where he lectured on spiritual matters. Like Lodge before him, Conan Doyle had also lost a son in the war. The famous escape artist Harry Houdini spent much of his time before his death in 1926 trying to disprove the spiritualist mediums and expose them as frauds. He fell out badly with Doyle while proving that a trick he had performed in front of him was no more than an illusion.

*   *   *

The Pennsylvania State government had built a monument in Varennes en Argonne, which was inaugurated on 30 May 1928. The monument stood near the site of Louis XVI's arrest and was in the Greek style. It overlooked the Aire valley and the Argonne Forest, and commemorated the troops of the 28th and 80th Divisions, many of whom died during the battles in the Argonne in September 1918, some liberating Varennes in 1918.

The name Roland Garros is nowadays better known as the venue where the French Open Tennis Championship is held every year. The championship is held in the Stade Roland Garros, on land originally donated by the French Rugby Union and Sports Club, Stade Francais. The land was given to build a stadium to host the return Davis Cup tennis match in

1928, after France had won it in the USA in 1927. The Stade Francais Club was chaired by Emile Lesieur, who had served with Garros in the First World War. He gave the land to the French Lawn Tennis Federation on the condition that the new stadium was named after his old wartime comrade Roland Garros. He had been killed ten years earlier, just a few weeks before the end of the war.

Eugène Adrien Roland Georges Garros was a run-of-the-mill pre-First World War civilian pilot, who shot to fame on 23 September 1913 when he made aviation history. Setting off from Fréjus on the French Riviera, he flew 700km over the Mediterranean to Bizerte in Tunisia, so becoming the first person to fly across the Mediterranean. It took him 7 hours, 53 minutes. On his return to France he was greeted as a national hero by the press.

In 1914 he volunteered as a *Poilu*, serving in the 'Stork Squadron' as a pilot, primarily for the aerial observation of advancing German troops and artillery locations. He went on to pioneer work that enabled a machine gun to fire through the propeller blades, so becoming France's first real fighter pilot.

He continued developing his prototype, which led to him shooting down five German planes in early 1915 and the American press christened him an 'Ace' – the term that would be applied to all pilots in the future who gained five kills or more.

On 19 April 1915 Garros was on a patrol looking for German aircraft, but the Germans were now well versed with this new French invention and kept well away. He saw a train that he tried to bomb; when the bombs fell wide, he returned to strafe the train, again the first pilot to do so. This time his luck ran out and the *Bahnschutzwache* (train guards) brought him down with small arms fire. Garros managed to land the plane but as he sought to set fire to it, to prevent the Germans from gaining the new technology, he was knocked unconscious. Thus one of the great wartime inventions fell into German hands.

For three years Garros was a prisoner of war, eventually joining Lieutenant Anselme Marchal, a pre-war friend. In 1916 Marchal had been sent to bomb Berlin with propaganda leaflets. After dropping the sheets, he was to fly on to the Russian lines, making the whole journey non-stop. His Nieuport was specially adapted with extra fuel tanks to make the long journey. Once refuelled, he would then return to Italy. After successfully navigating his way to Berlin, mainly in the dark, he dropped his payload of propaganda over the city. He then set off eastwards for the Russian front line. His engine failed because of dirty spark plugs, a problem that had been anticipated. He managed to land in a remote spot, 60km short of the Russian trenches, where he was unable to change all the plugs in time before he was captured by the Austrians. They were incredulous that such a long flight had been undertaken: over 1400km, which established a new world record.

Marchal was fluent in German, so the two of them devised an escape plan. Garros sent a coded message to France, and they were sent by return two tennis rackets, one of which had a map of Germany in the handle and the other a felt hat in the handle to wear whilst escaping. Dressed as high-ranking Germans officers, they strode out of the Scharnhorst POW camp at Magdeburg in eastern Germany on 24 February 1918 under cover of darkness. After an incredible journey across Germany, they managed to cross the Dutch border and back to England, becoming two of only twenty-two prisoners who managed to escape from a POW camp during the First World War.

On their return to France they were both hailed as national heroes and awarded the *Légion d'Honneur* at a ceremony in the Somme. Marchel was promoted and went on to survive the war. Garros was also promoted, but instead of taking a technical support job, as the French Premier Clemenceau wanted, he went back to front-line flying.

On 5 October 1918 he was flying over the northern end of the Argonne Forest with four other aircraft when they sighted several German aircraft and gave chase. Garros was left on his own and then attacked by six Fokker planes, and during the ensuing dogfight he was shot down and killed near Vouziers. He is buried there and a memorial marks the spot where his plane crashed in nearby St Morel.

*   *   *

On 21 April 1932 a monument to the dead Garibaldis was officially unveiled by Mr Mario Roustan, the French Minister of Education, and Count Manzoni, the Italian Ambassador to France, opposite the Abbey at Lachalade. It was located on the former burial site of the Garibaldis killed in the Argonne Forest in the First World War. On the monument are two brass effigies, one of Bruno and the other of Costante. The monument was made by the sculptor Sergio Vatteroni, famous for his Italian marble sculptures. In Latin is inscribed '*Optatum Foedus Amoris*' ('The wish for an alliance of love').

*   *   *

Since the early 1920s French veterans had started to assemble every summer in Verdun to commemorate the epic battle. To coincide with the twentieth anniversary, a Peace Rally was organised for the summer of 1936. The date chosen was 12 July: the day in 1916 when the French repulsed the final German assault of Operation Judgement, to take Fort Souville. It was also fittingly a rather wet and overcast day.

For the first time officially sanctioned veteran groups arrived from Germany and Italy to join French, British and American veterans. Hitler and Mussolini were both keen to burnish their country's peaceful intentions to the world's press; Hitler in March that year had reoccupied the Rhineland and therefore broken the Treaty of Versailles, while Mussolini the previous year had invaded Ethiopia and annexed it in May 1936. Somewhat controversially, though, several Italian and German veterans gave the Fascist salute during the commemorations.

At dusk 20,000 veterans marched sombrely from the ruins of the Sainte-Fine Chapel. National anthems, marching bands and weapons were not permitted. It was from this chapel, on 25 June 1916, that the final German offensive was launched. The long procession marched in complete silence up to the Douaumont Ossuary to lay wreaths. The men then dispersed across the adjacent cemetery and mounted a torchlight vigil and collectively swore an oath for global peace. Stillness prevailed for three hours, as 20,000 flickering torchlights danced over the crosses marking the graves. Men contemplated in silence the immense sacrifices made on the heights above Verdun, and their pledge for global peace.

Away from the limelight of the world's press assembled at Verdun to witness the former adversaries swearing the oath for peace, Hitler and Mussolini in reality had very different plans. During July both started supplying General Franco with troops and other military hardware to fight the civil war now raging in Spain. It was here that the Axis tactics that would dominate the early stages of the Second World War would be honed.

* * *

The ABMC monuments were all complete by 1937, including the three principal monuments at Montfaucon, Montsec (St Mihiel) and Château-Thierry. American Legion members sailed to Europe for a tour of the monument sites and the inauguration ceremonies. Nine battle monuments were inaugurated during August 1937. By this time the storm clouds of another war, just as Pershing had forecast nearly twenty years earlier, were gathering on the horizon. On 1 August 1937, twenty years after Pershing had first arrived in France, he was present for the inauguration of the main Meuse-Argonne battlefield monument at Montfaucon.

Montfaucon had also caught the eye of the French as a potential site for a monument, as much French blood had been shed in trying to recapture it early in the war. To them it was 'Little Gibraltar', in memory of a similarly futile Franco-Spanish siege against the British garrison on the Rock of Gibraltar from 1779 to 1783. For over three-and-a-half years they had tried to dislodge the well-engineered and defended positions of the British dug into deep into the Rock, without success. Under Montfaucon lay a network of tunnels and bunkers that had allowed the German defenders to move around with relative impunity from French artillery shellfire, while hidden observation posts on the top allowed them to rain down artillery fire at the first sign of movement on the plains below. It was the Americans, though, who ultimately captured 'Little Gibraltar' and Pershing was determined that it should be their memorial. Nevertheless, since the French had declared the top of the hill *'une vestige de guerre'* – 'a remnant of war', the American monument had to be constructed on adjacent land acquired by the ABMC. The destroyed village which had previously sat on the hilltop was rebuilt a short distance away, near the bottom of the hill.

John Russell Pope had been commissioned to design the Montfaucon monument. Like his IWGC contemporaries, he was one of the leading architects of his time. He had designed American churches, colleges, railway stations and even the Jefferson Memorial, which was completed after his death. Pope had a free rein and proposed three separate schemes. The one chosen by the ABMC had a 200-ft tall victory tower in the Doric style, on which stood the figure of 'Liberty', olive branches in hand, looking across the plains towards where the great AEF had assembled. Access to the viewing tower below Liberty is via 234 steps winding their way up the tower. Huge flights of stone stairs in front of the tower added grandeur to the memorial. Behind the memorial, set amid the trees, stand the remains of the village church and a camouflaged German observation post. At the base is a crypt in which are maps and an inscription. On the wall outside are engraved the names of the four most important areas of the American offensive: the Meuse Heights, Barricourt Heights, Romagne Heights and the Argonne Forest. At the bottom is a list of the divisions that made up the First US Army, which fought here, along with a tribute to their French comrades.

In front is an inscription on the ground which says

ERECTED BY THE VNITED STATES OF AMERICA
TO COMMEMORATE THE BRILLIANT VICTORY OF
HER FIRST AMERICAN ARMY IN THE MEVSE-ARGONNE OFFENSIVE
SEPTEMBER 26 – NOVEMBER 11 1918, AND TO HONOR
THE HEROIC SERVICES OF THE ARMIES OF FRANCE
ON THIS IMPORTANT BATTLE FRONT DVRING
THE WORLD WAR

During the inauguration ceremony a giant American flag was raised, using the 200-ft Doric tower as a flag pole. President Roosevelt gave an address from his yacht moored on the Potomac river in the USA, which was broadcast over loudspeakers situated around Montfaucon. In recognition of the French blood that had been spilt on the hill earlier in the war, Pershing then dedicated the memorial to the 'American and French soldiers who died here and the ties of friendship that exist between France and America'.

Chapter 6

The Argonne Forest in the
Second World War and beyond

Along with the awful destruction of their villages and lands during the war, the Argonne villagers had to deal with the reality of rebuilding their lives amid ruins. Given the numbers of men killed and families deciding not to return, there was an acute population shortage to help rebuild the Argonne. Even with the inclusion of Alsace-Lorraine, the overall French population struggled; over a million men had been killed and a further million were injured and unable to resume their work. Adult women in France now outnumbered men by over a million. Alsace-Lorraine also had another problem; having been in German hands for the best part of fifty years, the language and customs there had become Germanic. It would take a considerable amount of time and money to reintegrate them into French society.

France set a course of encouraging immigration from across Europe between 1921 and 1926. During that time more than 2.5 million people arrived and another half a million resided illegally. The arrival of Italians and Polish immigrants can be traced in the forest region today, where in some villages Italian and Polish names are as common, if not more so, than local French names. This policy was to have repercussions during the period of the Great Depression (1930–2), when France deported large numbers of immigrants. But as fast as France removed the immigrants, more arrived as Hitler allowed people to leave or expelled Jews and other groups from Germany and the territories he annexed. Refugees arrived from Spain after the Fascist victory in the Spanish Civil War.

By the summer of 1939, though, the Argonne villages were rebuilt, the population had stabilised and the forest was cleared and had started to regrow. Life appeared to have resumed its normal pre-war rural rhythm. The initial Argonne Forest management programme intended that the pines would start to be cut down after thirty years and hardwoods planted to replace them. With so many trees having been planted at once, there were concerns that, as they matured, they would all need cutting at the same time. The felling programme was halted in 1939 by the outbreak of the Second World War, which meant that the reforestation with hardwoods did not begin in earnest until the 1950s.

On 3 September 1939 France and Britain once more declared war on Germany, which had invaded Poland. The Argonne villagers could only nervously watch and wait to see if, for the third time in seventy years, they would be in the path of an invading German Army. France placed a great deal of faith in the Maginot Line, a network of fortifications built along its borders. Based on First World War strategy, the French believed that this network of forts would protect them and buy valuable time in which to mobilise the army. The Germans, though, had pioneered a new form of warfare: *Blitzkrieg*, using two of the last war's major inventions, planes and tanks, now much improved and coordinated in attack. These were placed in the vanguard and supported by motorised troops. Their attacks were sudden, overwhelming and fast-moving – very different from the static warfare of the First World War.

For many months, and well into the spring of 1940, a so-called 'phoney war' existed. In May 1940 villagers living in the Argonne were ordered to evacuate. By 11 June Les Islettes was empty, along with most of the other surrounding villages. A few hardy villagers, who, like their predecessors in September 1914 refused to leave, were all that remained. The Germans simply worked round the Maginot Line to the north and used *Blitzkrieg* tactics to advance back towards the Argonne. Once again, although the French Army put up stiff resistance around the Argonne on 13 and 14 June, the German advance was unstoppable.

On 23 June 1940 the Germans once more entered St Ménéhould and this time raised the Swastika flag. Paris had already been occupied on 14 June. The Argonne roadsides were littered with unburied French dead, while nearby were neat German graves. The remaining villagers were rounded up to help retrieve the French dead, who were wrapped in their tents and buried. Although not on the scale of 1914, the Argonne villages were again damaged by artillery and air strikes, particularly Les Islettes.

The Argonne Forest was immediately declared part of a 'Forbidden Zone'; those who had left could not return, and those who had stayed could not leave. To the east, Alsace-Lorraine was once more annexed into Germany on 30 November 1940. On 1 January 1942 the residents were again made German citizens, although Hitler had concerns about their racial purity after twenty years in French hands. In August the men were forcibly conscripted to fight on the Eastern Front; 120,000 men went to fight and over a third of them failed to return. The land to the east of Les

Islettes was now in the new 'Forbidden Zone' and was officially designated a German 'Settlement Zone', to be redistributed to German farmers.

The people left in the Argonne villages were effectively stuck; leaving even to go to St Ménéhould required special passes and negotiating a border crossing post outside Les Islettes. This continued for another twelve to eighteen months before the region once again became part of France. The conquered lands to the east, in Ukraine and Russia, could be now given to the German farmers, and the lands around the Argonne were no longer needed.

Unlike in the First World War, though, this time the war for the most part passed the region by quietly, although there were some French resistance attacks on Germans in the area. Three incidents, though, brought home the reality of the war to the villagers.

In the evening of Thursday, 14 October 1943 an American B17 bomber returning from a daylight raid on Germany was shot down near Nubécourt, the former President Poincaré's family seat. The bomber was based at RAF Grafton Underwood, home of the American 8th Air Force, which was charged with flying daylight bombing raids into Germany. The raid was on the German ballbearing factories at Schweinfurt, making parts used by the German Luftwaffe. It was the second raid on the factories, the first having taken place on 17 August. Then, 376 bombers had taken part, and an hour from their targets flew out of the range of their P-47 Thunderbolt fighter support aircraft. As a result sixty bombers were lost and many that did return were damaged beyond economical repair. With so many aircraft lost and damaged, the follow-up raid was postponed until replacements could be found. On 14 October, with new aircraft and fresh crews in place, the Americans tried again. On what became known as 'Black Thursday', the same problems beset the raid. The 291 bombers left behind their P-47 fighter support aircraft an hour from the target and were vulnerable to German fighter attack and anti-aircraft fire. Once again sixty bombers were shot down or ditched, and many more returned damaged beyond economical repair.

It was one of these planes, B17 42-31059, 'Patches', from the 384th Bomb Group, that was shot down near Nubécourt by a German Focke-Wulf FW 190A-6 at 4.30pm, just as it was getting dark. The plane's bomb aimer, Lieutenant William H. Wilson, died (possibly as a result of a parachute failure) and was later buried in the American cemetery in Luxembourg City. Nine crew members managed to parachute to safety. First Lieutenant Donald P. Ogilvie, the pilot, and Second Lieutenant Robert B. Kilmer, junior co-pilot, were captured soon afterwards, but the seven remaining crew members were picked up by local resistance fighters. They were then helped to escape to Switzerland, where they were detained for the duration of the war. A monument to this crew and other American aircrew who died for the liberation of France was erected in the cemetery at Nubécourt.

Five weeks later, on 18 November 1943, a British Stirling bomber, EF128 D of 622 Squadron based at RAF Mildenhall, was on a routine night bombing mission to the German city of Mannheim. On the flight out the Stirling was shot down by Helmet Bergmann, one of the top Luftwaffe fighter aces, flying from St Dizier. (He would later be credited with shooting down seven Lancasters in less than an hour on the night of 10/11 April 1944.) The order to bale out was given, but the only person to successfully jump from the Stirling was bomb aimer Bob Harper. He landed among the trees in the Argonne Forest but cut himself down and the following morning was picked up by two forestry workers. They took him to the doctor's house in Varennes, where his head and leg injuries were treated. He was then moved by the villagers to another house in Varennes, and he remained on the run until 31 December 1943, when he was betrayed and arrested by the Gestapo in the village of Fismes in Champagne. He survived the war.

That same night the villagers in Lachalade had heard a huge crash and seen a ball of fire on the forest horizon, but were not allowed to go and look. On the morning of 19 November the Mayor of Lachalade, Monsieur Marizier, went to the site opposite the *Cimetière National de la Forestière* with German police officers from Verdun. The wreckage, with ammunition still 'cooking off', was smouldering and lay scattered around an oak tree, felled by the crash. The carbonised bodies of the seven dead crew members – a mixture of British, Australian and New Zealand airmen – and a blood-stained parachute lay around the wreckage. The remains of the crew were carried down to Lachalade and buried in the cemetery by the villagers. A monument to the crashed Stirling and its crew was erected by the mayor and residents of Lachalade in 2003 opposite the *Cimetière National de la Forestière*, near the bomber's crash site. The remaining crew members lie in Commonwealth War Graves in the Abbey at Lachalade Cemetery.

On Saturday, 29 July 1944, at about 5pm, just a month before Paris fell to the French, Argonne *Maquis* (Resistance fighters) ambushed a Gestapo car driving through Clermont en Argonne. A German officer was killed and a soldier injured. The following day, 30 July, the Gestapo surrounded the town and terrorised the inhabitants. They dragged 112 male villagers to the town centre, including some men unfortunate enough to have just been passing through or nearby at the time. Assembled in the centre of Clermont at the Place de l'Hotel de Ville, they were loaded onto trucks in front of distraught relatives. Most would never be seen by their families again. They were sent either to Charles III prison in Nancy or to the Ecrouves camp. Around a hundred were later deported to the Natzweiler-Struthof concentration camp, where they arrived on 19 August. Seventy-two of these men would not return to Clermont, many dying in Dachau concentration camp. One survivor, Albert Champion, reported later: 'The worst was the executions. Towards the end, on 8 April 1945, twenty-two deportees were killed at Dautmergen plus one who was hanged because he stole a piece of bread.'

In August 1944 a German ammunition train exploded in Les Islettes, causing extensive damage. Whether it was an accident or was the result of an American air strike remains a matter of some debate. Just over four years after the German occupation, the Argonne region was once again freed, again by the Americans. By the end of August 1944 General George Patton's American Third Army arrived on their way to Metz. He subsequently died as a result of a car accident in Germany on 21 December 1945 and is buried in the American cemetery in Luxembourg.

This had not been Patton's first visit to the Argonne. As Lieutenant Colonel George Patton, he had been involved in the build-up and training for one of the great military breakthroughs of the First World War: the use of tanks. He had been instrumental in building the American tank units and their training in France in 1917. During the St Mihiel offensive, his courage and leadership under fire with his tanks marked him out as a leader. On the opening day of the Meuse-Argonne offensive, on 26 September 1918, he commanded the 344th Tank Battalion on the advance to the village of Cheppy. He arrived in the area on foot and could hear his tanks out in front in the early morning mist. But his tanks became bogged down, so Patton leapt forward and, under continuous heavy fire, remonstrated with infantry soldiers until they agreed to start digging out the tanks. At about this point he was shot in the arm and forced to leave the battlefield. His decisive action had got the tanks moving again and the tank advance was able to continue on to Cheppy and take the town. Patton did not recover from his wounds in time to take any further part in the Meuse-Argonne offensive.

Other famous Second World War American commanders also had their first experience of modern industrial warfare during the Meuse-Argonne offensive in the autumn of 1918. One was the ebullient Brigadier General

Douglas MacArthur, who rose to command the 42nd 'Rainbow' Division during the offensive (so called due to its make-up of National Guardsmen from twenty-six different states, an idea of MacArthur himself). The 42nd fought under General Gouraud with his French Fourth Army in Champagne and the St Mihiel and Meuse-Argonne offensives. In the Second World War MacArthur masterminded the American Pacific campaign.

Major Julius Ochs Adler, company commander of H Company, 306th Regiment, 77th Division, led the attack on St-Juvin on 14 October 1918, for which he was awarded a Distinguished Service Cross. In May 1919 he returned to the *New York Times*, serving as vice president and treasurer, before becoming general manager in 1935. He served as a divisional commander in the Pacific in the Second World War.

Captain Harry Truman served as an Army artillery officer with the 35th Division during the Meuse-Argonne offensive. He took part in several of the actions during the offensive, including the attack on Cheppy, where his men supported Patton's tanks. He entered American politics in the 1930s and became President Roosevelt's deputy, taking over when he died in April 1945. Truman then became the 33rd President of the United States of America. During his first term as president, life was far from quiet. The war in Europe had been successfully concluded on 5 May 1945, but conflict in the east still raged. It was Truman who permitted the use of the two atomic bombs against Japan in August 1945 in order to shorten the war. He oversaw the Marshall Plan for Europe, the reconstruction of Japan and the Berlin Airlift in 1948, and played in role in containing the Soviet postwar expansion. He also recognised the founding of the Jewish State of Israel in 1948 and supported the League of Nations.

George C. Marshall had organised the American Army's move from the St Mihiel salient to the Meuse-Argonne front in September 1918 for General Pershing. He later undertook a number of postwar army command and planning appointments, culminating in his appointment as army chief of staff in 1939. Planning was his forte, and he oversaw the planning of Operation Overlord, the invasion of Europe in 1944. Many saw him as the likely Supreme Allied Commander for the mainland campaign, although that honour went to President Roosevelt's choice, Dwight 'Ike' Eisenhower, an officer Marshall had picked out earlier in the war. Roosevelt said he didn't want to see Marshall leave Washington, such was his dependence on him, and this meant that a new job had to be invented for him. Marshall was duly made 'General of the Army'. This allowed him to play a central role in the planning of both the European and Pacific campaigns until the end of the war.

Back in America by January 1947, Truman appointed Marshall Secretary of State, the role in which he would achieve global fame with what was to become known as the Marshall Plan. This was concerned with the rebuilding of Europe after the Second World War, and saw America giving huge amounts of money to Europe to rebuild, including Germany. It also saw the removal of trade barriers and the modernisation of manufacturing in Europe. Although aid was offered to Russia, it was declined as the Russians would not allow any American control over their economy or rebuilding plans. The plan went ahead at the end of 1947 and American money started to appear in Europe in early 1948, and continued until 1952. Britain became the largest recipient of loans and grants, followed by the French. Marshall was awarded the Nobel Peace Prize in 1953 for his plan.

* * *

The arrival in the Argonne of the dashing French general Leclerc in September 1944 sent French hearts soaring, as he raced to relieve Strasbourg, fulfilling a vow he had made in North Africa after taking the Libyan desert oasis of Kufra. Here, with his nascent Free French Army, he had sworn 'not to abandon the fight until the Free French Tricolour shall fly again over Metz and Strasbourg'.

Philippe François Marie de Hauteclocque was a French aristocrat and cavalry officer who had survived the French defeat of 1940 and escaped to join General Charles de Gaulle in exile in London, where he changed his name to Leclerc to avoid any German retribution against his family, still living in France. Despatched by de Gaulle to French North Africa, he had raised a force of Free French under the Cross of Lorraine. They fought their way north from Chad to join the British Army in North Africa, taking part in the desert campaign from El Alamein to Tunis. His 2nd French Armoured Division (or Deuxième DB as it was known to its members) had arrived in France on 1 August 1944 and took part in the Normandy campaign. He then led the charge into Paris, accepting the German surrender at 3.15pm on 25 August at Gare Montparnasse.

By lunchtime on 22 November 1944 Leclerc had raised his Free French Tricolour over Strasbourg Cathedral, just as he had vowed to do on 1 March 1941 at Kufra in Libya. The route of his advance through Alsace-Lorraine is marked with yellow-topped bollards, some of which can still be seen on the roadside of the D163 heading east towards Verdun.

* * *

Given the post-First World War bureaucratic nightmare regarding the building of memorials, mayors and villagers not unsurprisingly decided not to go through it again. The names of the civil and military dead of the Second World War were just added to the First World War memorials in each village. Clermont residents also looked to commemorate separately the deported men lost in the concentration camps. A monument was decided on and thousands of postcards depicting 'The Final Departure' by Paul Lemagny were printed and sold to raise funds for the memorial. On 7 September 1947 the monument to the deportees was inaugurated, listing the names of all those who did not return to Clermont. The monument erected to their memory was designed by the engraver Paul Lemagny and carved by Henri Lagriffoul, both Grand Prix of Rome. In 1954 an urn filled with ashes from Dachau concentration camp was placed to the rear of the memorial. The urn remains but the ashes have now been removed to the crypt of remembrance at Saint-Didier Church, Clermont.

* * *

The late 1950s and 1960s were perhaps the golden period for the forest and the First World War veterans. Houses had been rebuilt, roads made good, electricity restored, hotels constructed, all the cemeteries were complete, the forests grown and managed. It was said that during this period hundreds of thousands of veterans, widows and their families visited the Argonne and Verdun region each year.

On 22 January 1963 the French President Charles de Gaulle began the first official healing of the long-standing enmity between France and Germany that stretched back to the 1870/71 war. A joint text was signed with German Chancellor Konrad Adenauer at the *Élysée* Palace in Paris. The '*Élysée* Treaty', as it became known, pledged both sides to meet regularly and coordinate defence and security matters.

* * *

In March 1966 the French president Charles de Gaulle, removed the French armed forces from the North Atlantic Treaty Organisation (NATO) and demanded that other NATO members remove their troops from France, particularly the Americans, who still had a large number of bases in the country. US President Lyndon Johnson asked Dean Rusk, his Secretary of State, to ask de Gaulle about the American dead – more than 60,000 American dead from two wars lay buried in numerous cemeteries. Rusk felt this was not a question that could be asked of de Gaulle, but Johnson insisted: 'Ask them about the cemeteries, Dean!' Dean could not refuse a presidential order, so he asked de Gaulle if his order included the 60,000-plus dead Americans in the cemeteries? De Gaulle, embarrassed, got up and left, and never answered the question. The American military bases were cleared, but in their own time. The American dead still lie in France to this day.

Later in 1966, during the fiftieth anniversary commemorations in Verdun, the deputy mayor of Verdun added a new element; remarking that in 1916 Verdun was the epicentre of the 'Glorious' French dead, so now in 1966 it should become a symbol of peace. But it was not until 1994 that part of the Bishop's Palace located in the city formally became the World Centre for Peace, Liberty and Human Rights.

In 1973, at the site of the Haute Chevauchée memorial, a large wooden 'Cross of Reconciliation' was erected on the lip of the huge crater created by the mine blast on 12 December 1916. The cross commemorates the 300,000 men of all sides who died during the fighting in the Argonne Forest between 1914 and 1918. It was erected to commemorate the tenth anniversary of the '*Élysée* Treaty'.

It was to be another forty-eight years before the old enmity was to be officially laid to rest at Verdun. On 22 September 1984 the German Chancellor Helmut Kohl met the French President François Mitterrand at the Douaumont cemetery at Verdun and they held hands for several minutes. The scene was all the more potent as Mitterrand had been injured and captured nearby in 1940 and Kohl's father had fought there in 1916. The two men stood in the rain to commemorate the 70th anniversary of the start of the First World War and the extraordinary losses of life endured by both sides during the epic battles around Verdun during 1916–17.

* * *

On 12 March 2008 *Le Dernier Poilu* (the last French soldier) of the First World War died. At the age of 16 in 1914, Lazare Ponticelli joined the Garibaldis, along with his older brother. Lazare's regimental number was 19718, and he served in the Argonne Forest with the 1st Battalion in 1914–15. After one of the Garibaldi attacks he was out in no man's land in the dark, looking for injured men, when he came across a German, whom he carried to the German trenches. As Ponticelli was not a French citizen, when Italy joined the war he was forcibly repatriated to Italy, despite his wish to join another Foreign Legion unit, and was conscripted into the Italian Army. He fought on the Austrian Front for the remainder of the war, where he was injured and in 1918 was gassed in an Austrian attack that killed hundreds of his comrades.

After the losses during the war, France was glad to accept immigrant labour and in 1920 Ponticelli returned to France, where he built up a metalworking business with two of his younger brothers. In 1939 he became a French citizen and served in the Second World War as a member of the Resistance. Later in life he was claimed to have said about the First World War, 'It was such a terrible waste of life.'

Only a handful of First World War *Poilus* were still alive at the start of the twenty-first century, and the French government wanted *Le Dernier Poilu* to have a state funeral. This Lazare initially declined, saying there were too many unrecognised men who had died, but he later relented when he officially became *Le Dernier Poilu* in February 2008, having outlived the other 8.4 million *Poilus* who fought in the First World War. His agreement was conditional on official recognition of all the *Poilus* who had served their country. French Foreign Legionnaires carried his coffin at his funeral on 17 March 2008.

Chapter 7

Travel Guide

If this book has whetted your appetite to visit the region, then there's still plenty to see, despite more than a century passing since the guns fell silent. Famous First World War sites, forest walks, cycling, bird watching or fishing, it's all there in this little known, rural and sparsely populated backwater. Unfortunately public transport does not reach most of the places, so a car is essential to make the most of a visit. It's a four or five hour drive south from Calais on the A26 Payage to Reims and then east on the A4 Payage to Metz, taking the turning at junction 29 to St Ménéhould. The main town and gateway to the region, **St Ménéhould** is famous as the birthplace in *c.*1638 of Dom Perignon, later a Benedictine monk, who made improvements to the locally produced Champagne wine, a brand of which later bore his name. It has petrol stations, cafés, restaurants and supermarkets. In the main square stands the beautiful eighteenth-century mayor's office, and opposite is the First World War memorial of the *Poilu* with his dog, looking towards *Haute Chevauchée*. There is also a library which offers free internet access and a tourist office, where English is spoken.

Alternatively, from Paris it's about two to three hours' driving east on the A4 Payage to Metz. If you follow this route, take time to stop at the wonderful First World War museum at Meaux, the largest of its kind in Europe (https://www.museedelagrandeguerre.eu/en.html). From Luxembourg Airport it's a two hour drive south on the A31, then west on the A4 Payage to Paris, turning off at the exits to Clermont en Argonne or St Ménéhould. (Drivers should be aware that the French police are vigilant, with speed traps and regular breathalyser testing. They expect to see paper car documents, not virtual documents on a tablet.) For travellers without a car, regular rail and TGV services run from Paris to Reims, Châlons en Champagne and Meuse, but thereafter the journey becomes more difficult. Coaches will get you as far as Les Islettes, but no further.

During the winter (November–March) the villages tend to be rather bleak and very quiet, and most facilities are closed. Many of the houses are now second homes, only occupied from June to September and during public holidays. From May to June the fields are filled with wild flowers and a myriad of birds, either nesting or migrating to northern Europe. Accommodation can be found via the Internet and now there are a few Airbnb rooms opening up.

The principal First World War sites are well signposted, albeit in French. Most sites have explanatory panels, with some English. All can be easily reached within 30–45 minutes' drive of Les Islettes and there is little traffic on the road.

In **Les Islettes** all the activity, such as it is, centres on the main square. Here you will find the war memorial, a local convenience store open seven days a week, and a pizza restaurant, open at lunch times and evenings, Tuesday to Sunday. It is closed all day Monday. There is a small hotel and another B&B on the outskirts of the town. During the summer months (early May to the end of September) the Glass Museum situated in the main street is open. It tells the story of the region's rich glass- and pottery-making history and holds regular workshops during the summer (http://www.verre-argonne.org/). Opposite is a small bakery. On the edge of the town is the austere French First World War cemetery. Here are also buried several of the men who were executed during the French Army mutiny of 1917.

Biesme valley, north of Les Islettes

Although **Le Neufour** was partially destroyed during the First World War, much of it has been rebuilt in the old Argonnaise style. The church has beautiful postwar memorial stained-glass windows. The memorial windows in many of the Argonne churches were paid for through public subscriptions and donations from relatives of the dead after the war. Well known glass-makers were selected to carry out the work, maintaining the spirit of the ancient Argonne glass-making tradition. If the church is not open, access can be sought via the mayor's office, opposite. Stained-glass commemorative windows proved popular not only around the Argonne, but as far afield as the Washington County courthouse in America, which also included the Red Cross and the YMCA in their designs, and there are more than 1,800 commemorative windows in Britain, mainly in churches.

Le Claon is a small village in the Argonnaise style. Costante Garibaldi was brought back to the church here in 1915.

Lachalade was another village destroyed in the war and rebuilt in several different styles. The centrepiece here is the Cistercian abbey dating back to the fourteenth century, which has recently undergone considerable renovation. In the First World War it was used by the French as a

Divisional Army HQ and by the Americans as a hospital. It is usually open seven days a week; uniquely, the bells are still rung by hand at noon every day to inform agricultural workers that it's time to return home for lunch. In the cemetery are the graves of the crew of the Second World War RAF Stirling bomber which crashed into the forest in 1943. Next to their plot is another grave that tells a tragic story. Two sons were killed in the Argonne during the First World War and were buried there; their father, unable to bear his grief, came to the cemetery after the war and shot himself. They are now all buried together. Opposite the abbey is the memorial to the Garibaldis and a sign indicating their former burial ground. It is possible to drive up into the Argonne Forest from the village, following the signs to the *Cimetière National de la Forestière*, but take care as it is a rough track and has some deep pot-holes.

Four de Paris has undergone several incarnations through history. Initially it was a roadside guesthouse, then a glass factory ('Four de Paris' meaning it made glass to the Paris standard) and latterly a Château for the family Granrut. The small settlement was entirely destroyed in the war. All that is left now to commemorate the epicentre of the Bois de la Gruerie struggle that took place in the forest behind during 1914 and 1915 is a large cross. Erected in 1926, *La Calvaire du Four de Paris* commemorates the dead of Bois de la Gruerie. It also commemorates the fourteen extended family members of the Granrut family killed in the First World War. On 18 March 2008 a ceremony was held here to celebrate Lazare Ponticello, the Garibaldi and *Dernier Poilu*. The forest behind is now in private hands and access is not permitted. The wartime sites were all destroyed when the forest was cleared and replanted in the 1920s and 1930s.

La Harazée is a very small village that now consists of about six houses and a rebuilt chapel, which has some memorial windows commissioned after the war. It also has a military cemetery, the *Necropole la Harazée*, which is one of the finest French cemeteries in the Argonne area. Some 1,700 men lie buried on the hillside site, which is particularly picturesque in the evening sunlight. From here, continue along the metalled track to Abri Guyard, named after a French Army engineer officer, killed early in the war. An engineer camp was dug into the hillside near here, making use of the local bricks, beams and other materials from the destroyed houses and outbuildings. After the war it became known as the Chinese Camp, where Annamites (French Colonial soldiers from Indochina) stayed while they cleared the battlefield and searched for the dead for reburial.

Vienne-le-Château was largely destroyed during the war and rebuilt afterwards; the church, which survived, still bears the scars of the fighting. Towards the edge of the village on the D63, on the left, is one of the last postwar *Maison Adrian*, a very small house now covered in tin. The road climbs a hill and as you near the brow there is a large military cemetery on your left, with parking on the right. On the right is the *Necropole National – Vienne-le-Château* memorial, which stands over the mass grave of 10,000 unknown soldiers killed in the area. Opposite is the *Necropole National – Sainte Thomas en Argonne*, where a further 8,000 plus men are buried. There are descriptive panels in both locations, with a small section in English.

Continue north on the D63 for a mile or so until you see a sign for the village of Sevron-Melzicourt on the D266. Turn left and continue through the woods for about 200 yards, past the 4km road marker, and stop opposite a small track. There are two memorials on the right. The left-hand one is to Bernard Citroën, André's brother, who was killed in 1914. It is in the same style as the roadside markers of the *Via Sacra*, marking the furthest advances of the Germans.

Bernard Citroën enlisted in the 51st Infantry Regiment, despite his poor health, and was based in Montmédy. The regiment moved north to meet the German advance through Belgium, where he took part in the Battle of Vitron on 22 August 1914. They then retreated to the Marne, with Bernard suffering from the great deprivations during the march. His unit was then posted to the Argonne, near Vienne-le-Château. Here he took part in the dreadful battles in Bois de la Gruerie. On Friday, 9 October 1914 Corporal Bernard Citroën was killed while going to rescue one of his comrades wounded during an attack. He received a posthumous *Croix de Guerre* with palm. On 15 October at Triaucourt-en-Argonne André received news of his brother's death and collapsed in shock. Bernard had always been the elder brother he looked up to, lived with, who had shown him the bright lights of Paris. André was always in awe of his charm and easy-going nature.

As you drive into the village of **Servon-Melzincourt** follow the signs to the German war cemetery. Here lie more than 10,000 German soldiers, mostly unidentified in mass graves. Beech and silver birch trees keep watch over the men.

Uncle Bob served at **Massiges** with General Gouraud from January 1915 until April 1915, amid the bitter and bloody fighting for the hilltop. Sadly no correspondence from this period survives. It is well worth a visit on two counts. First, on a small hill above the village is a wonderful trench system dug out of the chalk, using old aerial photos, over the last ten or so years. It is one of the few places on the Western Front that still has a very real First World War feel to it, particularly when the nearby army artillery ranges are firing. It is a well-known location for TV First World War documentaries (http://www.lamaindemassiges.com/). Even though it is only a small hill, the view it commands over the area illustrates why so much blood was spilt over it and similar small hilltops. There are descriptive panels at the site and it is open seven days a week.

The second reason is the Eco Museum in the village, which is open at weekends and during public and school holidays. Run by Raymond Kneip, who speaks only French, the wonderful museum hosts local artefacts going back centuries. His work on the two principal buildings, rebuilt in the old style, is a masterpiece of skill, love and dedication to the old master-craftsmen (https://www.lesgirouettes.fr/).

Driving north on the D63 from Vienne-le-Château beyond the Sevron-Melzincourt turn, you will see French and German flags on your left. Take care turning into the site as it is on a blind bend into oncoming traffic. This is **Camp Moreau,** the wonderful Third Line German Army rest camp. The camp has been lovingly restored by local enthusiasts and is open to the public on Saturday mornings from 10am until noon. Guides speaking French and German give conducted tours, but English is not always spoken. The tour explains the German rest and recuperation routine, camp buildings and their use. It is a unique attraction along the old Western Front (https://www.valleemoreau.com/en/).

North of Camp Moreau is the small village of **Binarville**. From there continue north, turning right on to the D66 at the sign for the German war cemetery at Apremont. The turning is marked by a memorial to the 9th Cuirassiers, a much-decorated French unit which captured Binarville on 8 October 1918, just before the men of the American 'Buffalo' Division arrived. Continue on the D66 from the memorial, dropping down quite a steep hill, and near the old Charleveaux Mill is the **memorial to the Lost Battalion**. There are explanations in French and English, providing a detailed explanation of the heroic action. It is not, though, the actual site. To find this, continue east along the D66/D442 until you see a large stone block on the right-hand side of the road with a directional arrow pointing down. Inscribed on the block is 'Lost Battalion'. A steep scramble down the hillside and you're in the Pocket; nothing remains of the old site, but it gives some understanding of the almost untenable position the men found themselves in and you can only wonder how they managed to hold out. Continuing along the road (now the D442) you will find a sign for the

Apremont German military cemetery. It is the one that probably best encapsulates the trees that 'Watch over the eternal rest of soldiers'.

Chatel-Chéhéry village, like most German-occupied villages, served as a place of rest and hospital care. As a result of this, it was largely destroyed during the war and rebuilt afterwards. Sergeant York has a commemorative memorial in the town, outside the town hall. Following the trail signs, which is best done on foot, takes you up to the start of the Sergeant York trail. This route is not suitable for any form of motorised transport. There is a 2–3 mile signed footpath that follows the route of Sergeant York's famous action. Suitable footwear is needed, as the going is undulating. At key points along the way are display panels in English describing the main events of the famous action (http://gb.ardennes.com/chatel-chehery/circuit-historique-du-sergeant-york/tabid/5421/offreid/8f8363db-6807-468c-9398-688954c24fc2).

*   *   *

For those who have more time (4 to 6 hours), you can continue north on the D4 to Cornay, which has numerous photographs on village houses showing them both during and after the war. A battlefield panorama has been placed on the hill above the village, La Croix Du Bayle. Continue to Fléville, where a memorial to the 16th American Infantry Regiment stands in the village centre. Continuing north on the D946 you pass the American First Division Memorial, on which is a recently attached plaque listing the American dead, at the road junction with the D54, and at St-Juvin there is the magnificently restored fortified church, which has three specially commissioned Argonne-style glass windows. Further along the D946 you pass through Grandpré, taken by the 77th Division. Carry on towards Vouziers, and just before entering the town is a combined French and German war cemetery at Chestres. Here soldiers of France and Germany lie side by side, with no dividing wall. In the cemetery is also a memorial to two Czechoslovakian units, which fought in the region in 1918. In Vouziers, there are road signs to the tomb of Roland Garros. He is buried in a French and Russian military section of the town cemetery. Next to the same cemetery is a German First World War military cemetery, with its unique metal pages listing the dead; the entrance to both is on Rue de Syrienne. Returning to the D946, head west towards Bourcq; just beyond it is a major roundabout, where you take the D977 south towards Sommepy-Tahure. At the village of Sommepy there are signs to the 'Monument Americain du Blanc Mont', the ABMC American Second Division memorial to men who fought under General Gouraud's Fourth

French Army. The monument, about 2 miles outside the village, is a stone tower with commanding views over the former battlefield. It is only open during the summer months, usually at weekends.

From the memorial proceed back to Sommepy-Tahure and take the D6 east through Aure and Manre to Ardeuil-et-Montfauxelles. Above Ardeuil is one of the most inaccessible and isolated memorials, surrounded now by farming land. It is an important memorial, though. On the stone are the names of the men of the 371st Infantry Regiment, 93rd Division, who took the hill. They fought here under General Henri Gouraud's Fourth French Army. One of the names, all but rubbed off, is that of Corporal Freddie Stowers, who was belatedly awarded a Medal of Honor in 1991 – the first African American to be awarded the medal in the First World War. He was buried in the Meuse-Argonne American Cemetery at Romagne after the war.

His Medal of Honor citation reads:

Corporal Stowers distinguished himself by exceptional heroism on 28 September 1918 while serving as a squad leader in Company C, 371st Infantry Regiment, 93rd Division. His company was the lead company during the attack on Hill 188, Champagne Marne Sector, France, during World War I. A few minutes after the attack began, the enemy ceased firing and began climbing up onto the parapets of the trenches, holding up their arms as if wishing to surrender. The enemy's actions caused the American forces to cease fire and to come out into the open. As the company started forward and when within about 100 metres of the trench line, the enemy jumped back into their trenches and greeted Corporal Stowers' company with interlocking bands of machine-gun fire and mortar fire causing well over 50 per cent casualties. Faced with incredible enemy resistance, Corporal Stowers took charge, setting such a courageous example of personal bravery and leadership that he inspired his men to follow him in the attack. With extraordinary heroism and complete disregard of personal danger under devastating fire, he crawled forward leading his squad toward an enemy machine-gun nest, which was causing heavy casualties to his company. After fierce fighting, the machine-gun position was destroyed and the enemy soldiers were killed. Displaying great courage and intrepidity Corporal Stowers continued to press the attack against a determined enemy. While crawling forward and urging his men to continue the attack on a second trench line, he was gravely wounded by machine-gun fire. Although Corporal Stowers was mortally wounded, he pressed forward, urging on the members of his squad, until he died. Inspired by the heroism and display of bravery of Corporal Stowers, his company continued the attack against incredible odds, contributing to the capture of Hill 188 and causing heavy enemy casualties. Corporal Stowers' conspicuous gallantry, extraordinary heroism, and supreme devotion to his men were well above and beyond the call of duty, follow the finest traditions of military service, and reflect the utmost credit on him and the United States Army.

Just outside the village, heading towards Séchault on the D6, is a roadside marker, D6, under which is 72. Park here and look south towards the hilltop covered in forest, with a clump of distinct pines on the corner. A track appears to lead towards it; walk up the track to the wood, then follow the wood round to the left to the summit. Here is the stone memorial to the 371st and Freddie Stowers.

From here, drive to the road junction at Séchault, where there is a memorial to the African American 369th Infantry Regiment ('Harlem Hellfighters') of the American 93rd Division.

Nearby another incident took place which resulted in the posthumous award of a Medal of Honor in 2015, although the actual site is unknown and therefore unmarked. The second African American to be awarded the medal in the First World War was Private Henry Johnson of the 369th Infantry Regiment, 93rd American Division. His Medal of Honor citation reads:

Private Johnson distinguished himself by acts of gallantry and intrepidity above and beyond the call of duty while serving as a member of Company C, 369th Infantry Regiment, 93rd Division, American Expeditionary Forces, during combat operations against the enemy on the front lines of the Western Front in France on May 15, 1918. Private Johnson and another soldier were on sentry duty at a forward outpost when they received a surprise attack from a German raiding party consisting of at least 12 soldiers.

While under intense enemy fire and despite receiving significant wounds, Private Johnson mounted a brave retaliation, resulting in several enemy casualties. When his fellow soldier was badly wounded, Private Johnson prevented him from being taken prisoner by German forces.

Private Johnson exposed himself to grave danger by advancing from his position to engage an enemy soldier in hand-to-hand combat.

Wielding only a knife, and gravely wounded himself, Private Johnson continued fighting and took his Bolo knife and stabbed it through an enemy soldier's head. Displaying great courage, Private Johnson held back the enemy force until they retreated. Private Johnson's extra-ordinary heroism and selflessness above and beyond the call of duty are in keeping with the highest traditions of military service and reflect great credit upon himself, his unit and the United States Army.

Ten minutes' drive south from Séchault brings you to Ville-sur-Tourbe, where you can either go west on the D566 to Main de Massiges or turn east onto the D66 towards Servon–Melzicourt. Alternatively, you can continue south for a further fifteen minutes on the D982 to St Ménéhould.

Four de Paris–Varennes Road

Turn right at the Four de Paris onto the D38 to Varennes en Argonne, driving up through the forest. After half a mile on the left as you climb up the hill is one of the last undamaged or stolen pink granite road pillars marking the German Army's furthest advance west in July 1918. It is often hidden in the dappled shade and hard to spot, and care should be exercised if you stop to look at it, owing to traffic. As you climb further up the hill, on the right-hand side you see dropping away the Ravin des Meurrissons, the scene of so much bitter fighting. Further along the same road is the former German military war cemetery, which is signposted and has a parking space opposite and just beyond it. Although it was cleared after the First World War and the central obelisk taken to the Servon-Melzincourt German war cemetery, there are still some physical remnants. Sadly in the last few years the wrought-iron gates were stolen.

At the top of the hill a sign directs you right into the forest and the *Haute Chevauchée*. Continue east to Varennes, passing the crossroads approximately where Erwin Rommel was shot in September 1914. Continuing east, the next stop is marked as the *Abri de Kronprinz*, named after the German Fifth Army commander. Follow the signs to the car park. A short walk away are a number of German bunkers, including *Champ Mahout*. There is also a marked forest walk around an arboretum. The actual *Kronprinz* HQ was some distance away in the town of Stenay, further north. Continuing east you arrive at the entrance to **Varennes**. Turn left and almost immediately you will see the sign for the Museum of Argonne (https://www.museesgrandest.org/les-musees/musee-dargonne/). This is open at weekends and during the summer holidays (May to September). It contains local artefacts, First World War items and the story of the capture of Louis XVI. Also, starting in the car park is a numbered panel tour guide of the town, outlining the story of Louis XVI's capture; each panel has an English section. Immediately to the right of the museum is the massive American Pennsylvania Monument, with its views across the old battlefield. On the right below the memorial you should be able to see one of the last wooden *Maison Adrian* in a garden.

Carry on by car or foot into the town centre. It has two bakeries, a municipal campsite and three restaurants, and there is a small supermarket with petrol just beyond the town. In the centre of the town is the rebuilt church, which still has visible war damage externally. If it is open, inside there is a small display of postwar artefacts, including a bill of damages from September 1914. The rebuilt church also has specially commissioned glass windows in the Argonne spirit. The external panels continue to tell the story of the capture of Louis XVI. Just across the bridge is the town war memorial, somewhat unusually in the form of an obelisk. Opposite that is a stone panel marking the site of the destroyed house where Louis XVI was held. On leaving Varennes, take the D38 in the main square to Vauquois; shortly you will see a sign to the American Missouri Memorial. Like the Pennsylvania Memorial at Varennes, this was not sanctioned by Pershing and the American Battle Monuments Commission (ABMC).

The fighting around **Vauquois** is not covered in any detail in this book, except for Edith Wharton's description, but it was very bitter and later degenerated into a vicious mining war. The village was relocated after the war to the bottom of the hill; the original village stood on the top of the hill but was destroyed in the war by the intense fighting and the mines. The village is rich in history, dating back to AD 888 when the Vikings were beaten here by the French king Eudes, who had been guided to them by a local hunter named Godbet. During the First World War men from the French city of Orléans fought here with distinction; after the war they adopted the town and helped fund its rebuilding.

Taking the road up to the top of the hill (*Butte*) the awful nature of the war of mines becomes fully apparent. There are panels with English explanations. On the first Sunday of the month from 9.30am to 11am you can go on a guided tour down into the mineshafts. This is one of the most realistic war experiences along the whole former Western Front. Again this site is a familiar TV backdrop (http://butte-vauquois.fr/en/).

Neuvilly-en-Argonne, situated on the main road between Varennes and Clermont, was largely destroyed during the war, as it lay just behind the French front line. Rebuilt now, its church has another wonderful series of postwar stained-glass windows. An interesting artefact on display is a crucifix that was taken as a souvenir by the American Alfred Hayes, a medic serving at the field hospital inside the church ruins in the autumn of 1918. His granddaughter undertook years of research trying to find where her grandfather had served before being able to return the crucifix to its rightful place in 2013.

The church was also the place where sisters Alice and Violet Mcallister, two 'Lassies' (as female Salvation Army workers were then known) comforted American servicemen amid the horrors of the Meuse-Argonne offensive in September 1918. Sitting on boxes in the ruins of the church, around a fire, they sang and played their guitars to hundreds of men who were either injured or on their way to the front.

The *Haute Chevauchée* ('High Road') follows the line of the old Roman road, which dissects the Argonne Forest from north to south. Driving up through the forest from the south (Les Islettes), on your right opposite a camping site is a large complex of buildings, one of which now houses a huge collection of local ceramics of all descriptions made between 1765 and 1848. It's open every day except public holidays, 10am–4pm, 1 October to 30 April and 10am–7pm, 2 May to 30 September. Its website address is www.seisaam.fr/esat/.

Past the museum, as the ground levels out, just before a track and road junction, there is a small stone cross – *St Pierre Croix* – on your right-hand side. Here men used to stop and cross themselves before going up to the front. One man described it as like entering a cemetery at night. There is a descriptive panel nearby. A small concrete First World War bunker then appears on the right, with signage.

Continuing north, you arrive at the *Cimetière National de la Forestière*, which was overseen by the Countess de Martimprey in 1924. There are panels (some in English) to explain the site. Opposite, on the rough track to Lachalade, you will see the memorial to the British Lancaster bomber shot down near here in 1943.

Carry on north to **Ravin du Génie**, a partially restored First World War French engineer and rest camp. Again there are descriptive panels here, some in English. There is a walk around the camp with signage, which takes half an hour to an hour. Leaving the camp, continue north. As you reach the high ground you will find the Countess de Martimprey's *Haute Chevauchée* Memorial. There are a number of descriptive panels here, with some English. At the rear of the memorial is a giant crater, which was blown by the Germans under Côte 283 in December 1916. On the far side is a Cross of Reconciliation between the Germans and French. With the memorial and crater to your back, on the right, amid the pine trees, is the location of the German front line from 1915 to 1918. On the left, at the edge of the pines, is the French front line. It is the pine trees here and in other similar sites around Verdun that create the 'cathedral effect', small shafts of light, which allowed veterans to sit in quiet reflection.

Although it is now closed due to safety concerns, you will see signs for the *Kaiser tunnel*. This was one of a number of tunnels built to bring German troops up to the front line in safety. With French troops still holding the high ground of Bolante and Fille Morte, they were able to call in artillery fire on movement below. Allow an hour here as there is much to see and good descriptive panels with enough in English to explain the site. Driving north from here, you are now effectively behind the old German front line and amid their support trenches and camps. At the T-junction with the D38, you can either turn left to Four de Paris or right for Varennes.

On the way to the village of **Romagne-sous-Montfaucon** from Varennes, you will pass the German First World War military cemetery at Eponville. It is worth stopping here, as it is another fine example of the tree spirit 'Watching over the eternal rest of soldiers'. Here great oak trees stand guard over the lines of dark steel crosses and mass graves.

The story of Romagne in the First World War is typical of the region. Most residents evacuated before the Germans arrived, and the hardy few who stayed suffered either immediate deportation to Germany or severe deprivation before finally being forced to leave their homes. The village housed six German hospitals during the Verdun campaign. A German cemetery was built at the edge of the village for the soldiers who died in the hospitals. By the end of the war 157 of the 174 houses in the village had been destroyed. In 1921 the village was awarded the *Croix de Guerre* for its suffering. A commemorative plaque with some English has recently been placed outside the church. Opposite is a new village war memorial to the civilians and soldiers from the village who died.

The German cemetery has undergone recent renovation work and is unusual on several counts. It was personally designed by Robert Tischler, Germany's principal First World War cemetery architect. You enter through a single-width gate, and the cemetery contains mainly the dead from the Verdun campaign. The crosses are made of dark stone, which is also somewhat unusual, as they are generally made of steel.

The village of Romagne has a small campsite and B&B just outside the village, while in the village itself is a small hotel and the world-famous Romagne 14–18 Museum. This offers a truly unique visitor experience, and cold meals and drinks are available (https://www.romagne14-18.com).

From the museum follow the signs to the American military cemetery of Romagne. This is a beautiful site and the largest American military cemetery in Europe. On the right the graves stretch endlessly up the hill towards the chapel. On either side of the chapel are inscribed on the walls the names of the men with no known grave, including those lost in the ill-fated Russian campaign of 1918/19. In the chapel the Argonne glass spirit sees the windows decorated with American divisional emblems. On the opposite hill is a visitor centre, which has regular exhibitions. The two main days of commemoration each year are Memorial Day in May and 11 November (https://www.abmc.gov/cemeteries-memorials/europe/meuse-argonne-american-cemetery).

Leaving the American cemetery by the opposite entrance, take the road to the somewhat austere village of **Cunel**. On the outside wall of the village church is something of a mystery: an inscribed memorial to three dead Americans from the First World War, on a water trough. Pershing permitted such public utilities as war memorials. The common feature appears to be that they all came from Boston, although this is incorrect. They all, though, did attend Harvard. How the three men came to be commemorated here together in this way, as none died near here, remains something of an enigma, the explanation lost in the passage of time.

On the outskirts of the village under a tree stands a white stone memorial with a red diamond. This is the insignia of the American Fifth Division, and it is one of more than twenty memorials they left in France, to the chagrin of Pershing and the ABMC.

Nantillois is home to the region's other wonderful private First World War Museum, 14–18 Nantillois, which also offers accommodation. The museum is open Thursdays to Sundays from 12.30pm to 6pm. Next to the museum is a village hall provided by Americans of the 315th Infantry Regiment, 79th Division, as a memorial. In the centre of the town is another Pennsylvania Memorial to the 80th Division.

Opposite is the town memorial is an obelisk commemorating the civil and military dead of the First World War. In the main square is another memorial, to Ernst Boulanger, born in the village, who was a local senator and government minister in the late nineteenth century and early part of the twentieth. The bust was shot at least twice in the head during the First World War hostilities; one, which hit the eye, now appears to host a bird's nest (http://www.14-18nantillois.com/index.php?lang=en).

Butte de Montfaucon is Pershing's primary Meuse-Argonne memorial. On top of the hill are the remnants of the old village, which was destroyed in the war. Adjacent to it, and towering over the former village, is the

200ft Doric tower, with its commanding view of the American front line on 26 September 1918. The long climb up inside the tower (there is no lift) to the viewing platform is not for the faint-hearted! On a clear day, though, the panoramic view over the former battlefield is well worth the effort.

South of Les Islettes

South of Les Islettes on the D2 is a somewhat unusual chapel, **Ermitage St Rouin**, which was built in concrete block form in 1950 but has wonderful stained-glass windows. It's also worth strolling the grounds and looking at the folly.

At **Passavant-en-Argonne** is the now-restored 'headless' memorial to the 1870 *Mobile* massacre. There is also a wonderful restaurant, and the last remaining pottery in the region. Just past the turning to the village is another to the left, the D2B to the village of Beaulieu en Argonne, which is one of the most picturesque in the region.

The church at **Triaucourt-en-Argonne** was safeguarded from fire in the First World War, but burnt in 1940. This is the village where the picture of Uncle Bob with André Citroën was taken at Christmas 1914, after the advancing Germans had destroyed much of the village.

Nubécourt was the family seat of the Poincaré family. In the cemetery her is the *Sepulture du President Poincaré*, where he and his family are buried. There is also a memorial in the church cemetery to the American B17 bomber 'Patches', shot down in 1943. The church was one of the few in the Argonne not destroyed in the First World War and dates back to the sixteenth century. Inside are many interesting religious artefacts and wonderful old stained-glass windows. In 1922 a memorial to the dead of the First World War was officially blessed inside the church. Outside the church you can see a small *Lavoire* (village washhouse).

The town of **Clermont-en-Argonne** has been much improved in recent years. Its central square is attractively lit in the colours of the French Tricolour at night. The main square contains the First and Second World War memorial and the memorial to the deported of the Second World War. There are two café/restaurants, plus a shop, a bakery and a tourist office where English is spoken. On the outskirts is a supermarket and 24/7 petrol station. On the hill above the village is the St Didier Church (he was the patron saint of Clermont), now restored with beautiful stained-glass windows in the Argonne style. Inside are six religious figures, one of which is known as the 'Holy Woman in a Peasant's Bonnet'. This has been attributed to the famous medieval French (Lorraine) sculptor Ligier Richier, and was carved in the early sixteenth century. For those interested in his work, there is a brochure and a trail around the region to see his other pieces. Carrying on up the hill you come to the town cemetery, where the redoubtable Sister Gabrielle is buried in a marked grave.

On the top of the hill, now a preserved First World War site, is the small chapel of St Anne. At the extreme eastern end is a viewing platform, with famous places in the distance marked. This provides a commanding view of the entire American Meuse-Argonne front and the direction of the autumn 1918 offensive.

Back in the town, the former hospital where Sister Gabrielle did her valuable work is still there but is now closed. Next to it, and sadly only open periodically for concerts and exhibitions, is the small chapel. Its Argonne glass windows are visible from outside and tell the story of the First World War in Clermont and the work of Sister Gabrielle.

Taking the D998 south from the centre of Clermont leads to a small number of attractions. The next village, **Rarécourt**, has a wonderful pottery museum open on Sundays during the summer (http://tourisme-argonne.com/musee-de-faience/). Just outside the village on the main road south, in a slightly awkward position opposite a picnic sign, is a layby marked 'no entry'. In the layby is a stone carved obelisk memorial to the 150 people from Meuse who lost their lives in the French Resistance in the Second World War.

Lavoye is a small village with a historic washhouse, complete with artefacts and a description of their use, which is open from May to September. There is also a small artisanal shop open at weekends during July and August. Hot and cold drinks and snacks can be purchased here and eaten overlooking the river.

Further south, just before the village of Fleury-sur-Aire, at the junction with the D20 is a huge stone monument dedicated to the medical services and the injured of France and America in the First World War. Included on the memorial plaque is John Verplank Newlin, AFS, who was injured in Esnes by a shell and later died in a hospital near the memorial.

From Fleury, head back to Les Islettes. About 30 minutes' drive east from Les Islettes is **Verdun**, now the World Peace Centre, which hosts a number of attractions, shops, restaurants and riverside cafés. In the city centre you can take a rail tour of the old underground citadel, where Private Thin selected the French Unknown Soldier. On the heights above the city is the main site where the awful battle raged throughout 1916.

There is a museum and the famous **Douaumont Ossuary** containing the skeletal remains of over 130,000 unknown French and German soldiers.

About 30 minutes' drive west from Les Islettes is **Valmy**, the site of the famous 1792 battle which saw the end of the monarchy and France's birth as a Republic. The main site, with its famous windmill, is open every day and it has descriptive panels with some English. The museum is open at weekends (https://www.valmy1792.com/).

Bibliography

Books and Journals

Amal, Jean-Paul, *Les Forets de la Grande Guerre* (University Press Sorbonne, France, 2015).

Arlen, J. Hansen, *Gentlemen Volunteers* (Arcade Publishing, New York, 1966).

Barbusse, Henri, *Le Feu* (Flammarion, France, 1917).

Best, William B., *The Fight for the Argonne* (Abingdon Press, New York & Cincinnati, 1919).

Bliss, Major Paul S., *The History of the 805th Pioneer Infantry Regiment, American Expeditionary Forces* (St Paul, Minnesota, 1919).

Bloch, Marc, *Memoires of War*, trans. Carole Fink (Cornel University Press, Ithaca & London, 1980).

Budreau, Lisa M., *Bodies of War* (New York University Press, New York, 2010).

Clodfetter, Michael, *The Lost Battalion and the Meuse Argonne, 1918, America's Deadliest Battle* (McFarland & Co., USA, 2012).

Clout, Hugh, *After the Ruins: Restoring the Countryside of Northern France After the Great War* (University of Exeter Press, Exeter, 1996).

Cooke, James J., *The All-Americans at War: the 82nd Division in the Great War, 1917–1918* (Praeger, USA, 1999).

Crane, David, *Empires of the Dead* (William Collins, London, 2014).

Ferrell, Robert H., *Unjustly Dishonored, an African-American Division in World War 1* (University of Missouri Press, USA, 2011).

Friends of France, described by its members (Houghton Mifflin Co., New York & Boston, 1916).

Garibaldi, Giuseppe, *A Toast to Rebellion* (John Lane, Bodley Head, 1936).

Garibaldi, Ricciotti, *I Fratelli Garibaldi* (ENEB, Milan, Italy, 1933).

Gavin, Lettie, *American Women in World War 1 – They also served* (University Press of Colorado, USA, 2006).

Geller, L.D., *The American Field Service Archives of World War 1, 1914–1917* (Greenwood Press, Connecticut, USA, 1989).

Gubert, Betty, Sawyer, Miriam and Fannin, Caroline, *Distinguished African-Americans in Aviation and Space Science* (Greenwood Press, Connecticut, USA, 2001).

Hardouin, Henry Jacques, *L'Epoppée Garibaldienne* (Debresse, Paris, France, 1939).

Hastings, Max, *Catastrophe, Europe Goes To War 1914* (Williams Collins, 2013).

History of the 77th Division, August 25th 1917– November 11th 1918 (Designed and written in the field, France).

History of the American Field Service in France – Told by its Members, vols 1–3 (Riverside Press, Cambridge, USA, 1920).

'The History of the Negro in the War' (*The Crisis*, vol. 18, no. 2, June 1919).

Hunton, Addie W. and Johnson, Kathryn M., *Two Colored Women With The Expeditionary Forces* (Brooklyn Eagle Press, 1920).

Johnson, Thomas M. and Pratt, Fletcher, *The Lost Battalion* (University of Nebraska Press, Lincoln & London, 2000).

Judd, Dr James R., *With the American Ambulance in France* (SicPress.com).

Lengel, Edward G., *To Conquer Hell* (Aurum Press, London, 2008).

Lunard, Phillippe, *Infantry Attack, the Desert Fox in the Argonne Forest*, trans. from German original by P. Lunard, 1937 (Potsdam, Germany, 1998).

McCollum, Private 'Buck', *The History and Rhymes of the Lost Battalion* (USA, 1929).

Marcosson, Isaac F., *SOS. America's Miracle in France* (John Lane Co., New York & London, 1919).

Mastriano, Douglas V., *Alvin York* (University Press of Kentucky, USA, 2014).

Official History of the 82nd Division AEF – written by Divisional Officers.

Quinlan, Mark, *Remembrance* (Authors OnLine Ltd, Hertford, 2005).

Schmidt, Major A.D., *Band 18 Argonnen* (Didenburg, Berlin, Germany, 1927).

Schneider, Jean-Jacques, *Nicole Mangin* (Editions Place Stanislas, Nancy, France, 2011).

Scott, Emmett J., *The American Negro in the World War* (http://net.lib.byu.edu/~rdh7/wwi/comment/Scott/ScottTC.htm).

Sheldon, Jack, *The German Army on the Western Front 1915* (Pen & Sword, Barnsley, 2012).

Sherman, Daniel J., *The Construction of Memory in Post War France* (University of Chicago Press, Chicago & London, 1999).

Smythe, Donald, 'Five days in June 1917', *Army Quarterly & Defence Journal* (West of England Press, Tavistock, 1974), vol. 104, no. 2.

Southcott, E.J. (ed.), *The First Fifty Years of the Catford Cycling Club* (C.T. Foulis, 1939).

Triplet, William S., *A Youth in the Meuse Argonne* (University of Missouri Press, Colombia & London, 2000).

Websites

https://largonnealheure1418.wordpress.com/
https://www.morthomme.com/
http://chtimiste.com/
http://centenaire.org/fr
http://amislucienjacques.fr/
http://www.guerredesgaz.fr/index.htm
http://www.historynet.com/weaponry-use-of-chlorine-gas-cylinders-in-world-war-i.htm
http://le-souvenir-francais.fr/
http://www.westernfrontassociation.com/
https://www.ymca.org.uk/
https://france3-regions.francetvinfo.fr/bourgogne-franche-comte/doubs/histoires-14-18-ymca-foyer-du-soldat-1388675.html
http://www.ourstory.info/library/2-ww1/AmHosp15/ahp1915.html
https://apps.dtic.mil/dtic/tr/fulltext/u2/a241174.pdf
https://medium.com/iowa-history/women-filled-key-roles-in-world-war-i-5556b9a19f79
http://www.ourstory.info/library/2-ww1/AmHosp15/ahp1915.html
https://apps.dtic.mil/dtic/tr/fulltext/u2/a241174.pdf
https://www.abmc.gov/
https://www.goldstarmoms.com/

https://www.volksbund.de/en/volksbund.html
https://poppyladymadameguerin.wordpress.com/
https://www.britishlegion.org.uk/
https://www.legion.org/
https://journals.openedition.org/rha/185
https://www.worldwar1centennial.org

Index